WASHINGTON MERRY-GO-ROUND

And as a result he is in the $25,000-a-year class. Unlike Snure he does not have to work from early morning until well into the night in an intense competitive field. He turns out his three syndicated articles a week, leisurely and comfortably, and leaves his cozy office close by the White House only to attend the semi-weekly Presidential press conference or when summoned by Mr. Hoover to talk over an idea or two.

In Charles G. Ross, chief of the bureau, Paul Y. Anderson, and Raymond P. Brandt, the St. Louis *Post Dispatch,* the most enlightened, courageous and forceful metropolitan newspaper in the United States, has a Washington staff that in every respect is worthy of its high standards.

For all-around competence, high integrity and fairness, these men are matched only by two other staffs, those of the Baltimore *Sun,* and the Scripps-Howard Newspaper Alliance. They afford that now practically extinct spectacle in American journalism of honest and independent reporters working for honorable and brilliant newspapers.

Ross is the finest type of correspondent in the press corps. He is a thorough scholar of national affairs, is widely read, and a keen and fearless analyst and writer. Anderson is the crusading reporter, hard-boiled and pugnacious. His work on the Teapot Dome oil scandals won him the Pulitzer Journalism Prize several years ago. He is at his best in a senatorial investigation and in many of them he has taken a more active and effective part than most members of the committees.

The brilliant work of the staff of the Baltimore *Sun* papers, because of the large circulation of the papers in Washington, has a considerable influence in the capital. This is particularly true in the field of political and foreign affairs.

J. Fred Essary, head of the morning *Sun* bureau, is that most laudable of newspaper executives, a stanch and loyal defender of his reporters. Essary always backs his men to the limit, not hesitating on occasion to brave Presidential displeasure to do so.

He is also one of the few large bureau managers who never takes a story from a member of his staff and writes it under his own by-line. The stories that carry Essary's name are stories he obtains by his own efforts. He is particularly well informed on railroad consolidation and has had considerable experience abroad.

He is one of the few correspondents who has written books about Washington. He is the author of three volumes throwing much light on personalities and behind-the-scenes history.

Drew Pearson, the *Sun's* expert on foreign affairs, has the reputation of knowing more about the State Department than most of the people who run it, and to a considerable extent this is true. He has been a fixture at the State Department for so many years that few people realize he was once a sailor, circus hand and vagabond journalist working his way around odd corners of the world. He was, that is, until he married Countess Felicia Gizycka and came to Washington to get a veneer of respectability. Divorced some years later, Pearson stuck it out in Washington and takes cynical delight in lampooning some of the diplomats who once high-hatted him when he enjoyed less fortuitous circumstances. He is the State Department's severest critic, yet because its members either fear him or value his opinion, he is taken into their confidence on many important international moves. Because of his independence he is either loved or hated; there is no middle ground of affection where Pearson is concerned.

M. Farmer Murphy, the *Sun's* Senate reporter, is one of the most widely experienced and forceful correspondents in Washington. For many years he was a foreign correspondent in the important European capitals. His Senate dispatches are unique for their vigor and outspokenness, and he has had the unusual experience of having United States Senators plead with him to "lay off" of them.

Franklyn Waltman, Jr., and Newton Aiken, the other members of the *Sun* staff, are keen reporters whose initiative and conscientiousness are constantly giving the *Sun* exclusive and significant stories.

Frederick R. Barkley and Henry M. Hyde of the *Evening Sun* staff are equally zealous correspondents. Hyde's daily "running" stories of the most important news development in the capital rank among the finest pieces of workmanship in the press corps. His articles have a literary quality that is rare in American political writing.

Only in one respect are the *Sun* papers behind the St. Louis *Post Dispatch* and the Scripps-Howard papers and that is in the very important matter of salaries. The *Sun* papers are skimping when it comes to the pay envelope.

Frank R. Kent, the political columnist and commentator of the Baltimore *Sun,* is not a member of the Washington staff, although he usually writes his column under that date-line. He presents the sad spectacle of a man possessed of a rare opportunity for performing a desperately needed public service in exposing official incompetence, duplicity, and dishonesty, stultifying himself by unworthy personalities, social contacts, and stupid obstinacy.

In his daily front-page column, "The Great Game of Politics," Kent is his own master. It is the only column of its kind in the country. In making this space available to Kent and giving him full control over it, the *Sun* gives expression to the highest ideals of a free press.

It may disagree with Kent's views, in fact it practically always does, both in its news and editorial columns, but it never in any way interferes or limits Kent's freedom of expression.

This extraordinary opportunity, Kent, in the past several years, has sorrowfully misused. Formerly a caustic commentator on Presidential hypocrisy and dishonesty, since the incumbency of Hoover, he has become the militant defender of the very things he once so bitterly denounced and ridiculed.

With glaring misstatements of fact and half-truths, he has strained and labored to alibi and explain away the President's colossal failure while at the same time impugning the sincerity and principles of the Insurgents and Democrats who have had the courage to challenge the President.

Their refusal to fall for the Hooverian lure and swallow, as he has, the myth of a Great Leader, he attributes wholly to personal malice and vindictiveness. Only base motives and demagoguery prompt them to challenge vicious appointments, and speak out against Mr. Hoover's incompetence, duplicity, and reactionarism, in Kent's opinion.

Do the Insurgents and Democrats refuse to confirm a fifth rate politician appointed by Mr. Hoover to the United States Supreme Court, then they are depriving the poor, patient South of representation on the high tribunal.

Do they try to enact vital economic and political reform legislation, which Mr. Hoover characteristically secretly opposes, and against which, under cover, he makes use of a servile and Tory Republican House leadership to emasculate and defeat, then they are obstructionists and conspirators, bent on embarrassing an innocent and pure Executive, and the House bosses are forceful men with an active "sense of direction."

Does the Senate frankly admit it erred and attempt to reconsider the confirmation of three undesirable Federal Power Commissioners on the ground that they displayed undue solicitude for private power interests, then Kent rushes forth with a "powerful piece" ridiculing the idea of a power trust.

Who has ever seen the power trust, he demanded. He hadn't. Talk of it was all sham heroics on the part of the "breast-beating" Insurgents.

But when a few days later this non-existent power trust ironically enough manifested its reality by broadcasting far and wide Kent's article, he came to with a pained shock. In great distress he rushed to newspaper friends to find out just what the power question was all about.

At great length and with full details, they informed him, and he began to see light. A week or so later he admitted in his column there really was such a thing as a power trust, and a little later when Martin Insull, brother of Samuel Insull, the great water-power magnate, delivered a radio talk in which he quoted Kent's first article, Kent waxed righteously indignant and flayed him in a vitriolic attack that was gloriously reminiscent of his one-time crusading days.

Kent was early taken in by Hoover. So were many other newspapermen. But whereas practically all of them soon recovered from their gullibility, Kent, who should not have been duped in the first place, has been the most persistent in refusing to admit his stupidity.

He has hung on, trying to make it appear that he is right and every one else wrong and malicious for not agreeing with him. The result has been that much that he writes is influenced by this distorted view, and his resentment at those who refuse to believe as he does.

The high repute and standing Kent once had in all quarters in the capital he has considerably forfeited. Senator Tom Heflin, who once fiercely denounced him because of Kent's biting characterization of him as a clown and buffoon, has acclaimed him as a friend and comrade, and where Washington once read Kent with respect, it now laughs at him.

Kent's obstinancy in persisting in the Hoover myth arises out of his inherent lack of a broad and comprehensive grasp of vital economic and political issues. Nothing could be more significant than his article denying the existence of a power trust, followed by his rushing to newspaper friends to learn from them, for the first time, that it actually exists.

His whole approach is that of the ward politician—personal. He believes in personal politics and knows it only from that viewpoint. When Kent is attacking an individual he is always at his best. When he gets on issues and principles, he is muddle-headed, inaccurate, and uninformed.

As long as he was a good Democrat and was blasting the Republicans under Coolidge, his writing attracted attention. But when he became a Hoover advocate and, upon the collapse of his hero, attempted to keep him afloat by attacking the opposition, Kent's weaknesses and inadequacies stood out in glaring sharpness.

Kent for a number of years was one of the *Sun* editors. He does no news writing, confining his work wholly to his column of comment and opinion. He spends a few days a week in Washington, gathering "dope" for this purpose and the rest of the time in Baltimore.

Kent is credited with cherishing Maryland senatorial ambitions. Several years ago it was reported he was offered the Democratic nomination, but declined for financial reasons. Now he is said to be in a position to accept such an invitation but it is doubtful if it will again come to him.

Democrats are alienated by his pro-Hoover views and the hostile attitude he has assumed toward national Democratic leaders. And from the mass of protesting letters that have poured in upon the *Sun,* denouncing his articles, it is apparent that there is a considerable body of Maryland voters who also feel anything but cordial toward him.

The Scripps-Howard Newspaper Alliance is made up of twenty-four dailies located in every section of the country. The papers are the most liberal and independent in their communities.

On labor, enlightened and advanced social legislation, on economic issues and international affairs, the Scripps-Howard papers are leaders in sound and progressive thought. This is due chiefly to the excellence and fine character of the members of its Washington staff.

On national politics, particularly on Presidential candidates, the Scripps-Howard record is not so commendable. This is due to some of the organization's business executives.

After the Alliance had given the elder LaFollette powerful and devoted support in his independent political race in 1924, these executives, in spite of the warning of their Washington staff, decided in 1928 to back Hoover, and then campaigned for him on his Democratic opponent's liberal platform.

That election campaign, and a period afterward, was a

trying time for the Alliance's Washington staff. Its members had no illusions about Mr. Hoover and were sick at heart at the action of their superiors.

To the latters' credit, they eventually saw the error of their ways and had the courage and honesty to admit their mistake. To-day there is no more plain-spoken press critic of the Hoover Administration than the Scripps-Howard Alliance.

The Washington staff of the Alliance is made up of distinguished correspondents who are leaders in their fields. They supply the twenty-four papers of the group with their editorials and special articles on national and international affairs.

Lowell Mellett, chief of the staff and editor of the Washington paper of the Alliance, the *News,* is one of the finest figures in American journalism. He is a man of wide learning, exceptional executive and writing ability, and a gentleman.

During the LaFollette Presidential campaign he accompanied the Insurgent crusader throughout his electioneering as the Alliance's correspondent, but actually he was the candidate's most valued counselor and advisor. Under his editorship the Scripps-Howard Alliance is giving the nation's capital the only liberal and interesting daily in the city.

Although one of the five greatest capitals of the world, Washington's newspapers, with the exception of the Scripps-Howard publication, are dull, flabby, provincial and stupid. There isn't a first-class paper in the city. This need is supplied by the Baltimore *Sun* and the New York papers.

The *News,* the Scripps-Howard paper, is the nearest approach to a first-class paper in the capital. It is handicapped by its tabloid size. In its editorial page, the *News* is one of the strongest papers in the country.

John M. Gleissner, managing editor; Ludwell Denny, chief editorial writer; and William Philip Simms, foreign affairs editor, contribute largely to the high order of the editorial and special feature material of the Alliance.

Denny has had extensive press experience both in the United

States and in Europe. For many years he covered the State Department for the United Press. He is the author of two volumes on international economics and finance, "We Fight for Oil" and "America Conquers Britain." These exhaustive studies have a world-wide reputation and have been translated into several languages.

Attached to the Alliance staff are eight correspondents who represent one or more Scripps-Howard papers. They are all reporters of force and ability.

Leo R. Sack, correspondent for the powerful Ohio and Pennsylvania group of Alliance papers, made the disclosures concerning 1926 senatorial campaign expenditures that brought about the Reed committee and the subsequent loss to two aspirants of their Senate seats. Ray T. Tucker, correspondent for the two New York papers, writes extensively on Washington for several magazines.

The Washington staff of the Chicago *Tribune* also presents the spectacle of a happy rapport between paper and reporters, in viewpoint and ideas. But this is a far different kind than that which exists on the Baltimore *Sun* papers, the St. Louis *Post Dispatch,* and the Scripps-Howard group.

The *Tribune* is ultra-reactionary, Republican, and jingoistic. Every member of its Washington staff is a sincere and earnest believer in the *Tribune's* economic, political, and international views.

No open or secret dissidents are to be found on the *Tribune's* staff. All heartily concur in their paper's ideas, and enthusiastically turn out the news copy needed to support them.

As reporters, the members of the staff are competent and able. Arthur Sears Henning, the chief, is one of the best in the press corps. His principal job is writing articles that propagate the *Tribune's* various reactionary policies.

During the London Naval Conference, Henning, writing turgid big-navy propaganda—information for which was supplied him by naval members of the American delegation—undertook to pump up Charles Francis Adams, the Navy

Department's mentally becalmed civilian chief, into the proportions of a national hero who was standing out against his colleagues for American naval supremacy. The *Tribune's* idea was to precipitate a rift in the American delegation and thereby, perhaps, disrupt the conference.

Henning gave his best. One dispatch began with these inspiring words: "Like his ancestors at Bunker Hill, Secretary Adams is holding his fire until he sees the whites of their eyes."

Despite this talented prompting, Adams failed the *Tribune*. The other members of the American delegation slyly showed him up by asking him to conduct a press conference one morning. The result was so dismal that Henning, responding to the good-natured jeers of his colleagues, remarked: "My White Hope has club feet."

Clinton W. Gilbert, chief of the Curtis Philadelphia *Public Ledger* and New York *Evening Post* bureau, is one of the few nationally known Washington correspondents who, despite the handicap of a partisan and biased publisher, has not compromised his personal or professional integrity. He has been prevented from doing much that he could have done had he had a free hand, but he has never fawned or groveled because of pressure or because it paid better and was so much more comfortable.

Gilbert is one of the best confidentially-informed men in Washington. He is outstanding for his exclusive stories. He is author of the delightful and best-selling "Mirrors of Washington," and the most entertaining weekly magazine column in the capital, "The Man at the Keyhole," in *Collier's*.

Robert B. Smith, Warren Wheaton and Harold Brayman, members of the staff, are upright, able, hard-working reporters compelled by economic necessity to write the sort of stuff that is to be found under their names in the Curtis papers.

Brayman, correspondent of the Evening *Post*, unearthed the story of Mr. Hoover's duplicity about naval construction. He found that contrary to the President's public announcement several months previous, the navy had received no orders to hold up building operations on three cruisers, and had been proceeding all along with this work. Brayman received no thanks from his paper for his enterprise. His story was a clean beat and was picked up by the entire press of the country the next day. But instead of receiving congratulations, he was sharply admonished for his unfriendly administration attitude.

The *Christian Science Monitor* has one of the larger Washington news bureaus. It is manned by competent and conscientious reporters who are held down by the conservative views and many prohibitions of their organization. Robert S. Allen, head of the staff, is the youngest large bureau chief in the capital. Despite his youth, he has had important newspaper experience both in the United States and abroad.

Another talented correspondent who is hedged in by editorial policy is Henry Suydam of the Brooklyn *Eagle,* one of the Frank E. Gannett group of newspapers. Suydam gave up reporting for a while to become head of the press section of the State Department when Charles Evans Hughes was Secretary of State. He left the diplomatic field, however, soon after Hughes resigned. He is an excellent musician, and the Gridiron Club's most versatile composer and playwright.

Ulric Bell, correspondent for the Louisville *Courier-Journal,* is also unusually gifted. In addition to being a sterling and forthright reporter, he is a fine painter. Some of his work has attracted considerable attention. His paper is Democratic and conservative, but Bell is allowed wide latitude. He avails himself fully of this to write forceful and frank dispatches which are often at variance with the timid views of the paper's editorial writers.

Theodore C. Alford, of the Kansas City *Star;* George F. Authier, of the Minneapolis *Tribune* and Davenport *Democrat;* and Alfred D. Stedman, of the St. Paul *Pioneer Press* are the agricultural experts of the corps. These men know more about the farm problem than all the professional farm

relievers and the present and last few Secretaries of Agriculture put together.

Their reporting is reliable and fair, and while held down
by the editorial policies and prohibitions of their papers, they
do much effective work.

Stedman's conscientiousness, in spite of the timidity of his
paper, in vigorously covering charges of Representative Maas,
of Minneapolis, that the Post Office Department was condon-
ing a scandalous local postal lease, was an important factor
in arousing public sentiment and bringing about the sweeping
senatorial investigation of such long-standing abuses.

Lawrence Todd, correspondent of the Federated Press which
serves radical and labor papers, and the Washington representative of Tass, the Soviet Russian news agency, is the so-
called "Red" of the corps.

Actually he is one of the mildest-mannered and most
courteous of men. He is also one of the few correspondents
who is financially independent. He has been in Washington
many years, is widely known, and universally held in high
regard and respect.

Like many of the most prominent newspapermen in the
capital, Frederic William Wile got his start in Chicago.
Although a Jew, he is a graduate of Notre Dame University
and one of its best known non-athletic alumni.

Wile went abroad early in his press career and there made
his reputation as the Berlin correspondent of Lord North-
cliffe's *Daily Mail*. During his foreign service, Wile traveled
extensively and in high official circles.

After the War, he came back to the United States as a
Chautauqua lecturer and then became chief of the *Public
Ledger* bureau. He lost this job. He promptly set up his own
press syndicate and concentrated on radio news broadcasting.
In both these fields, his acute eulogistic faculties have had
unlimited scope and he has prospered handsomely.

Wile is one of the most industrious men in the press corps.
He is always ferreting out new ways of earning a friendly

dollar. In addition to his news broadcasting, he writes a thrice-weekly column that goes to a string of papers, and does special articles and editorials on foreign affairs for the Washington *Star*. These adhere loyally to the *Star's* unbroken policy of never saying anything of any importance or vigor on any subject.

For his weekly fifteen-minute news broadcasts over the Columbia system, Wile gets $250 a week. He left the National Broadcasting Company, with which he got his start as a radio news discourser, to go to Columbia when they offered him an increase in pay which National refused to meet. Wile is also a zealous public speaker and makes numerous talks about the country on Washington, for the best fee he can get.

"Freddy," as he is known in the capital, is the most successful and persistent goer-out in the press corps. There are few functions that go off without his presence. And he always repays these favors with eulogistic pats-on-the-back in his gossip column.

This column is the sweetest and most sugary writing in the capital. It exists only to bloom dear little buttercups of compliments and good wishes. If by rare inadvertence, an inferential note of criticism should creep into it, Wile more than makes up for it in his following dispatch.

Once he had a paragraph about Senator "Jim" Reed that a friend of the Senator's jokingly told Wile might make him angry. In his next column, Wile extended himself in acclaiming Reed and enumerating all his sterling qualities.

One of Wile's greatest gifts is his ability to discover administration victories. So successful has he been in this respect that he proudly displays on his office wall a letter signed by Mr. Hoover commending him for his great assistance.

Naturally all this industry and these exceptional talents have paid Wile well. He has his own limousine and chauffeur and is one of the foremost of the select group of $25,000-a-year correspondents.

David Lawrence is an even more shining example of what

unremitting application, business acumen, and respectful regard for high authority and position will do for an ambitious man.

Lawrence was a reporter once—and one of the very best in the game, too—but to-day as the result of the happy combination of the aforementioned talents, he is an editor, owner, and publisher. He owns a home off fashionable Massachusetts Avenue, which is not surpassed by that of any Cabinet member, commands his own yacht, and has a limousine for his wife and a gleaming roadster for himself, both of the most expensive make.

He is very much of the $25,000-a-year group, but with an income that is nearer $125,000.

Lawrence began life as a newsboy in Buffalo. He obtained his education strictly by his own toil and ingenuity as a reporter. It was as a student at Princeton that he formed the friendship with Woodrow Wilson which stood him in such good stead when, years later, he was a Washington correspondent and the professor was President of the United States.

After the War, Lawrence had the business genius to see that a boom was rapidly crystallizing and that there would be enormous popular interest in stock market quotations and special business articles. At that time only a small number of afternoon papers carried a full stock market report or any kind of a business service.

Lawrence organized such a service. He gathered a staff of experts, set up a fast stock report, and hammered away at editors until he sold his idea. With the rising tide of "prosperity" and stock speculation, his service became a success and he cashed in.

He then turned to establishing the *United States Daily,* the idea for which he got from a colleague. Despite large doubts among newspapermen, Lawrence has kept the unusual paper going for more than five years. At times it has been reported to be in hard straits, but so far he has kept its head above water. Early this year it was reported that he obtained $1,000,000 from the Laura Spelman Fund. This did not, however, prevent him from cutting the salaries of his staff in March.

Lawrence is absolutely ruthless in keeping himself to the fore in his organization. No one else, not even William Hard, who works for him, is allowed to use the daily leased wire for transmission of articles. No one is permitted to dim the standing of the chief.

Yet, despite this sensitiveness, Lawrence is devoted to his friends. He may have curtly discharged, with a two weeks' notice, the man who gave him the idea for the *United States Daily,* when the latter absented himself without notice for a week from his work, but two of Lawrence's boyhood school chums who defended him when bullies baited him as a Jew hold lucrative life jobs in his organization.

With all his material success and extraordinary business achievement Lawrence is not a particularly happy man. For one thing he is not popular among the correspondents. He is too commercial for the taste of the true reporter.

Then he is trying to do too much. Besides publishing the *United States Daily,* speaking over the radio once a week, and running a news syndicate, he attempts to keep up his daily Washington dispatches, which are now little more than editorialized re-writes of the morning papers.

The result is that he who once was renowned for his exclusive Washington dispatches is now shoved onto a back page or not used at all, even by the Washington *Star.* And the Hoover Administration, despite his tenacious fealty, has publicly rebuked him for inaccuracy.

"Bill" Hard has been too popular for his own good.

His rare charm and personality, the brilliance and power of his intellect, his loyalty and sincerity, have won him too many political friends. And these friendships, because of his kindliness, have taken their toll at times in pulling his punches.

In business, politics, and society, such a rare talent for friendship may be a desirable asset. But no independent news-paperman can be steadfastly true to himself and have the sort of friendships that wormed their way into Hard's confidence. A President, particularly of the extreme sensitiveness and suspicious egotism of Mr. Hoover, cannot put up with robustness of thought and expression in a friend.

All of which Hard, after several years of wholehearted de-votion to Mr. Hoover, finally and grimly learned to be true.

It was characteristic of Hard that once he realized the true situation, he frankly and freely admitted his misjudgment, and, regardless of material cost, set about righting himself. He is as outspoken and fearlessly critical of the Administra-tion now as he once was wholeheartedly a supporter of Mr. Hoover, in the face of the ridicule and abuse of his oldest friends.

Hard also sprang from Chicago newspaperdom. His first journalistic experience was as an editorial writer for the Chicago *Tribune*. Here he met Medill McCormick, one of the owners of the paper, and afterward United States Senator from Illinois. They became lifelong friends.

When the latter died, following his defeat for reëlection, it was Hard who discovered his body; and to-day McCormick's long fur overcoat, cut down to fit Hard's diminutive size, is a familiar and amusing sight in the capital.

It was this friendship that in many ways was responsible for the period in Hard's life that cost him for a time the regard of his oldest and stanchest friends. For many years he was nationally known as the most independent cor-respondent in the capital. He was famous as a journalistic fighter and thinker. Through sheer brilliance he actually made independence pay, building up a news syndicate that brought him a good income.

After McCormick's death, Ruth Hanna McCormick, his widow, who tried in 1930 to win a Senate seat with one of the sorriest exhibitions of demagoguery of that year, induced

Hard, who was deeply shocked at his friend's death and intensely devoted to him, to give up his newspaper work and write the history of her husband's fight against the League of Nations.

She paid Hard the equivalent of his newspaper income. Two years passed and no book appeared. What became of it is not known. The suspicion is that no publisher would print it.

Hard was left high and dry. He had lost his syndicate and naturally could not go on accepting money from Mrs. McCormick even if she would have paid him. He went through a difficult time.

It was during this period that Hard fell for the Hoover propaganda, and step by step drifted into the Hoover camp. The President made full use of Hard's exceptional ability. In his campaign and for a long time afterward, Hard was consulted on every important matter, and his writings were among the President's chief solaces.

Hard's suspicions about Mr. Hoover were first aroused when, returning from Mrs. McCormick's nomination campaign in the spring of 1930, he frankly told the President that he ought to stop pussy-footing on prohibition and the World Court, and take a definite stand against both.

Mr. Hoover never got over the shock. From then on Hard was made to feel he was suspect. On Hard's part, as the economic depression intensified and the President did nothing except attempt to deny the seriousness of conditions, the realization became increasingly clear that the man he had believed in was unfit.

It would doubtless have been much easier for Hard to have kept silent about this discovery and to have made his peace with the White House. But he refused to do that and to-day in his articles and radio broadcasts he is doing some of the keenest and most plain-spoken reporting in the capital.

He is again standing on his old independent ground. He *is*

again the comrade of his old fighting friends and newspapermen. And he is having the time of his life and showing it.

American journalism needs its outspoken Hards in the
Washington press corps. There was never a time when an
enlightened, liberal, and intrepid press was more urgently and
vitally demanded in the interest of good government in the
United States than to-day. In the atmosphere of reaction,
cowardice, bigotry, incompetence, and even worse, that pervades the capital to-day, a militant and fearless press could
render invaluable service to the cause of a desperately needed
political and economic reformation.

Such a press could be the leader of public opinion instead
of the misleader. It could tonic the whole body politic of the
nation.

Its columns would not be filled with White House propaganda and idiotic blurbs about Strong Silent Men and Great
Engineers. The House of Representatives, the most ludicrous,
boss-ridden and inefficient legislative body in the entire land
would not be acclaimed as "businesslike and alert," and Senate investigators exposing corruption, infamy, and chicanery
would not be denounced and assailed as "invaders of private
affairs" and irresponsible disturbers of the peace and of business stability.

But until the majority of American newspapers are rid of
their business and money-drawer domination, it is futile to
expect any betterment in the Washington press corps. There
is no reason why there should be any improvement.

Better correspondents are not the most urgent need. As it is,
a majority of the correspondents are better than the papers
they work for.

Even if the personnel of the corps was appreciably improved, it would meet no demand and find no opportunity
for expression. The American press is stifling and thwarting
what little idealism and honesty still exists in its ranks.

The problem is far more fundamental than improving the Washington press corps. More independent, honest, enlightened, and courageous newspapers are what is desperately needed.

THE END

WASHINGTON
MERRY-GO-ROUND

BLUE RIBBON BOOKS, Inc.
New York City

Published, July, 1931
Second printing, July, 1931
Third printing, July, 1931
Fourth printing, July, 1931
Fifth printing, July, 1931
Sixth printing, August, 1931
Seventh printing, August, 1931
Eighth printing, August, 1931
Ninth printing, August, 1931
Tenth printing, August, 1931
Eleventh printing, September, 1931
Twelfth printing, September, 1931
Thirteenth printing, September, 1931
Fourteenth printing, September, 1931
Fifteenth printing, October, 1931
Sixteenth printing, October, 1931
Seventeenth printing, October, 1931
Eighteenth printing, November, 1931
Nineteenth printing, November, 1931
Twentieth printing, December, 1931
Twenty-first printing, December, 1931
Twenty-second printing, January, 1932
Twenty-third printing, May, 1932

Printed and Bound by The Cornwall Press, Inc., for
Blue Ribbon Books, Inc., 448 Fourth Ave., New York City

TO THOSE WHO STILL REACH
FOR THE BRASS RING

CONTENTS

WASHINGTON
MERRY-GO-ROUND

CHAPTER ONE

BOILED BOSOMS

*W*ITH the exception of Peking, no other capital in the world equals Washington for the relentless brilliancy with which the spotlight of public attention is fixed upon the comings and goings, the cocktail parties and the amours of the petty people who run the official and social life of the capital of these United States.

If Nick Longworth came back from Cincinnati unexpectedly one autumn night to find himself locked out of his house on Massachusetts Avenue; should Dolly Curtis Gann stop to adjust a slipping stocking before a crowd of shoppers at Woodward and Lothrop's; or should Mrs. Hoover have a dispute with her secretary, Polly Randolph, over flowers for the White House table, most of the dinners and tea parties of Washington are buzzing over the incident twenty-four hours later.

There are two reasons for this. In the first place, Washington is small, and the group which runs its social and official life is even smaller. In the second place, Washington has only one industry—politics.

London, Berlin, Paris, Rome, Moscow, Vienna—all the other great capitals of the world are also vast industrial and commercial centers in which the pompous preening of society is almost swallowed up. Were the capital of the United States located in New York, much of the material for the merry-go-round of Washington would be non-existent. But the capital is not in New York. Instead, it has been plumped down in a placid agricultural community, surrounded by the remnants of a Southern aristocracy which still prides itself on its hounds, hunters and mint-juleps, and which boasts no industry other than the Bureau of Printing and Engraving plus a few river boats which chug sleepily up the Potomac, bringing oysters, Norfolk honeymooners and split pine logs.

Not only is the sole industry of the capital politics, but this industry is concentrated among a very few. Fifty percent of Washington's half million population is of a race which, except when it gathers to cheer Paul Robeson or its lone congressional champion, Oscar De Priest, is neither interested nor admitted into high society.

Of the remaining quarter million people, most are government clerks and the trades-people who support them, leaving the capital's social life almost exclusively in the hands of those who live in the fashionable northwest. This is an area, which, socially speaking, begins at the White House and stretches out Pennsylvania Avenue and Sixteenth Street toward ancient Georgetown to the west and toward *nouveau riche* Chevy Chase on the north.

Within this orbit, divided into many cliques and schisms, throbs a social life as gay, as superficial and as futile as in any capital of Europe.

Broadly speaking, Washington society can be divided into two classes: Those who want to get their names in the papers and those who want to keep them out.

The Cabinet members, the congressional climbers, the Army and Navy, and the professional pushers are all more or less in the first category, while the Young Set, the intellectuals and the fast-riding, hard-drinking poker players are in the second.

There are in Washington a half dozen middle-aged or aging ladies who absolutely dominate the social stage. Their arrival in the fall and their departure in the spring is the order for the ringing up or down of the curtain for the social season. They put the social lions through their tricks—pull them in and out of the social ring. They crack the whip, and they crack it with all the grimness of the tamer who must inspire fawning obedience or retire from the ring.

Most fawned upon among Washington's social whip-crackers are:

MRS. JOSEPH (JULIETTE) LEITER, big, blonde, and the most domineering whip-cracker of them all. Just after the turn of the century she married Joe Leiter, whose boast is that he was "the largest individual holder of wheat in the history of the grain trade," but who, finding it easier to control wheat than his wife, now leaves his enormous mansion on du Pont Circle entirely to her and to the fabulous parties which she gives in the manner but not the quality of the Vanderbilts.

MRS. JAMES F. (LAURA) CURTIS, patron saint of those who play for a thousand-dollar limit. She has swallowed her pride just once. Although she left her husband, only to take him back again, Jimmie has gone to live in New York, from which point of vantage he supplies the cash and watches her crack the whip over her little clique as relentlessly as she once cracked it over him.

ELEANOR MEDILL PATTERSON, formerly Mrs. Eleanor Schlesinger, formerly Countess Gizycka, formerly Eleanor Medill Patterson, one of the most gifted women in Washington but who has dissipated her gifts, for the most part on trivialities.

ALICE ROOSEVELT LONGWORTH, brilliant if not gifted, who through the prestige of her position and the vitriol of her tongue dominates Washington's ultra-fashionable official group more completely than any other whip-cracker in the capital.

One of the most charming things about Washington is that it is almost never without a social, diplomatic or matrimonial war, and as in all one-industry villages these feuds are waged so earnestly that before they are over they line up on one side or the other almost every one in town. Within less than the past twelve months there have been:

THE EDWARD B. McLEAN-PRINCE DE LIGNE WAR over an alleged dinner-table prank, as the result of which the Belgian

Ambassador, although later forced to retire, received a personal apology from Secretary of State Stimson, and the publisher of the Washington *Post* got a personal apology from the Philadelphia *Record*.

THE PRADO-POINDEXTER WAR over a servant imported from Lima by the wife of the American Ambassador to Peru, which resulted in Counselor Prado, of the Peruvian Embassy in Washington, resigning his post and taking the servant off with him to London.

THE TOTO MACIA-ITALIAN EMBASSY WAR over the unimportant question of incompatibility, which resulted in the beautiful Senora Macia rising up in all her Canadian wrath, fleeing her house at midnight, and secreting her baby in Baltimore.

THE SIAMESE LIQUOR WAR over the right of a legation to transport beverages from Baltimore, which resulted in the entire Diplomatic Corps rebelling against the capital police, with the exception of the gentle British Ambassador, Sir Esme Howard, who promptly announced he would import no more liquor.

THE SALVADOREAN LEGATION-POLICE WAR over the failure of the latter to prevent hi-jackers from absconding with seventeen cases of liquor, and which caused Don Carlos Leiva, having been severely beaten over the head with a flashlight, to sit up in bed and issue scathing statements about repeated attempts to rob his Legation, against which the police offered no protection.

THE DAISY HARRIMAN-RAY BAKER WAR, between two of the most charming and once friendly Democrats of the capital, which resulted when the former came back from Bermuda to find that the latter had dumped 5,000 tons of dirt from the cellar of his new house in the middle of her front lawn.

None of these, of course, could compare with the Dolly Curtis Gann-Alice Roosevelt Longworth precedence war, a war which stirred Washington to the depths of its sensation-loving soul. Unfortunately, this feud, except when Edward Everett Gann calls up the Washington *Daily News* to complain that he is not a "meek" husband, is in a completely comatose stage. Fortunately, however, its place was taken, just before it breathed its last, by the Patterson-Longworth War.

This was not a new battle. Intimate friends of both Eleanor Patterson and Alice Longworth knew that it had been smoldering ever since their debutante days when they had competed for the most eligible men in town. One of them married a young Congressman from Cincinnati, and the other Count Joseph Gizycka, a dashing young Polish cavalryman in Emperor Franz Ferdinand's army.

Later, Cissie Gizycka came back from Warsaw once again to cramp Alice's style and in later years to tell a story on herself—which may or may not be true—about a young nobleman who sat at Alice's right at dinner one evening. After dinner Cissie monopolized him in an upstairs library. The following morning she received a note from her hostess which read as follows:

"Dear Cissie:

"Upon sweeping up the library this morning, the maid found several hair-pins which I thought you might need and which I am returning.

"ALICE."

To which Cissie says she replied:

"Dear Alice:

"Many thanks for the hair-pins. If you had looked on the chandelier you might also have sent back my shoes and chewing gum.

"Love,

"CISSIE."

It was at the Republican National Convention of 1920, held in Chicago, that the first real breach occurred. Cissie Gizycka had taken a house for the period of the convention, and had invited as one of her guests William Edgar Borah, shaggy-maned and shaggy-browed Senator from Idaho. She was writing a series of human-interest stories on the convention for the Hearst papers and devoted one of them to a more than laudatory sketch of Borah. Her house-guest explained that this was highly embarrassing and cautioned her against any repetition of her flattery. A day or two later and with all the ear-marks of having been inspired by an irate Countess Gizycka, her brother's newspaper, the Chicago Tribune, published a scathing editorial, headed "Borah and Blah." Borah's hostess had no connection with the editorial, but both he and Alice Longworth, even then one of his most intimate friends, thought she had. They never forgave Cissie.

Simultaneous with her marriage to Elmer Schlesinger, five years later, Countess Gizycka shook Washington out of its usual slumber by publishing her first book, "Glass Houses." In it she painted, so deftly that no one could mistake them and so brazenly that every one gasped, her old friend and her arch-enemy, Borah and Alice. This widened the breach beyond all repair.

The climax came after Cissie Schlesinger, widowed, always too active to be idle and too intelligent to be content with the routine of society, became editor-in-chief of Hearst's Washington *Herald*. A few weeks later there appeared tucked away at the bottom of the first page an insignificant looking box which brought the *Herald* more circulation in one week than it had ever gained before in years. The box read:

"INTERESTING BUT NOT TRUE

"The news is that Mrs. Alice Longworth will not only be the confidential advisor to Mrs. Ruth Hanna McCormick, but that she will campaign publicly for her lifelong friend. Interesting but not true.

"Mrs. McCormick takes no advice, political or otherwise, from Mrs. Longworth.

"Mrs. Longworth gives no interviews to the press.

"Mrs. Longworth cannot utter in public.

"Her assistance will, therefore, resolve itself, as usual, into posing for photographs."

Letters of approval and protest followed. Washington beamed. A sequel to the Gann-Longworth War had broken out. Editor Patterson, who by that time had resumed her maiden name, tried it again. The majority of her friends frowned and her enemies raved. But as a circulation-getter it was a wow.

It had only one fault. In order to create a first-class row there must be two parties to a dispute. In this case, however, there was only one. Alice refused to hit back. She continued to grant no interviews, make no speeches. She confined her activities to the thing she has always done best, posing for photographs. There is no fun in punching a deflated punching-bag, and Editor Patterson quit.

Since then she has had to be content with giving pretentious dinner parties for Mrs. William Randolph Hearst, interviewing Al Capone and Dr. Einstein, and pretending to enjoy coarse newspaper revelries at which she tries hard to be one of the gang.

*

ALICE LONGWORTH is one of those rare women who is really absorbed in politics. There are a large number of Washington ladies who flock to the Hill whenever they hear that Borah is going to blast the World Court, or Millard Tydings, Beau Brummel of the Senate, is scheduled to bait the prohibitionists, but not one of them is a regular and consistent follower of all the important things the Senate does. Alice is the sole exception. She not only attends the outstanding Senate debates and committee hearings, but behind the scenes she pulls the wires, as far as she is able, against such pet hates as the World Court, the League of Nations, and the London Naval Treaty.

The part which Mrs. Longworth plays on Capitol Hill, the prestige which she commands throughout Washington, is, of course, resented by other congressional wives, most of whom lead a dull and pompous existence in the red-plush drawing-rooms of the second class hotels which cluster around the Hill, or attend excessively stodgy teas, the guest lists of which they phone at great length to society editors.

It was natural, therefore, that a large number of these estimable ladies should have sided with Dolly Curtis Gann in the social-precedence war against her much more charming and socially powerful opponent, Alice Longworth. Not that they liked Mrs. Gann more; they merely thought of her as one of their own kind.

What was not natural, however, was that Edward Everett Gann, socially unimportant brother-in-law of the Vice President, and Nicholas Longworth, standing at the peak of social supremacy, both should have aided, abetted, spurred and egged on their respective wives in a controversy which for a time rivaled a back-alley cat fight. Edward Everett Gann has been pictured as an "unassuming man" who practised law, never troubled his head about society and led a quiet, happy life until his strapping, titian-haired wife became the official hostess of her half-brother, the Vice President. Then his wife moved him from a vine-clad home in Cleveland Park to a ten-room suite at the Mayflower Hotel, and Mr. Gann's troubles began.

All this was undoubtedly true. But to assume that Mr. Gann objected to his wife's fight for her social rights is equivalent to assuming that Herbert Hoover objects to an adjournment of Congress. Mr. Gann may be shorter and less prepossessing than his wife, he may sidle into inconspicuous corners of drawing-rooms and speak only when spoken to, but he never flinched at the major social war whirling disturbingly around his head. On the contrary, he loved it. He set his jaws and egged his wife into the fray. He subscribed to clipping bureaus. He read with avidity everything written about his wife. If he did not like it, he complained to editors. Most especially he complained about the adjectives "meek" and "mild" when prefixed to his own name. He became Washington's only rival to Italian Ambassador Martino for complaints to the newspapers.

Speaker Longworth, although more thick-skinned about the press, took the controversy just as seriously. He considered his wife's war his war, a war to uphold the dignity of the Speakership. Furthermore, it was a war on behalf of the American people. The Government of the United States, he pointed out, is vested in the people. The Constitution says so. The people are represented by the House of Representatives. It is the body closest to the people. Over this body presides the Speaker. Therefore, the Speaker should go in to dinner ahead of every one except the President.

Longworth, however, overlooked one fact. He, as Speaker of the House of Representatives, was a tremendously powerful individual. He controlled legislation in the House. He was a busy man. He had other things to do than dine out.

Charlie Curtis, on the other hand, wields no more power as presiding officer of the Senate than that of annoying its members with his gavel, as a gnat annoys a horse. To the Vice President, therefore, is given the compensating distinction of being the Administration's chief diner-out.

Actually this is not much of a compensation. Most of the dinners he is called upon to attend are given by such distinguished dowagers as Mrs. Henry F. Dimock, who wears a plumed hat and rides about in a victoria; Mrs. Clarence Crittendon Calhoun, who claims the Earl of Mar as an ancestor and gives Scotch evenings at which she displays her Tennessee husband in kilts; Mrs. François Berger Moran, who claims to be a lineal descendant of George Washington and goes marketing in ermine; Mrs. Larz Anderson, enthusiastic joiner of all possible patriotic societies; plus other starchy affairs at which the Vice President has to sit beside the wives of the Second Assistant Postmaster General, the Commander of the Army Air Corps or the Chief of the Division of International Conferences.

Smart hostesses do not fawn upon Charlie these days. His half-sister, although amiable, tries to hide her mid-western background but every so often reveals it with such abrupt indiscretions as: "Oh, Charley, come kiss me," accompanied by gestures with plump arms. Then, too, when one invites the Vice President to dinner these days it means inviting a small army, since Mr. Gann also must come along. A shadow seems to darken an otherwise scintillating party whenever the vice-presidential trio heaves into sight, and the result is that those who crack the whip with greatest success look to livelier pastures for their dinner guests.

In the official field, grazing is not so good. Among the Cabinet members, Stimson, because he gets up at five-thirty and because of his wife's health, dines out only when diplomatic decency compels it. Secretary of Agriculture Hyde gives stiff and expansive parties at the Mayflower for which he imports potted palms from the Botanical Gardens, and the tall Secretary of the Interior, Ray Lyman Wilbur, although intellectual and witty, is more ill at ease in smoothing the rough edges off a dinner conversation than when facing a senatorial committee on the Federal Power Commission. Frequently, he does not know his guests' names and behind their backs asks whispered advice from other guests as to who they are.

Of the others, Charles Francis Adams, although as taciturn as his Northampton neighbor; Andrew W. Mellon, who loves Washington society so much he is willing to take orders from Hoover; and Attorney General Mitchell are booked well in advance. Patrick Jay Hurley, Hoover's very young, very handsome and very energetic Secretary of War, however, is the Beau Brummel of the Cabinet. Hurley studied in Washington, represented the Choctaw Indian Nation in Washington and before he had reached the age of forty-five had made about $15,000,000, chiefly in Washington. Finally, he married tall, blonde and determined Ruth Wilson, daughter of a rear-admiral and from Washington. Hurley, therefore, despite the fact that he entered the Cabinet late, had a running start on the rest of his colleagues, as far as Washington society is concerned. In order to maintain his lead, he took a swank house next to Eugene Meyer's on Crescent Place, and every Wednesday his wife dutifully pours tea for itinerant Oklahomans and any others who may grace her drawing-room. The gathering is dull but politically necessary to Pat's vice-presidential ambitions.

It has been a long time since Oklahoma was honored by having a native son in the Cabinet and the State expects its

Cabinet representative to know his social onions. The neighbors from Tulsa follow every dinner and tea which Ruth and Pat attend and a whole carload of them came up for the first dinner which the Secretary of War gave to the President of the United States. They arrived a day or two earlier in order to rest up before the big event, and although showered with invitations from other less-favored Oklahomans during the two days prior to the party, they declined all of them. If there were any jaded complexions, heavy heads, or dark circles under eyes at the Hurley-Hoover dinner it was an Act of God and no fault of the Oklahoma delegation.

Ruth and Pat Hurley smiled benignly upon their neighbors and did not disclose the fact that when they first came to Washington they had been so in awe of high society that they had rehearsed their entrances and exits, their conversation and their bows, before every big party.

It is not to the Cabinet, however, that the smart hostess of Washington turns for members of officialdom who will give the right touch to her dinner parties. The Senate offers a much wider range, but out of its ninety-six members, only about a dozen are in real demand. They are: Reed of Pennsylvania, Moses of New Hampshire, Tydings of Maryland, Shipstead of Minnesota, Bingham of Connecticut, Johnson of California, Wagner of New York, Capper of Kansas and Bulkley of Ohio.

David Aiken Reed, especially since he built a palace in the neighborhood of Mr. Hoover's S Street home, put murals in his dining room and installed a telephone with a private number, has been in greater social demand than any of his senatorial colleagues.

Reed goes in for society as hard as he goes in for the Senate. He is indefatigable in regard to both. In the winter he dines out, in the spring he spends his Sundays yachting on the Potomac, in the summer he goes to Bar Harbor, and in the fall he shoots ducks. His wife, sweet-tempered and considerate, nurses her senatorial husband like the small boy he sometimes is.

Reed's only social rival is George Moses. Moses lacks the house, the murals and the private telephone, but he has two other assets—his face is not so lugubrious as Reed's nor his conversation so earnest; and, much more important, one can never tell when Moses will be subject to one of his fits of indiscretion and wax vituperative in regard to his chief *bête noir,* Herbert Hoover. Such moments, weeks later, still make a dinner party the talk of the town. Mrs. Moses, silent and self-effacing, wears a look of loyal martyrdom.

Millard Tydings, brilliant bachelor, has been known to offend sedate Georgetown ladies by playing "footie" with them under the table, but among the younger set he remains the Senate's most dined-out member. He also holds the Senate's heart-throb record. He has caused more capital beauties to dream of hooking a senatorial husband than any member of that body in years. One of them even took a trip to Reno with that in mind. Probably the secret of this is the fact that Tydings gives them no encouragement. The thought of him, clad in purple dressing-gown, painting hunting scenes in his attic studio at midnight, is enough to bring out the sacrifice complex in any woman. What could be more useful than to help a lonely Senator mold his great career?

Arthur Capper, sixty-six-year-old widower and millionaire publisher of moral journals, is not only one of the Senate's prime diners-out but probably its chief dancer-out. Debutantes flock around him like lame-ducks around a job. And despite the fact that his fox-trot has a hop in it reminiscent of a gay-nineties two-step, the debs continue to dance with him and to buy new evening slippers.

Robert Johns Bulkley is the Senate's latest contribution to the hostess's insatiable demand for something new in dinner guests. Successful wet senatorial candidate in the dry State of Ohio, he is being touted as Democratic presidential timber, and, as a result, every capital hostess is booking advance space on the Senator's friendship list. As a prosecutor in the capital's latest mystery game—"Murder"—the Senator from Ohio is a washout. The lights are turned out. There is a scream. The lights are turned on again. The prostrate figure of the murdered guest is found lying on the floor and the other guests are lined up for questioning. Then as the *pièce de résistance* of her evening, the hostess brings forth the leading attorney of Ohio and asks him to expose the guilty. He pokes a pudgy finger at each witness and inquires with mild mannered amiability: "Did you commit this crime?"

He has never yet found the criminal.

The House of Representatives, with its four hundred and thirty-five members, proportionately has even less to offer Washington hostesses than the Senate. Topping the list of eligibles are Piatt Andrew and Dick Wigglesworth of Massachusetts, Ruth McCormick of Illinois, Simms of New Mexico, Ruth Bryan Owen of Florida, Dick Aldrich of Rhode Island and Jack Wainwright, Bob Bacon, Ham Fish and Ruth Pratt, all of New York.

Piatt Andrew is the most sought-after member of the House. He is that body's most eligible and elusive bachelor. He has a mansion at Gloucester, Massachusetts, famous for a lounging room reached only by a ladder, which, to insure complete privacy, can be pulled in. His notoriety was increased when Ruth Bryan Owen, just arrived in Washington, was reputed to have thrown roses to him from the gallery of the House. The rumor that there was to be a Republican-Democratic alliance between the Representatives from Massachusetts and Florida has now been shattered.

Mrs. Owen, daughter of William Jennings Bryan, has been played up to Washington hostesses as the Congresswoman with sex appeal. Mrs. Owen is a grandmother. Before reaching the age of discretion, she eloped with a missionary named Leavitt, and later, exquisitely unhappy, was taken by her mother to Egypt where she met and married a British officer, Major Reginald Owen. Her oldest children grew up unaware that they bore the name of Leavitt. Mrs. Owen stays reasonably late at parties, is not a bad dancer and refuted the charge of being the only British subject elected to Congress.

Since her defeat for the United States Senate, the Widow McCormick has consoled herself with introducing a debutante daughter to high society and building a whoopee house in the garden of her Georgetown home, in which she dances with Congressman Simms, another lame-duck. Mrs. McCormick prefers to dine at home rather than at large, and gives intimate dinner parties, to which she invites a mixture of Senators, newspapermen and would-be intellectuals, serving them with tomato-juice cocktails and champagne cider. Chiefly because her late husband, Medill McCormick, was a famous wet, she is the strictest dry in Washington society.

Outside of these cases, the expert hostess finds Capitol Hill a dry and sterile desert. Nor is there more abundant harvest in other official fields. The Army and the Navy move in a social world all their own. Their wealthier members drink mint-juleps on summer evenings at the Chevy Chase Club and the less wealthy do the same thing at the Army, Navy and Marine Corps Country Club. With a few exceptions, their conversation is as inspiring as that of the Army's ex-Chief-of-Staff, General Charles P. Summerall, who, when he sits beside a young and beautiful lady, invariably expounds the glories of a military career.

Among the few exceptions are Admiral William V. Pratt, who is so original in his thinking that he is always about five laps ahead of the State Department and ten ahead of the Navy; General Douglas MacArthur, young, bald, and a great glad-hander, whose promotion to be Chief-of-Staff brought fleeting pangs of pain to the present Mrs. Lionel Atwill (the former Mrs. MacArthur); General Charles Laurie McCawley, charming and diminutive Marine Corps officer; and Colonel Louis McNulty Little, who, with his wife, the former Elsie Cobb Wilson, make one of the most delightful couples in Washington.

With them, although not strictly military, should be included Trubee Davison, and David Sinton Ingalls, Assistant Secretaries of War and the Navy for Aviation. Together with Lou Douglas, lone Congressman from the State of Arizona, they are seen at most of the smart dinner tables and even more frequently in each other's company.

Trubee Davison has started early to do what his late father, partner in the firm of J. P. Morgan, always wanted to do—use his wealth and ability in some public service. As a result, Trubee works at his "little cabinet" job as if it were the most important in the world and the Air Corps is devoted to him. His wife, once Dorothy Peabody, is the daughter of the head of Groton where Trubee went to school, and she has never been able quite to get accustomed to spending money after the manner of those born with silver spoons in their mouths. As a result she requisitions army trucks and soldiers to move her household goods and sends army airplanes from her Long Island home to bring silver she has forgotten to take with her from Washington. She smokes a pipe through preference rather than affectation and is an extremely efficient mother to four small children.

Trubee, sometimes inclined to be as precocious as his six-year-old, has developed the trick of getting himself out of a locked mail-bag, which he will demonstrate when sufficiently urged. Once when his neighbor, Mrs. Maud Torr, had gone off to the movies, leaving her husband, Secretary of the British Embassy, enthralled with the brilliant chit-chat and suppressed desires of Nancy Hoyt, Trubee decided to play the rôle of Protector of the Home. Getting Lou Douglas to drag him, locked inside his mail bag, into the Torr home, Trubee flounced all over the room, upset chairs, knocked down the fire screen trying to extract himself. Finally, red-faced and almost suffocated, Douglas had to extract him. The trick catch on the lock had slipped.

The social sterility of the official field causes the capital's most successful whip-crackers to do a great deal of shopping on the outside. Their constant problem is to find a combination of State Department, diplomatic, congressional, George

town and journalistic dinner guests who will put sufficient
snap into the evening without precipitating any severe social
ructions. Each hostess usually has her own dinner pets, with
the result that people find themselves gravitating into groups
whose members see increasingly more of one another, and,
perhaps as a commentary on their breadth of vision, never
seem to be bored.

There are, of course, groups within groups, cliques within
cliques, and overlapping of cliques and groups, but probably
the three most interesting and well-recognized of these self-
gravitating sets are those who until Nick's death played for
high stakes under the slap-dash inspiration of Laura Curtis
and the Longworths; those who go in for political conversation at the prodding of Mrs. Borden Harriman and Mrs.
Frank West; and those who go in for conservative drinking,
conservative dancing and conservative love-making when sufficiently chaperoned by the younger Britishers, the Canadi-
ans and the H.B.V.'s.

The Curtis-Longworth parties were always wringing wet and
usually terminated in poker, although frequently not until
Nick had yielded to a demand that he play his violin. Alice
and Nick long ago had reached a very amicable understanding that each could go more or less his or her own way, with
the result that the two frequently turned up at entirely different parties, or, if they came together, Alice sometimes left
long before Nick remembered that somehow or other he had
to wield the gavel in the Speaker's chair at twelve o'clock sharp
the next morning. This was one of the things that Cissie Patterson upset with her blast against Alice in the Washington
Herald. Nick used to be a regular visitor at the Patterson du
Pont Circle home, but the open attack on his wife was even
more than his amiable indifference could tolerate.

Other ladies who move only in the highest circles have
equally amicable arrangements worked out with their husbands, provided they still retain such appendages. Among these
are Mrs. Truxton Beale, who, although devoted to her aging

husband, sometimes leaves him for airplane jaunts over Egypt and the Arabian desert; and Mrs. Tracy Dows, who went off to Europe several years ago a gray-haired, plump, and somewhat sedentary matron, to come back a few months later with golden hair and a vanished waistline. She promptly left her husband in New York, and, except when he comes down for Thanksgiving or Christmas, leads the life of a grass widow, dabbling her fingers into the Washington social stream where it runs hot but not too swift.

Alice Dows and Marie Beale both moved with grace and dignity in the Laura Curtis-Nick Longworth set, and, along with Cornelia Mayo, were sometimes referred to as Nick's girls, although the first two never asked the Speaker's intervention to get them an invitation to a costume ball.

In the same set also move Mr. and Mrs. John Philip Hill, the former being Baltimore's most ardent wet and the man who, by fermenting grape juice in his cellar and daring the prohibition officials to prevent him, won back for the American people their biblical right to make wine out of water.

Not exactly in this group, but not exactly outside it, are two families for whose parties a good many people break their necks to wangle invitations. They are the Henry Leonards, famous for the Butler-Mussolini court martial case, and Mr. and Mrs. Eugene Meyer, the former famous as the only man who never lost his temper with Senator Brookhart.

Eugene Meyer has been a perpetual official-holder ever since the Wilson Administration and he has been an able one. Why he puts up with the senatorial brick-bats that come his way, as a reward for accepting an insignificant salary for doing a $50,000 a year job, is what some of his New York friends cannot understand. The secret is that Meyer has all the money he wants and gets no thrill at all out of making more. His wife, Agnes, goes in for Chinese art, Mayan architecture and dinner-dances, one of which touched off the Gann-Longworth row.

Ellen Warder Leonard, sister of Alice Garrett, American

Ambassadress in Rome, has the most attractive garden in Georgetown, one of the most attractive husbands in Washington, four grandchildren and the patience of Job. Her husband, a one-armed and retired Major in the Marine Corps, can outride, outbluff and outcourt any man between Colorado, where he spends his summers, and Virginia, where he is in constant demand as a horse-show judge. It was Leonard who bluffed Hoover and the State Department out of the Smedley Butler court martial.

A whip-cracker in her own right, Mrs. Edward B. McLean was also once a member of the Poker Players. Now she sits alone at "Friendship," the vast McLean estate on the northwest edge of the city, leads a hermit existence in Florida, or swears out warrants to have her husband prevented from divorcing her in Mexico.

There was a day when two bands imported from New York jazzed alternately at the opposite ends of the McLean ballroom, when several hundred bottles of champagne were opened in an evening and when the most select of social Washington uncertainly danced the New Year into the dawn. There was also a day when Ned McLean dined regularly at the White House, and on such days that he didn't, Warren Gamaliel Harding dined or cocktailed with him at the Little Green House on K Street. There was a day when the Washington *Post* influenced administration policy and brought both Evelyn and Ned power and prestige. Those days are now over. Mrs. McLean still has the Hope diamond but wears it almost never. Ned McLean is rarely seen at the White House and has auctioned off his famous racing stable in Virginia.

The end came with their marital break. Together they were a power in Washington. Diplomats, the State Department, even the White House, feared them. Alone they are nothing —nothing more than divorce and alimony news blurted out on the front page of the McLean newspapers.

*

LIKE every other social group in the capital, the politico-intellectuals are dominated by widowed ladies bored with New York, San Francisco and Chicago who have settled in Washington to amuse themselves with the profundities of politicians and the jingles of journalists. Probably the most interesting and only semi-serious social group in Washington, it is led by the Widow Harriman, godmother of the Democratic Party, by the Widow West, a newcomer into Democracy who takes it most seriously, and by two such irreconcilable Republicans as the Widows Keep and McCormick.

Daisy Harriman has a disposition so magnanimous that she has seldom been known to say an unkind word about any one except members of the reigning Republican Party. But there are two things Daisy loves almost as much as she does the Democratic Party. These are: to bait Tom Walsh and to give deliciously scrambled dinner parties at which the Republican Administration is dissected piece by piece and pronounced unfit ever again to regain the voters' confidence.

There was a day when Washington expected Daisy Harriman to marry Senator Walsh. There was also a day when Daisy herself thought rather seriously about it. At first it was his mustache which deterred her. It was of the long, weeping-willow variety so fashionable among prospectors who have long been away from both civilization and scissors in the Senator's home state. It used to strain the vegetables from the soup and gather globules of mayonnaise that glistened in the candle-light. Finally Daisy persuaded the Senator to trim it. There is a suspicion among her friends that she achieved this only on the promise that she would marry him and that, after achieving it, she went back on her word.

Walsh was decidedly difficult after this and it took Daisy several years of persuasion to score with him again. Her next goal was his great protruding eyebrows that jutted out from his forehead as sagebrush off a cliff. They gave his eyes a cadaverous effect, and when he hammered on the table and demanded the facts regarding Teapot Dome, it seemed to

Harry F. Sinclair that Walsh was looking at him from a long way off and peering right straight down into his harassed soul.

But Daisy didn't appreciate this, and eventually she took her own scissors and sheared the Senator, as Samson was shorn of yore.

Walsh is milder and fairly manageable now. Occasionally, when Daisy has over-exploited him for the benefit of her dinner guests, he sulks a little and boycotts her parties. But for the most part, he performs grimly and dutifully and loves it. A strange couple, they have all the affection for each other that a purely platonic friendship can have without the chafing of married life.

Gravitating in the same politico-intellectual orbit is Birne West, wealthy California widow, beautiful, witty, greedily on the lookout for unexploited dinner guests, a specialist at mixing soup and Senators, always able to get the maximum kick out of her own jokes; Mrs. Frederick (Florence) Keep, gentle, considerate, gracious, with one of the few well-stocked cellars in Washington, and a sister, Miss Mabel Boardman, whom the Prince of Wales once mistook for his royal mother; Adolph and Mary Miller, the former solemn and always ready to expound on the Federal Reserve Board on which he sits; a scattering of newspapermen—the Oulahans, the Hards and the Ned Lowrys plus the Edward Burlings, whose log cabin up the Potomac is the rendezvous every Sunday for most of the above.

Most of them will not admit they are intellectuals. They affect a sense of humor about life, but if they ever got frank with themselves they would confess to a considerable amount of intellectual egocentricism. And, as a matter of fact, they come closest to being the only intellectuals able to exist in the rarefied atmosphere of social Washington.

*

SOCIAL life among the younger set is never static in the capital. It ebbs and flows. Debutantes bud, blossom, marry and move away, to come back years later when they are divorced, to settle down and eventually take over the place of some exalted society whip-cracker who has retired from the ring. In the same way, the fledglings of the State Department's white-spat corps are ordered to Callao, Singapore and Cape Town, to come back years later as always available last-minute dinner guests for distracted hostesses. In general, however, it is safe to assume that the perennial Leander Goodhart McCormick and his charming wife Janet will always be on hand, and that the really select members of the younger crowd will be dominated by the attachés of the British Embassy, the Canadian Legation and the H.B.V.'s, which used to be considered very shocking and very secret initials, but which now are blurted out across any dinner table as the "High Bosomed Virgins."

CHAPTER TWO

STARCHED FUTILITY

*F*ROM the point of view of the Diplomatic Corps, Washington is the most unique capital in the world.

It is, for instance, the only capital where the Minister of Guatemala is more important to a foreign office than the Ambassador of Spain.

It is, for instance, the only capital where the Minister of Nicaragua is more important to a foreign office than the envoys from Finland, Latvia, Esthonia, Lithuania and Denmark, all put together.

It is for instance, the only capital where the Minister of Panama may sit absolutely quiet in Washington and receive a telegram from his Supreme Court asking him to assume the Presidency of his country.

The secret of this, of course, is the United States' Economic Empire to the south. The total number of American dollars invested in the banana and coffee plantations of infinitesimal Guatemala just about equal those invested in the mines and street railways of much vaster and more populated Spain. And, in addition, Guatemala is much nearer the Panama Canal. Spain may suffer a revolution and it will not even occur to the State Department to send cruisers and marines. But if revolution breaks out in Guatemala, not only does the State Department immediately suffer a gunboat complex, but it also notifies the revolutionary leader that he cannot become President.

There are five other Central American countries, plus three in the Caribbean, plus twelve on the South American continent and Mexico, whose envoys get flowers, fruit and polite messages every time their President has a birthday, they leave on a vacation, or their wives give birth to twins.

All this, of course, is a mere matter of business routine. After the State Department closes its doors at four-thirty, its socially minded young men, with the exception of Francis White, who cannot help himself, are to be found, not in the homes of Latin-American envoys, whom they fête by day, but cocktailing and dining among those diplomats who seldom have to concern themselves with affairs of state but are skilled in saying the right word at the right time.

Washington's Diplomatic Corps, therefore, might be divided into two parts:

Those who dine out and those who dine at home.

Or to paraphrase, the Corps might be divided into those who dine out and those who work.

This, however, would not be strictly accurate. There would have to be noted such distinguished exceptions as:

> The British Ambassador, Sir Ronald Lindsay, who is invited out both because he is charming and because he represents His Majesty's far-flung Empire, and yet, despite all that, manages, in a dull, British sort of way, to turn out a reasonable amount of work.

> The Cuban Ambassador, Orestes Ferrara, who is invited out because of his wit rather than the importance of his country, but who none the less works early in the morning and late into the night.

> The Bolivian Minister, Diez de Medina, whom scarcely any one invites out, and who, having no work to do, manages to get involved in all kinds of remarkable and compromising situations.

For purposes of strict accuracy, therefore, it is necessary to divide the Diplomatic Corps into four groups, which, except when they attend the Secretary of State's breakfast on New Year's Day or the Diplomatic Reception at the White House, have about as much in common as Dolly Gann and Alice Longworth. They are:

The Smart Set, which includes the important European envoys who have to be invited out, regardless of their wealth or their wives, plus a lot of lesser lights who are asked out in order to counterbalance the deadheads and give a little leavening to the party.

The Latin Americans, whose leading Ambassadors rate just as high officially but not socially as the Big Five of Europe.

The Asiatics, who keep very much to themselves.

The Balkan, Near East and the Border States, beneath whose appearance of boredom run some of the most bizarre lives in Washington.

*

UNTIL the British Empire becomes infinitely more down-at-the-heel than it now is, its Ambassador, no matter whether he be prosaic or platitudinous, always will be the most dominant figure in the Diplomatic Corps. So to-day, the British Empire, still being one with which the United States has been able to achieve only paper naval parity, Sir Ronald Lindsay, outranks, in power and prestige, every other Ambassador in Washington. He achieves this despite the fact that Ambassador Tellez of Mexico, Dean of the Corps, is a much abler man; despite the fact that Sir Ronald is very new and a little green; despite the fact that he is deaf; and despite the fact that his wife, because of her illness, has an unhappy way of stepping on people's pet theories. The answer is that the British Empire is simply too powerful to take a back seat.

Sir Ronald would be a distinguished and dominant diplomat whatever country he represented. Somewhat less charming but far more canny than his predecessor, Sir Esme Howard, Lindsay would be the last one in the world to answer a letter written by a Virginia dry promising to import no more liquor for the British Embassy—a promise, which, although sincerely given by poor old Sir Esme, never got him any credit even from the drys, due to the fact that his irate undersecretaries let slip the fact that his cellar was stocked with much more than he could ever drink up before his retirement.

Nor would Sir Ronald Lindsay ever make the mistake of leaving Washington for the North Shore, as did Sir Esme in 1927, just on the eve of a naval conference which, due partially to his absence, was to make Anglo-American history by marring Anglo-American friendship. Lindsay has made only one break so far and that was a very minor and rather amusing one which occurred when he met Drew Pearson, of the Baltimore *Sun,* in the halls of the State Department, and, thinking he was an assistant of Secretary Stimson's, told him about the very confidential steps Great Britain and the United States were taking to bring France and Italy into the London Naval Conference. Pearson never published the news until some days later, when he received permission from both Ambassador Lindsay and the State Department, but for the moment, Sir Ronald was as embarrassed as a third secretary who has spilled ice cream down the neck of his Ambassadress.

Lindsay is a Scotsman whose six feet eight inches, in Highland kilts and bare knees, make a rare figure of a man. Washington has never seen him thus garbed, but it would like to. He has a great drooping mustache of the Senator Walsh type before Daisy Harriman induced him to trim it, and his deafness makes him incline his massive shoulders slightly nearer the earth in order to catch the words of those who would talk with him from below.

Lady Lindsay is a nervous and irritable lady who spent one of the hottest summers Washington has ever known moving furniture to the new British Embassy on Massachusetts Avenue and telling curious people who insisted on getting early glimpses of the establishment to "please do not track up the rugs" or "please don't move those chairs," with the result that by midsummer she had to be taken to Long Island in an ambulance.

The British Embassy, until a Socialist Government came into power, used to be the social arbiter of Washington, and a bid to dine there was more coveted by some than an invitation to the White House. Those days are now about as antiquated as the White House cocktail parties of the Harding administration, due not only to the advent of the Labor Party but also to the departure of Sir Adrian Bailey and Henry Hopkinson, who, having no great talents in any other direction, concentrated upon dinners and debutantes. The British Embassy for the most part is now a cold and silent tomb perched upon the hill, to be lighted up only for such formal and stodgy occasions as diplomacy requires.

The other leaders of the Smart Set within the Diplomatic Corps include von Prittwitz of Germany, de Martino of Italy, Claudel of France, and, until the hurried exit of Alfonso, Padilla of Spain. Next to Claudel, the most celebrated of these is the small and wiry little personage who bears the name Nobile Giacomo de Martino, Ambassador of the Royal Italian Government.

The type of celebrity Martino has achieved is vastly different from Claudel's. It verges on notoriety. He won it, first, through the Fascist League of North America and its persecution of Italians in the United States; second, through Major General Smedley D. Butler, U.S.M.C.

Like many men of small stature, Martino makes up for his height by his pugnacious persistence. Long before General Butler put him on the map with the general public, Martino had come to have the same relation to State Department officials as a mosquito to a malarial patient.

He called at the Department on every possible occasion and pretext. If he could find no pretext, he called to chat about the weather. It is no exaggeration to say that he called and still calls more frequently than all the other members of the Diplomatic Corps put together. He subscribes to a most comprehensive clipping service and whenever he finds that an editor, even in Sioux City or Okmulgee, is maligning his

Fascist chief, Martino trots down to the State Department to complain. The fact that the State Department's reply is always the same—"The United States has no censorship as you do in Italy"—does not deter Martino a bit. He always comes back for more.

The State Department, therefore, did not show one glimmer of surprise when Martino turned up one morning with a clipping from the Philadelphia *Record* reporting that the most distinguished officer in the Marine Corps had branded the Dictator of Italy as a hit-and-run driver. The *Record* happens to have the smallest circulation of any Philadelphia newspaper. If Martino had not brought the clipping down to the State Department, probably no more than a mere handful of people would have noticed Butler's accusation. After he called, several million became firmly convinced that Mussolini did run over a child and did exclaim: "What is one life in the affairs of a State?"

But for Martino that clipping was a great opportunity. At last he had the State Department where he wanted it. No longer could Bill Castle turn him off with the reminder that there was no censorship in the United States. This was a commissioned officer in the service of the United States who had spoken. It was not only a great opportunity, but it was heaven-sent. The Fascist Consul in New York had been dimming Martino's luster. He had been getting credit in Rome for being the real Ambassador to the United States. Martino needed some such incident as this, and, sparing no cable costs, he promptly wired his Fascist Chief all the details.

No one, therefore, was more pleased with himself than the persistent little Ambassador when he came to the State Department to receive Secretary Stimson's note of "deep regret." He fell all over himself in his haste to get to the cable office and put the results of his victory on the wires to Rome.

His smug self-satisfaction lasted but two days. The court martial ordered by the Navy Department proved a boomerang. It hit back at Mussolini with a thousand times the force of the original Butler speech. It stripped away all of the kudos Martino had stored up for himself in Rome. It made people believe that Mussolini really was the bad man General Butler said he was.

Given facts like these, Martino did what he has always done. He called at the State Department. He expressed the view that as far as Italy was concerned the incident was not only "closed but forgotten." A court martial, he said, would be highly embarrassing. Mr. Stimson did the rest. Ambassador Martino achieved at least one victory. The court martial was dropped.

*

BETWEEN Friedrich W. von Prittwitz und Gaffron, Ambassador of Germany, and the amiable Otto Kiep, his Counselor, there was a rivalry that they scarcely took the trouble to conceal.

The Ambassador, sometimes called "von Nittwitz" by his less appreciative admirers, was awarded the Washington post in return for the many hours and days spent bowing low over the hand of Frau Stresemann. Frau Stresemann's husband, however, has now passed on to a place where he can no longer be Foreign Minister of Germany, and Von Prittwitz must stand on his own two feet.

Amiable Otto Kiep knew this probably as well as any one —perhaps better than Von Prittwitz. And, therefore, Otto, despite a wife who has been known to take him off a ballroom floor for cheek-dancing with a beautiful matron, continued to be amiable and to throw dinners famous for their roast goose, red cabbage, and Rhine wine.

And when the Ambassador went away on vacation—which he did regularly and at some length, Amiable Otto was in his element. He raked up armfuls of distinguished German visitors to present at the White House. He sent lengthy cables to the Foreign Office, reporting in detail what President Hoover told each visitor. And he sent even lengthier cables reporting what the American people, the American press, the American State Department and the American Diplomatic Corps were thinking and saying about Germany in general, and about Amiable Otto Kiep in particular. The Embassy's cable bills increased about threefold when Kiep took charge; but why should he worry when each cable was a step toward his greatest ambition—the under-Secretaryship of the Foreign Office.

Or so he thought.

His father-in-law was one of Prussia's prosperous barons of big business. His brother had designed the German greyhounds, Bremen and Europa. He himself had been offered a $60,000 job with a German-American business house. Nothing, apparently, could block the onward march of his ambition.

But something did. Either Von Prittwitz was more powerful than any one dreamed, or else Kiep's cable bills were higher than the Foreign Office could stomach. At any rate, he was demoted to be Consul General in New York, where he pretends to be highly pleased with an East Side pent house, submits reports which have to be approved by his arch-enemy, the Ambassador, and takes frequent and wistful trips to see his old friends in Washington.

The Ambassador is young and looks younger than he is. He has a young and attractive wife, and they have a young daughter. They make an attractive-appearing couple and if they were not so shy they would not be unattractive to talk to. As a glad-hander, the Ambassador is a washout. This is a calamity, because his predecessor, the late Von Maltzan, was an adept at this art, and his rival, Amiable Otto, has torn several pages out of Maltzan's book. Probably the unhappiest moments Von Prittwitz ever spent in Washington were when he attempted to glad-hand newspapermen at a beer *abend* and had to submit to the embrace and heavy-laden breathing of the most bibulous star in Hearst's diadem, while he expounded on the good-fellowship of the German people, despite their alleged atrocities in Belgium.

Whether he is responsible for it or not, Von Prittwitz heads the most efficient Embassy in Washington. No article unfavorable to Germany is written without the Embassy spotting it and approaching the author, if he is approachable, with a dinner or luncheon invitation. Rudolf Leitner, an Austrian, is unquestionably the brains of the Embassy, being ably supported by Emil Baer and Johann Lohmann. The staff is one of the hardest working and least social in the capital.

Probably the opposite is true of the Spanish Embassy, which, as before noted, is about as important to the State Department as the Guatemalan Legation, but which maintains eight full-fledged secretaries and attachés, as against Guatemala's two. The answer is that Spanish prestige requires an Embassy and, therefore, also, the military attachés, naval attachés and all the social personnel and paraphernalia that go with it.

Despite all its trappings, the Spanish Embassy is pleasantly and naturally social, and probably will continue to be just as much so under a republic as under a monarchy. Ambassador Padilla had little to do except look over his Madrid cable every morning, twirl his black mustache and announce excitedly: "Spain is quiet." Once in a long while he went down to the State Department to denounce the Treasury Department's restrictions against Spanish cork or to complain bitterly to Bill Castle that Spain should have been a charter member of the Kellogg-Briand Outlawry of War Society. Two or three times each winter he sallied forth to the Metropolis for an opening of the New York opera.

His one really great accomplishment was in forcing the State Department, after one hundred and ten years of obstinacy, to promise damages for Andrew Jackson's raid into West Florida in 1814, when Florida was then sovereign Spanish territory.

But on such rare occasions as Senor Don Alejandro was thus occupied, the social life of the Embassy ran smoothly and charmingly under the guidance of his son and two daughters, of whom Rosa, the eldest, was one of the most attractive girls in Washington. They gave dull and formal dinner parties in the winter and made up for it in the summer by doing the devil's dip at Glen Echo or staging midnight parties around the fountain that cools the Embassy patio. After all—Spanish temperament is very warm—and it has been a long time since the war of 1898.

*

THERE are numerous diplomats who wedge their way into the Smart Set, not through the weight and prestige of the governments they serve but through: one, the power of their money: two, the charm of their personalities: or three, the attraction of their reputations. Representative of these three categories in their respective order are Count Szechenyi of Hungary, Michael MacWhite of the Irish Free State, and Davila of Rumania.

Laszlo Szechenyi, Scots-Hungarian, with more of the Magyar in him than the Scot, counts diplomatically only because he married Gladys Vanderbilt and her accompanying millions. Heavy jowled, always with a black patch over one eye, Szechenyi is the most sinister-looking figure in the Diplomatic Corps, but one who, when sufficiently imbued with the spirit of the evening, has been known to doff his tail coat, drape a rug around his portly hips and imitate a bonny Scot clad in native tartan dancing the Highland Fling.

Szechenyi is the leader of a little group of diplomats, who, headed by the Red-baiting Bill Castle, have taken a solemn vow to wage unceasing international guerilla warfare against radicals. Szechenyi it was who prompted the State Department to bar for so many years the harmless Count Karolyi who later won the pity of lecture-loving old ladies when Secretary Stimson finally admitted him to the United States. And Szechenyi it was again who, when fourteen Jewish working girls came over from Baltimore to parade in front of his legation, jumped into his high-powered roadster and disappeared down Sixteenth Street.

Michael MacWhite has no mission in the United States

other than to exercise his personality, and this he does to the credit and glory of the Irish Free State. MacWhite is one of those engaging individuals with the usual Irish smile and a frankness that is rare even in an Irishman. When, as a member of the British Empire Delegation, he represented the Irish Free State at the Geneva Naval Conference in 1927, he remarked to an American journalist:

"This is the only time the British and you Yankees have sat down at a conference table side by side and the Yanks haven't been licked. I hope ye keep it up."

As a representative of the Irish Free State at the League of Nations for many years, MacWhite always refused to use English. Whenever he addressed the League Assembly, as he frequently did, he used French, because, as he explained it, "I can't speak my own language, and I'll be damned if I'll speak English."

Such a man performs exactly the duties the Free State Government and Irish-American Societies want an Irish Minister to perform, and as a result he is constantly on tour.

Charles A. Davila is socially there. As to how he got there, there are various stories. Some attribute his arrival to the contrast of his brown shoulders with his snow white bathing suit as he lounges in the sand at Bailey's Beach. Some say it is the same charm which won for him a betrothal with Belle Baruch, daughter of Bernard Baruch, or again the charm which beguiled the New York chorus lady who later cost him such embarrassing litigation.

At any rate, there can be no question that Davila has a fascinating reputation and that this reputation wins for him a place, albeit not the most sought-after place, but, nevertheless, a very refulgent place in Washington's diplomatic and social life.

Davila happened to come to Washington because as a member of a Rumanian financial mission in Paris, he wooed and won—temporarily, at least—Miss Belle Baruch, whose father was one of the monied mainstays of the Wilson Ad-

ministration. Miss Baruch was not satisfied with the prospect of marrying a mere financial attaché. She was interested
in bigger game, and, so the story goes, promised to wed the
young Rumanian if he bagged a major diplomatic post.
Davila promptly telegraphed Bucharest, reporting that he was
engaged to the daughter of the influential Mr. Baruch and
suggested that in view of the American prestige, which would
undoubtedly accrue through this alliance, the legation in
Washington should be his. Either the telegram was garbled
or else the Foreign Office did not know its United States
Senate, for Bucharest decided that any one who married the
daughter of the chairman of the Senate Foreign Relations
Committee certainly should be sent to Washington. Later,
Cretziano, who objected to being ousted from his comfortable
post by such a youngster, had the pleasure of writing to the
Foreign Office somewhat as follows:

"I beg to inform you that Senator Borah, Chairman of the
Foreign Relations Committee, has no children. It seems incredible, therefore, that the newly appointed Minister is to be
married to his daughter."

In the end, Miss Baruch let Davila down. The marriage
has never come off. There have been constant rumors of an
announcement, but so far the rumors have borne no crop
and Washington is beginning to wonder just what happened.
The most likely explanation is that Miss Baruch became
peeved over the triangular story of Davila, the chorus girl and
the ring.

It happened this way: Davila suggested to a lady with a
willing disposition that she go out and buy herself a trinket
—a ring, perhaps—anything reasonable. The lady went out,
but on the way consulted a male friend who was experienced
in these matters, and received the suggestion that she borrow
from him a ring belonging to another woman to whom he had
advanced $500. The lady with the willing disposition was
then to collect from Davila to the tune of $1,000 and bring
the ring back. All went well except for one hitch. The lady

with the willing disposition did not bring the ring back at all. She kept it. Shortly thereafter, its original owner went to the male friend who was experienced in these matters, placed $500 in his hands and demanded her bauble.

The whole thing came to light when the latter lady became overly insistent and sued Davila, as the original giver, for the return of her property.

The incident vexed only one person more than it did Miss Baruch. He was Carlos Davila, Ambassador of Chile, whose photograph appeared in the newspapers instead of that of Davila, the Rumanian.

*

THE line of demarcation between the Smart Set which dines out and the Latin Americans who work at home is not a straight one. It wavers in the cases of Ambassador Tellez of Mexico, Davila of Chile, Ferrara of Cuba and Amoral of Brazil. The first three are men of exceptional ability, considerable charm, and represent countries whose good will is supremely important to the Latin-American policy of the United States. Ambassador Gurgel do Amoral differed from them only in that his duties never sat very heavily upon his shoulders. He would rather feed his cats than read dispatches from Rio. In fact, he would almost rather feed his cats than make love, which any one who knows Amoral's past may consider an extreme statement.

The Ambassador is a colorful, soulful figure who moved with starched precision across Washington's official stage. He is charmingly, even naïvely, of the *vieille noblesse*. He bows exquisitely from the waist. His pet abominations are motorcycles and flies. In these, his maturer years, his chief love is cats.

Amoral's affection for cats began as a small child. His father preferred dogs. His mother favored cats. Gurgel, torn between two desires, finally decided that cats needed protection from their enemies. His mother's pet cat, Nyssah, was torn to death by two dogs when she lost her balance and fell from the wall of the Amoral home in Rio. Another pet, Bilontra, was instantly killed by a Great Dane. Saddened by their fate, young Amoral determined to be the champion and protector of all persecuted pussies in the future. He has kept his word. In Hyde Park, London, two of the Ambassador's cats rest under marble slabs. In Berlin a granite shaft adorned with a medallion in bronze commemorates a cat named Menina. When, in reward for Amoral's too great loyalty to the late Government of Brazil, the revolutionists demoted him to Tokyo, Flit, his pet pussy, went with him.

Only two rules govern Amoral's feline existence: no cat shall eat mice, and no cat has more than one life.

*

DURING that hectic period prior to 1923, when Charles Evans Hughes and Charles Beecher Warren were trying to jockey Mexico out of the victories won by her revolution in return for American recognition, there sat in the Mexican Embassy in Washington a black-haired, black-eyed youngster named Manuel C. Tellez, who, as far as Mexico was concerned, ran this end of the show.

Finally, after Hughes backed down, and—without a settlement of the petroleum or agrarian controversy—recognized Mexico, this youngster was selected to stay on in the Embassy at Washington as Ambassador. That selection nearly provoked a social revolution in Mexico City. The Washington post was looked upon as a prize political plum. A dozen or more politicians, some of them powerful, were clamoring for it as just reward for their aid to Plutarco Calles and the Revolution. But Calles wanted a man who knew how to handle the State Department and, despite the youth of the nominee, despite the clamor in Mexico City, Calles stuck to his original decision.

Two years passed—two years of bitter controversy. The irate and irascible Frank B. Kellogg had written note after note —all private—to his Ambassador in Mexico City, James R. Sheffield. They were filled with invective. Sheffield answered back in kind. Suddenly the notes fell into the hands of the Mexican Government. Tellez brought them down to the State Department and politely handed them back to Mr. Kellogg. The latter raged. His face was crimson. He claimed the notes were forgeries. Tellez knew they were not. Privately, Kellogg suspected Tellez of stealing them. He ordered every scrap of waste paper burned before it left the State Department. He ordered an investigation of his clerks, his diplomatic couriers, his translators. Tellez was one of the most suspected men in Washington. Members of the State Department scarcely would speak to him. Kellogg handed him a note, announcing that Mexico was on trial before the world. But he stayed on.

To-day, Ambassador Tellez—Dean of the Diplomatic Corps —still a young man—stands at the head of the line when the diplomats greet the President on New Year's morning. He is the first to enter the dining-room at almost every official dinner. He outranks the Senate, the Cabinet, the Secretary of State, and the Speaker of the House of Representatives.

All of which may be mere mush to some people, but to the State Department it means that the youngster who has won every diplomatic joust with the Colossus of the North is still guarding the Rio Grande.

*

ARGENTINA, most powerful nation of Latin America, ought to have in Washington an Ambassador of the Tellez type. It has not. Manuel Malbran is weak, flabby and full of vague ideas about powerful protests he expects some day to make to the State Department about the tariff on meat, wheat and flaxseed, but never effectually does. He is a career diplomat of the Latin-American type, which means an AA rating for phlegmatic inertia. Career diplomats of any nationality are bad enough, but the Latin-American variety mixes all the laziness of the professional dilettante with none of the social charm of his European colleague.

Malbran is now on his second tour of duty in Washington. The first tour ended in a way that few people know about and Malbran hates to recall. His pay was cut off by President Irigoyen; no diplomatic dispatches were routed to him by the Argentine Foreign Office; and he was left high and dry in Washington, not knowing whether he was Ambassador or totem pole.

An Ambassador does not object, usually, to being transferred, and sometimes, provided he can rise up in his wrath and get a lot of publicity for himself by a war of words with his home government, he does not even object to resigning. But to be totally ignored, to have the State Department take pity on your ignorance by sending you copies of the correspondence received direct from Buenos Aires, to have all your colleagues smile knowingly behind your back—that is the worst fate that can ever befall a diplomat. And that was the fate that befell Malbran. Loyal career man that he is, however, he has now swallowed his pride and is back in Washington working once more for the glory of his country and $25,000 a year.

Among the other Latin-American diplomats the most outstanding are the suave and urbane Don Manuel de Freyre y Santander, Ambassador of Peru, who needs only a monocle to make him the most complete Englishman in the United States, and who, although very new to Washington, is rapidly becoming one of the social satellites of the Corps; the ashen-faced Diez de Medina, of Bolivia, described by one of his colleagues as having the rank of Minister, the brains of a third secretary and the habits of a military attaché; and the tall and gawky Juan B. Sacasa, Minister of Nicaragua.

Sacasa had one of the greatest triumphs of his life when

he walked into the White House to present his credentials
as Minister to the United States. Three years before that
triumphal entry, Sacasa, then Vice President of Nicaragua,
had cooled his heels in the ante-room and corridors of the
State Department for months trying to persuade its officials
that he, rather than Chamorro, the revolutionist, should be
recognized as President of Nicaragua. He failed to get anything more than sympathy, and returned to Nicaragua. En
route he stopped in Mexico and, having become friendly in
Washington with Ambassador Tellez, he got from President
Calles more concrete encouragement—arms and ammunition.
The rest of the story was blazoned black and bold in the headlines of the newspapers of that day—how Frank B. Kellogg
sent fifteen warships and five thousand marines to quell Sacasa's forces, and how Henry L. Stimson finally went as
peacemaker, pledging supervision of the election by which
Sacasa's Liberals won a sweeping electoral victory, Jose Moncada becoming President, and Sacasa, Minister to Washington.

The Latin-American members of the Diplomatic Corps
for the most part are able men and work hard. They have to.
Next to the President and one or two Cabinet officers, they
hold the most important post in their government. They
represent their nation of one or two or perhaps ten million
people at the capital of the mightiest nation in the world, a
nation which controls most of the world's gold, a nation
whose tariff may overnight ruin their export trade, a nation
whose State Department may cause revolution by the mere
refusal of a loan, a nation which has proclaimed a Monroe
Doctrine by which it sets itself up as the protector of all the
Western Hemisphere, a nation which, in short, holds all but
the three largest governments of Latin America literally in
the palm of its hand.

No wonder then that Washington's Latin-American Diplomatic Corps works hard. No wonder, also, that when they
seek recreation they herd together, rarely mingling with

their European colleagues or the State Department's social satellites. A powerful enemy develops the herd instinct.

*

FROM a social, political and economic point of view, most of the diplomats representing the Asiatic, Balkan, and so-called Border States might just as well pack their rugs in moth balls, discharge their cooks, and cut down their national budgets by the cost of one Washington Legation per year. Except for the telephone girls in the Hotel Mayflower, almost nobody in the United States, not even the State Department, knows that there is an Albanian Minister in Washington. The same is true of the Latvian, the Lithuanian and the Finn, except that they lack even a following of telephone girls, unless they have been more subversive about it than most people guess. The same would also be true of the Siamese, were it not for the fact that a maladroit policeman seized a truckload of Siamese liquor about two years ago and kept the poor little Minister, Major General Prince Amoradat Kridakara, on the front pages so long that he scarcely had time to recover before the arrival of his King for eye treatment subjected him to a fresh deluge of publicity.

Not even the Japanese Ambassador is seen very much in Washington, despite the fact that he is a most charming individual. As far as prestige goes, Katsuji Debuchi is a big shot. He is invited to all the dinners that he should be invited to, but to few of such *intime* affairs as those at which the Widow McCormick or Daisy Harriman drag in the men who are really doing things and discuss the latest skulduggery of the capital.

The staff of the Japanese Embassy is the biggest in Washington. This is because the intricacies of the Japanese language make typewriting impossible and it is necessary for an immense retinue of secretaries to spend hours each day painting English into Japanese. As a result, the staff is so big that it could spend the entire winter more or less dining among its own members and not be fed up with quite all of them. Whether Ambassador Debuchi spends his time that way nobody knows. But unless naval negotiations or a Russo-Chinese row in Manchuria bring him out into the open he makes himself as scarce as the ground-hog in February.

Dr. C. C. Wu,* Debuchi's colleague from the Asiatic mainland, is much more in the limelight. This is both because the limelight brightens his soul as sunlight builds bonny babies and because he is more at home in Washington than in Shanghai, Peking or Canton.

Old Wu-ting-fang, the first Minister China sent to Washington and who delighted its inhabitants by regularly parading a long blue mandarin coat and a pig-tail down Connecticut Avenue, brought with him his son, C. C. Wu, then a mischievous Chinese youngster of eight. Young Wu attended Western High School, threw snowballs at its windows, and came to be as much of a rough-and-tumble American as any one in his class. Now that he has come back to Washington, he tells gullible women's clubs about China's modern progress in a slow American drawl, makes perennial trips to persuade Secretary Stimson to abolish extra-territoriality and is one of the few diplomats in the capital who is a fair match for the newspapermen who beleaguer him at the entrance of the State Department.

Ahmet Muhtar, Ambassador of Turkey, has been a great disappointment to the pious wives of all Congressmen who wanted to meet a man with a harem. Not only does he lack the four wives prescribed by Mohammed for all good Moslems, but he has no wife at all. Furthermore, he is a washout as a table companion as far as most congressional wives are concerned, for he talks about as much English as they do French.

---

* Dr. Wu has now resigned in protest against American shipments of munitions to the Chinese Government to be used against his fellow citizens in Canton.

Just across the street from the Turkish Embassy, however, is one of the most interesting foreign establishments in the capital. It gives no official receptions; it sends no envoys to the State Department. Its occupants are not registered in the Diplomatic List. But occasionally they do throw a dinner, with much caviar and vodka to a guest list which is the most carefully selected in town. And its Ambassador, unofficial though he may be, is unquestionably one of the ablest in or out of the Diplomatic Corps.

The Information Bureau of the Soviet Union has no diplomatic rating, but it is called, by those who know anything about it, the Soviet Embassy. Boris E. Skvirsky, its chief, is an employee of the Soviet Foreign Office and draws his salary from it just as does any Soviet Ambassador to any other part of the world. He came to Washington ten years ago as the representative of the Far Eastern Republic of Siberia, in an effort to put Soviet Siberia's claims before the Washington Conference. Although he failed in that, he has been here ever since, and this fact alone, taking into consideration the Red Menace investigation of Ham Fish and the anti-Russian complex of the State Department, is sufficient indication of his success.

Probably because they have nothing else to do, the envoys of the Balkan and Border States—those who are neither in nor out of high society—lead the most bizarre lives in Washington. The Persian and the Albanian, although ostensibly with little in common except Charley Hart who has been American Minister to both countries, have the reputation of staging parties equalled only along Broadway or the Bosporus. Bey, the old Egyptian Minister, is still being mourned by the capital's greatest guzzlers. Charalambos Simopoules, the Greek, and his wife, play for the highest stakes in town and are fully able, if they wish—and some of their friends ruefully contend that they do wish—to make enough each week to pay the upkeep of their legation.

Faik Konitza, the Albanian, and Mirza Davoud Khan

Meftah, the Persian, used to begin their parties very quietly, sometimes with an afternoon picnic in Rock Creek Park, featured by large onion sandwiches and little Persian pickled onions. Perhaps it was the mixture of onions and champagne or the unusual union of Albania and Persia, but as the afternoon and evening wore on, the parties gathered momentum and buoyancy.

Konitza now is a lonely man. His companion-in-relieving-the-monotony-of-the-Washington-vacuum has gone back to Persia. The why and wherefore of his going was sad and shrouded in mystery. Mirza Davoud Khan Meftah had an enemy—a young Persian of royal blood who was attached to his own staff. The attachment was purely nominal, for Mozaffar Mirza Firouz never did any work and it was over this that the two fell out. The stories of what subsequently happened differ, but this—for what it is worth—is the Minister's version of it.

Young Firouz wrote to the United States Customs officials stating that the Minister was taking advantage of his diplomatic immunity to smuggle opium into the United States. He even informed the customs authorities that a consignment of the drug was arriving at such and such a date. Then, according to Mirza, young Firouz had his friends in Persia send a package of opium to the Minister. The package arrived, was seized by the customs, and Mirza was confronted with the evidence. He pleaded a frame up and was recalled, together with Firouz. And so passed from the diplomatic stage one of those benign and soulful figures which Washington always associated with pickled onions and rouge inscriptions on the starched bosoms of sleeping plenipotentiaries.

CHAPTER THREE

THE PRESIDENT

No man ever came to the Presidency with a greater opportunity for constructive and courageous administration than Herbert Hoover.

The national temper, the economic and political situation were over-ripe for a vigorous and positive leadership. The country was ready, as it had rarely been, for a man of principle, purpose, and will.

Eight years of the criminalities, puerile mediocrity, and reactionary do-nothingness of the Harding and Coolidge régimes had crystallized a deep urge in the national consciousness for a man of really first class caliber. The country was sated with the pettiness, the tragic weaknesses, and the asinine posturing of its leaders. It wanted some one it could be honestly proud of.

There were many reasons for it to believe that Herbert Hoover was that man.

Liberal leaders had acclaimed him. Far and wide he was hailed as an executive and a doer. He was not a professional politician. He did not come from a class that produced politicians. He was an engineer who apparently had done well at his work.

His public service was heroic. The whole world had applauded his great humanitarian exploits. He had fed starving millions, succored whole nations. He had taken a small, little-known department, and made it the most potent and widely advertised agency of the government.

True, little of the man himself was known. Long periods of his life were utterly blank, except for studiously vague explanations. His business career and operations were carefully guarded and elaborately obscured.

About his various food administrations there was also much that was highly debatable. Farmers accused him of having deliberately favored grain operators as against their interests. Even Old Guard Republican leaders, such as Representative William R. Wood, of Indiana, Chairman of the Republican Congressional Campaign Committee, had risen on the floors of Congress and bitterly assailed his management.

In Europe it was related of his food administration that he and his subordinates had used vital food resources, given by a generous people to feed starving women and children, as a weapon to crush the uprisings of oppressed masses throwing off the yokes of the masters who had precipitated the catastrophic World War.

There was the fact also that while making the Department of Commerce a mighty instrument of trade and business he had sat silent and unperturbed among Cabinet colleagues whose gross crimes and corruptions are unparalleled in the history of the country.

But all this was brushed aside in the trusting belief that he was a man of action, of broad vision, of force of character and mind. Not even a Presidential campaign, significant only in its grim evasion and covert bigotry, could dissipate the profound confidence in his inherent integrity and ability.

The American people believed in Herbert Hoover, the hero. They believed in him as the Great Engineer, the Great Administrator, the Great Humanitarian, the Great Idealist. They believed in him so earnestly that he was able to do the impossible in Presidential history: come back after having been discarded by the politicians.

The people elected him President by the greatest majority in a national election. They installed him in the White House, cast in a lofty rôle. They were ready to follow him in a courageous, independent, enlightened administration. He had but to lead the way.

The scene, the rôle, the play, even the audience was his own making. All that was needed was the courage and intellectual integrity to live up to the personality he had the genius to imprint on the public mind. Nothing could have stopped him.

In less than two years after he had taken office he had fully revealed the true quality of his character. He wrote the record fast and for all time. It is to be found in every phase of his administration.

He began his term with a Congress overwhelmingly Republican in both branches. Twenty months later a disillusioned and bitter electorate swept these majorities away and placed the control of the national legislature in the hands of his opponents.

He took over the reins of a party flushed with victory and high in morale. To-day, it is furtive, besmirched, and disorganized, filling the Nation with the stench of its Claudius Hustons and Robert V. Lucases, whom he himself installed as the managers of its affairs.

He came in on the high tide of a prosperity which he claimed was wholly the act of the Republican Party. It was a golden era that under his ministrations would be broadened and deepened in its fruitfulness. He was the apostle of the New Economic Order, promising a chicken in every pot and two cars in every garage.

A year later millions were walking the streets out of work. Thousands of factories have been shut down. Thousands of concerns and businesses have gone into bankruptcy, and hundreds of banks have crashed and failed. Agricultural prices have sunk to the lowest levels in thirty years. Exports have fallen off hundreds of millions of dollars and throughout the length and breadth of the land there is want, hunger, despair, and tragedy.

When he entered the White House he was the hero of great humanitarian exploits. In Europe and Russia he had fed millions. He had never hesitated to come before Congress and ask for vast sums for this purpose.

When disaster overwhelmed millions of his own countrymen in the city and on the farm, he suddenly developed austere scruples. To feed the hungry by funds from the Federal Treasury was undesirable "charity" and a "dole." To do so by pitiful breadlines, by private and inadequate local charity, was not.

Violently and frantically he set his face against a Federal grant. While millions starved he talked of "self-reliance." And when finally he was compelled to give way and permit some relief, at least to drought-stricken farmers, he adamantly refused to allow the use of the word "food" and insisted upon "security" for the pittances reluctantly loaned them by the richest country in the world.

The three measures sponsored by Senator Wagner, of New York, projecting a sound program for dealing with depressions in the future, he secretly fought in the House of Representatives and when that chamber finally repudiated his leadership and enacted them, he vetoed the most vital, establishing a national employment exchange system.

His administration was to be one of great organizing and executive skill. He was the Great Engineer, the Great Executive. Confronted through depression, with one of the greatest opportunities in the history of the country for far-reaching social and economic reorganization, he completely blew up; and when a circus stunt, the so-called business conference he staged in the early days of the collapse, fell flat, he resorted to evasion, distorted statements and misrepresentations in a futile and hysterical effort to stem and belie the inexorable march of deflation.

His whole record throughout the great national disaster is

unbelievable for its abysmal incompetence, do-nothingness and reactionary stultification.

*

WITHIN a year after he had taken office, the country was asking the question, "Why has Hoover failed?" There were few, not even among the staunchest members of his own party, who would not admit that he had failed to live up to expectations.

Such irreconcilable Hoovercrats as Senator Simeon D. Fess, fawning chairman of the Republican National Committee, and Will Irwin, his old classmate at Leland Stanford University, attributed his collapse to bad breaks, the drought, the stock crash, politics. But to the country at large the mystery of why a man apparently so preëminently qualified and so successfully advertised as the executive of executives should have so completely missed fire remained unsolved.

The answer is fourfold. The Hoover myth, the picture of the great engineer, qualified beyond all others to lead the Nation, was built up by one of the most skilful propaganda machines in the history of American politics.

Again, Hoover spent most of his life among the coolies of China and the wage-slaves of the Far East, where he reaped a great fortune and reputation through the exercise of the autocratic right of hire and fire. When he came to be the head of a great Democracy he found he could not fire a Senator who opposed him, unless he appointed him to an Ambassadorship, and there were only five of these to go around.

Third, when the fact dawned on him that the United States was a Democracy and he tried to play politics, he surrounded himself with politicians of the lowest order and who have made his Administration famous for its political ineptitude.

Lastly, and perhaps the most important answer to Herbert Hoover's failure is the fact that deeply ingrained in his make-up are two unfortunate characteristics, fear and vacillation, which, coupled with a petty personal temper, sorely try even his most loyal friends.

That Herbert Hoover was beset by this petty temper was not disclosed to any except those who knew him intimately until after he received the Republican nomination for President. Then with the spotlight of public curiosity focused upon him as never before, his fatal weaknesses of character began to come to light publicly.

As Secretary of Commerce he had, of course, been "in the news," in fact was the member of the Harding and Coolidge Cabinets who kept his name more consistently on the front pages than any other. But it was always in a secondary and impersonal rôle. When he stepped into the Presidential spotlight everything he did, said, or thought became public property. The spotlight of publicity dodged back and forth over every move he made, sought out every crevice of his private life, illuminated even his soul.

This was nothing new. It was the same with Coolidge. It was the same with Harding. It was the same with Wilson. It will be the same as long as the United States has a President and as long as the people of the United States insist upon treating their President as one of themselves rather than as Europe treats its monarchs.

Under these circumstances it is inevitable that sooner or later every fault and blemish, every whim and eccentricity of a man's life will be uncovered, particularly if he has such vital inadequacies as Herbert Hoover had to hide.

The first revelation of the Presidential temper came some weeks after Hoover had been nominated at Kansas City. He was living at Palo Alto, preparing for his acceptance speech. At the urgent requests of the newspaper photographers a morning was set aside for them to snap various "stills" and "movies" of the Hoovers at home.

Mrs. Hoover was self-appointed master of ceremonies. After all, it was her home and if it was going to be photographed, she wanted it done right. She ordered photographers over here, there and everywhere. She wanted chairs placed this way and benches that. Nothing seemed to please her. The photographers perspired and struggled. The newspapermen stood by amused. It was not their show. Mr. Hoover grew irritated. True he was sorely tried. Every one's sympathies were with him. And half a hundred people were watching him.

Finally, despite his audience, Mr. Hoover turned to his wife. "You'd better run in the house now," he grumbled. "That will be all."

Mrs. Hoover looked a little startled. Then remembering how many people there were present, she smiled.

"All right," she replied cheerfully, and obeyed.

Another example of the Hoover temper was displayed on election night. Again he was in his home in Palo Alto. Election returns were being received and as the night went on and it became apparent that he was the victor, neighbors and friends dropped in to congratulate him. In the course of the chatter, some one laughingly remarked that the university vote showed a number of ballots for his opponent. Mr. Hoover immediately grew cold.

"I don't see how any intelligent person, especially a member of the Stanford faculty, could so misunderstand the issues of the campaign," he exclaimed indignantly, a dark scowl passing over his face.

A somewhat similar incident occurred when Mr. Hoover returned to his S Street home in Washington. One of his neighbors on S Street is Frederick A. Delano, prominent architect and once head of the opium commission to Persia. Mr. and Mrs. Delano are old friends of the Hoovers, and, after the latter's return to Washington, they called to pay their respects.

Tea was served. The conversation was vivacious. All went well until Fred Delano remarked:

"I must be quite frank with you, Mr. President. I voted for Al Smith. But now that you're elected, I'm extremely glad and I want to congratulate you."

Mr. Hoover did not reply. His conversation lagged. The coolness became so perceptible that the Delanos left within a few minutes.

Since entering the White House, Mr. Hoover has repeatedly revealed streaks of temper and pettiness.

One of his favorite pets was a massive police dog named "King Tut." The dog had the freedom of the White House grounds and frequently ran and walked with the President when the latter went back and forth between the residence and the executive offices.

One day the President on his way to lunch observed King Tut playing with one of the White House Guards. The President whistled. The dog looked up but did not come. Mr. Hoover whistled again. Still the dog remained with the guard. Mr. Hoover turned on his heel and went on.

That afternoon an order was issued that none of the White House staff should play with the White House pets.

Some time after this, the Baltimore *Sun* published an article reporting the fact that the bids for air mail contracts over certain western routes had been drawn up but were phrased in such a way that only one company could bid on them.

The article also called attention to the fact that Herbert Hoover, Jr. was employed with this firm.

At his next press conference, the President completely lost control of himself and denounced the article with a passion which few who know him have ever seen him display.

All these and many similar incidents, showing a streak of pettiness seldom before witnessed in the White House, contributed to the dissolution of the Hoover myth.

Even without them, however, the myth would have been dissolved. It rested on too artificial a foundation to stand the strain of the pitiless realities of the Presidency.

Every possible trick, every new device, known or capable of being invented by skilled publicity agents, had been invoked to make Hoover the Superman, the Great Executive, and a reputation thus made was all the more easily washed away.

How meticulous were not only Hoover's publicity experts but even he himself in building up this myth can be gauged from an incident which occurred in his office at the Department of Commerce. Mr. Hoover had been notified a few hours before that the Kansas City convention had nominated him for the Presidency and the photographers flocked in for a picture.

Mr. Hoover sat at his mahogany desk. No papers cluttered its shining surface. No mail remained to be answered. There was a silver inkwell, a row of push buttons. That was all. The stage was set for the filming of a picture of the Great Executive.

The cameramen took their first snap from a moderate distance, then picked up their tripods and swooped down for a close-up. The new nominee threw his hands in front of his face and fled from the room.

No close-ups for him! He knew his publicity game. He knew that in close-ups his face looked weak and flabby. It was not the face of the Great Executive, the Strong Man.

George Akerson, his secretary, inadvertently let this out while persuading the cameramen to retreat from the desk. Later he persuaded Mr. Hoover to return, and the cameramen took their pictures from a reasonable distance. What Mr. Hoover did not know, however, was that the cameramen during the confusion had put on their long distance lenses. They got their close-ups anyway.

Before he became President, Mr. Hoover got so in the habit of getting across his publicity in a big way, so accustomed to having the public believe, without challenging it, whatever he had to say, that it was the most natural thing in the world for him to believe he could continue to do this after he entered the White House.

He started out with his memorable announcement that the Presidential yacht, the Mayflower, would be scrapped. He explained that he took this step because the ship was too expensive and also because the men who manned her were needed in the service. Immediately after, he took not only the eighty marines who served on the Mayflower—and who were needed in the service—but twice that number to build his Rapidan

fishing camp, and later had a company of army engineers from
Fort Humphreys sent in to build roads for the place.

Again there was his memorable statement of 1929 that he
was going to pare army costs. It brought him loud cheers from
almost the entire press and the general public. But when some
months later the budget was submitted to Congress, it was
found that army costs had not been reduced. Few people
knew this, however, and all in all, the statement got just what
it was calculated to get—a generous amount of good Presidential publicity.

Most of Mr. Hoover's statements during the London naval
negotiations were on the same order. He started out with the
glamorous announcement that the United States would hold
up the building of three cruisers. He followed it with a statement trying to prove that the results of the London Conference had been real reduction, when, as a matter of fact, the
London Treaty fixed the total construction program at a figure higher than ever before.

By this time, however, the press in general and Congress
in particular had become suspicious of his high-sounding words
and had begun to inquire for themselves just what the facts
were. In the case of the alleged suspended cruisers, reporters
for the New York *Evening Post* and the New York *Sun* discovered that no orders had gone out to the Navy Department
to stop work on them, but, on the contrary, all preparation
for the construction of the vessels was going forward as per
schedule.

His statements summing up the work of the London Naval
Conference, in which he undertook to make the upward limi-
tation agreement appear as a momentous reduction achievement, aroused widespread protest. He undertook to set up the
wholly false comparison of the extreme big-navy figures of the
unsuccessful Geneva Naval Conference, held three years
previous, with the lesser tonnage of the London Treaty.

So completely untenable was this claim that it was never
once adverted to by Administration spokesmen throughout the

long committee hearings and the Senate debate on the pact.

At the beginning of the last session of the Seventy-first Congress, the President announced that the Treasury deficit would be about $185,000,000. A week later, when the Budget was published, it disclosed that actually the deficit was estimated as likely to be more than $500,000,000.

The time between the President's announcement and publication of the official estimate was so short that one of two conclusions was unavoidable: either Mr. Hoover was woefully ignorant of the fiscal affairs of the Government or was playing politics with figures.

As a result of these and many other such misrepresentations, every statement the President now makes is minutely scrutinized. As Secretary of Commerce he was accustomed to having his word accepted as gospel. The oracle spoke; every one listened. As President, his statements have attained such an unsavory reputation for being purely inspired, purely unfounded publicity blasts, that whenever he proclaims business to be picking up, the stock market goes down.

So regularly has this occurred that in September, 1930, when construction activities in the United States showed an upturn for the first time in many months, the Treasury Department advised the White House not to announce it for fear of an unfavorable repercussion on the stock market.

Despite the sweeping and unfounded statements he is in the habit of making in his own defense, the President is not only super-sensitive but literally quails and becomes hysterical when he himself is attacked.

Members of President Wilson's White House staff relate that during the War any unfriendly remark made in Congress about Mr. Hoover was sure to mean a visit from him. He would complain bitterly to Mr. Wilson and frequently threatened to resign unless protected from such congressional outbursts.

During the Coolidge Administration, when Henry C. Wallace was Secretary of Agriculture, Mr. Hoover once complained to Coolidge that Wallace's farm journal was attacking him. Coolidge, however, looked bored. He told his Secretary of Commerce about his own discovery—that it was much more comfortable not to read "things that are agin' you."

How Mr. Hoover came to build his political reputation on the shifting and uncertain sands of a propaganda machine is easy to understand. He had been doing this all his life.

The secret of his success as an engineer was promotion. Actually his work was not engineering. At the height of his business career he was receiving $5,000 a year as "mining expert," and $95,000 a year as a "financial expert."

His job was to promote, to organize and then pass on. In all that vast area which he ranged, from Siberia to Australia and from China to Africa, there is to be found to-day not a single engineering project which bears his name and the stamp of his handiwork. Of concessions with which he was connected, however, there are many.

When he retired from "engineering" he did so to become the organizer of his own concession-holding ventures in foreign lands. From an office in London he promoted a long list of mining enterprises, listed by the British Mining Manual of 1912 as the Burma Mines, Ltd., Inter-Argentina Syndicate, Ltd., Inter-Russian Syndicate, Ltd., Russo-Asiatic Corporation, Ltd., Yuanmi Gold Mines, Ltd., Babilonia Gold Mines, Ltd.

It was as a thirteen-year-old youngster in Oregon that Herbert Hoover first learned to become a promoter. He was associated with his uncle in jobbing off now relatively worthless real estate in Salem, Oregon, during one of those "California-Florida" land booms which are always promising an Eldorado to the American people. His uncle's company was out to sell land. It found it was losing sales to rival companies. Young Herbert conceived the idea of meeting newcomers at the station, settling them in private boarding houses, thus giving his uncle's salesmen an opportunity to talk to them without competition.

With the commission young Herbert got from renting the rooms, he helped finance himself through college. From that time on, he never ceased promoting.

*

It is not difficult to understand why Herbert Hoover has played politics ineptly, why he does not get along with people, and why he has surrounded himself with yes-men.

All of that period of his life during which a man's character and mental process are molded was spent far from the field of politics in isolated parts of the world. Months and years spent on the edge of the Australian desert or in the interior of China rob any man of that contact with his fellowmen so essential if he is to inspire leadership. Especially true is this when the people with whom he is surrounded on the edge of that desert or in the interior of China remain there subject to his whim and pleasure.

It was in these circumstances that Herbert Hoover developed the habits of autocracy which have so handicapped him in the White House. Because he had the power to command, he never developed the power to lead. His word was law. Once, expounding his views on labor troubles to a friend, he told how he had always found that chaining a Chinese coolie to a stake for a day in the hot sun was conducive to good discipline and a minimum of strikes.

How ruthless was Herbert Hoover's business conduct in China has been told in the High Court of Justice, Chancery Division, London, in the suit brought against his firm in 1905 by Chang Yen Mao, Director-General of mines for the Chinese Government. Chang accused Hoover and his associates of euchring him out of some valuable mining property, and Mr. Justice Joyce in rendering the decision against Hoover and his company said:

"Incidentally it appears by a letter of Mr. Hoover that he actually took possession of some title deeds of the property by main force. Under the circumstances, I am of opinion that to allow the defendant company, while they insist on retaining the benefits of the transfer, to escape from the obligations of the memorandum upon any such pretext as that Hoover or De-Wouters were not authorized to agree to its terms, or that it was impossible for the defendant company to perform some of these terms without altering its constitution, would be contrary to one of the plainest principles of equity. It would be to sanction such a flagrant breach of faith as, in my opinion, could not be tolerated by the law of any country."

And in conclusion, the Judge added these significant words:

"I think," he said, "that I ought to make one more observation, which is that, in the investigation taken before me of the transaction in question, it has not been shown to me that His Excellency Chang has been guilty of any breach of faith or of any impropriety at all, which is more than I can say for some of the other parties concerned."

A man cannot spend some twenty years of his life experiencing this unnatural relation toward his fellow-men without becoming permanently influenced by it, without becoming dictatorial, autocratic and a perpetual dependent upon the right of "hire and fire."

The result is that Mr. Hoover, both as Secretary of Commerce and as President, constantly has surrounded himself with inferiors, men who accept his word without challenge and carry it out.

When thrown in contact with equals, with men whom he could not discharge, he has failed abysmally. This factor is perhaps the greatest reason for the political turmoil which has attended every month of his administration.

Finding that he could not "fire" a Senator or a Representative, the President has alternated between abject surrender and weak, stupid bluffing, in which he has never yet been successful.

Early in his administration, Representative Bertram Snell, hard-boiled Chairman of the House Rules Committee, returned from a conference with the President regarding the latter's attempt to take control of New York State patronage and ribaldly reassured his colleagues.

"I have met the President and he is ours," Snell announced.

There is not a really significant Republican leader in Congress or the country at large who trusts or respects Mr. Hoover. Some of his bitterest critics are to be found among Republican Senate and House leaders who have confidential relations with him.

During the Arkansas food-relief controversy in the closing days of the Seventy-first Congress, Republican leaders refused to assume the responsibility of assuring the Democrats that the proceeds of the compromise $20,000,000 appropriation would be used for "human" relief as well as "animal" relief. Senator McNary, who had been double-crossed by the White House on the same issue at the beginning of the session, bluntly sent word to the President that he was through pledging his word for him and that if the President had any promises to make he would have to make them himself.

It was also during the course of the two months' struggle over the food-relief issue that there occurred the astounding spectacle of the President issuing a statement defending his policy and attacking the opposition, and when they turned on him and lashed him mercilessly, for a week straight, not one responsible Republican leader in the entire country rose to say a word in his behalf.

Most of Mr. Hoover's administration has been a series of surrenders to one political faction after another.

He has been cowed by petty state and local politicians into making appointments he was against. In Pennsylvania they bullied him into naming Albert L. Watson and, in Kansas, Richard J. Hopkins to Federal judgeships, despite the fact that his Attorney General pronounced both unfit for the Federal bench.

The Old Guard high-tariff gang cowed him into signing the Smoot-Hawley Tariff Act which in a thousand ways violated every view he had ever held on the tariff and which, up to a few hours before he furtively announced his approval, he had described to his friends as vicious, extortionate and obnoxious.

Even the Insurgents, whom he hates, on more than one occasion have forced the President to bow to their demands. Threatening a fight on confirmation, they forced him to withdraw the name of Lieutenant General Edgar Jadwin as Chairman of the Federal Power Commission, and, by defeating a fifth-rate appointment he attempted to foist upon the Supreme Court, compelled him to name Justice Owen J. Roberts, a man of outstanding ability.

So abject and tortuous has been the President's course, that even such slavish Republican newspapers as the Chicago *Tribune,* the New York *Evening Post* and the New York *Herald Tribune* have denounced and berated him with bitter indignation.

Elected on a platform of taking important appointments out of politics, Mr. Hoover has played politics with almost every appointment he has made.

Instead of merit, ability and character, political expediency alone has counted with him. His record in judicial appointments is unsurpassed for mediocrity and partisanship. As Minister to Canada, he sent a blatant super-patriot known among his fellow-service men as "Boob" McNider. As Ambassador to Berlin, he sent Senator Frederic M. Sackett, a machine politician who dared not face a reëlection contest in Kentucky. As Ambassador to France, he sent Senator Walter E. Edge, whose ownership of the Dorland Advertising Agency, vigorous competitor of the French official agency, somewhat embarrassed Franco-American relations.

A vacancy on the Supreme Court of the United States he attempted to use to strengthen a collapsing political machine in the South, and the International Joint Commission, which he had declared he would reorganize to carry out important American-Canadian negotiations, he has completely debased by packing it with decrepit lame-duck Senators and an unwanted Post Office official.

Afforded an exceptional opportunity to strengthen the government's regulation of the great water-power industry through the creation by Congress of the new Federal Power Commission, he ransacked the land for unknown and amenable mediocrities and appointed them to the Commission. Of all the outstanding experts and authorities that he could have obtained he picked these five wholly inexperienced and uninformed nonentities and turned this vital responsibility over to them.

Not only did he surround himself with one of the most mediocre, and most servile Cabinets in history, but during the first two years of his incumbency, he appointed three National Republican Committee Chairmen: Hubert M. Work, a blunderer; Claudius Huston, a lobbyist; and Simeon D. Fess, an Anti-Saloon League-ridden and reactionary Senator.

While Mr. Hoover has some precedent for playing politics with this type of appointment, there has been no President in recent history who has reached into the departments of his Cabinet officers and dictated the appointment of their assistants.

Mr. Hoover has done this repeatedly, the two most glaring instances being the appointment of William R. Castle, Jr., as Under Secretary of State, and of General Douglas MacArthur as Chief of Staff. Secretary Stimson, in the case of Castle, and Secretary Hurley, in the case of MacArthur, both vigorously opposed the appointments, and yet despite the fact that the success of their departments depends upon harmony with their chief assistants, Mr. Hoover insisted that these men be named.

No instance of the petty political prejudice of the President has been more revealing, however, than that of his veto of the Wagner Bill, proposing the establishment of a national employment exchange system.

The veto affords a profoundly illuminating insight into the

character of Herbert Hoover. It was inspired purely by personal and political dislike of the sponsor of the bill, Senator Wagner, a Tammany Democrat and an intimate friend of Alfred E. Smith.

In 1920-'21-'23-'24 Mr. Hoover specifically and categorically associated himself with recommendations for the establishment of exactly such an employment bureau system as Senator Wagner proposed.

In 1920, as Chairman of President Wilson's Industrial Conference, Mr. Hoover recommended "enactment of appropriate legislation by Congress making provision for an employment clearing house under Federal control." In 1921, as Chairman of President Harding's Conference on Unemployment, he recommended an "adequate permanent system of employment offices." In 1923 as Secretary of Commerce, he appointed a committee on business cycles which recommended "a national system of employment bureaus." In 1924 he appointed a Committee on Seasonal Operations which endorsed the previous recommendations.

He rejected the Wagner Bill, despite the repeated pleas of Colonel Arthur Woods, Chairman of his Unemployment Committee, that it be approved. He did so on the ground that the bill would abolish an already existing system that the year before had found jobs for 1,300,000 workers. That both statements were false was proven by the fact that exactly six weeks after he had killed the bill, he became alarmed at the growing volume of denunciation of his action, and undertook to set up, by Executive order, very much the same system.

The Wagner Bill specifically provided that the existing United States Employment Service should not be displaced until the new and more desirable system was in operation. Furthermore, the old Federal service had not found work for 1,300,000 applicants in 1930.

It had placed 700,000 seasonal workers, of the harvest hand type. In this field the problem is not finding jobs but workers who will take them. In the fields where the difficulty is finding employment, such as in industry, business, and offices, the Federal agency accomplished practically nothing.

The 1,300,000 that the President claimed for it was a deliberate misrepresentation. Six hundred thousand of these jobs were actually found by State Employment Bureaus whose only connection with the Federal system was through the designation of one of their staff as a Federal Employment Supervisor, for which he received $1 a year.

Of the same character was the President's refusal to permit Senator Wagner to be chairman of a special committee the Senate authorized on his motion to inquire into unemployment insurance measures. It is an unwritten Senate rule that the sponsor of a special committee is always named its chairman. In recognition of this precedent Vice President Curtis appointed Wagner as the first man on the committee, thus confirming his right to the chairmanship. But when Wagner, and the two Old Guard Senators named as his associates, met to organize the committee, they shamefacedly informed him that the President was opposed to his being chairman and they would have to unseat him. Being docile party hacks they proceeded to carry out their instructions, thus robbing Wagner of the opportunity of doing the constructive work he had planned.

*

WHEN Herbert Hoover was a small boy in Iowa, his father operated a barbed-wire factory, and, anxious to improve his product, he hit upon the idea of covering the steel strands with tar.

One day young Bertie, standing beside the steaming caldron of tar and wondering whether it would burn, tossed a flaming stick into it. The conflagration which resulted destroyed his father's plant and nearly wiped out the little town and his father's store.

"That night," according to Rose Wilder Lane, one of Hoover's most adulatory biographers, "he heard his father tell how the store, and perhaps the town had been saved. The fire, it was thought, had been caused by the unwatched kettle of tar, which must have boiled over. Bertie said nothing. If he had been asked, he would have told what he had done, but no one asked him.

"He sat unnoticed, eating silently. He was sorry and terrified, yet he was glad. It was such a strange feeling that when he had gone to bed he lay awake for a long time, hearing the katydid in the wild crab-apple tree outside his window. He had done a frightening thing; the shock of it was still in his nerves and the crime of it on his conscience, but he had not meant to do wrong. He had been innocently experimenting, and the result was not entirely disheartening.

" 'Anyway, I found out what it would do,' he thought. 'I found it out all by myself.' He wondered if he would be punished if he told. He thought not. But he decided that it was best to keep his own counsel in the matter.

"And for forty years he did so."

The story is one of the most revealing incidents in Herbert Hoover's life. It gives the key to many qualities in his character which both his friends and his enemies have been trying to explain.

It explains his vacillation, his indecision, the worry through which he passes before making up his mind. It explains his hesitancy in facing issues, a hesitancy which sometimes borders on outright cowardice. It explains why he privately denounced the oil scandals of the Harding Administration and yet sat unmoved throughout that régime, never denouncing it publicly. It explains why he hesitated three days before accepting the rôle of Belgian Food Administrator which the Allies had offered him. It explains his basic intellectual timidity, his inability to grapple in a straightforward and forthright manner with vital issues, why he is always resorting to such indirect devices as commissions to relieve him of the responsibility of acting on controversial questions.

It explains also why on such a moot question as prohibition, he has never once said one word that positively and definitely stated whether he is wet or dry. Senator Carter Glass of Vir-

ginia once offered to pay $1,000 to any one who could produce
a single categorical dry declaration by the President. Several
years have passed since then but no one has ever claimed the
reward.

From his "noble experiment" reply to Senator Borah, in the
pre-nomination campaign in 1928, to this day the President
has never made a positive statement of his stand, either for or
against prohibition. Throughout his campaign he lurked behind the screen of enforcement, while his managers and
spokesmen gave assurances to both sides, representing him dry
to the drys and wet to the wets.

From this policy he has never deviated. Every dry-by-impli-
cation statement he has made has been followed immediately
by an under-cover wet "interpretation." This occurred when
he gave out his pronouncement on the Wickersham Commission Prohibition Report and after his acceptance speech, at
Palo Alto, California, in the summer of 1928.

In that address his remarks regarding prohibition were
widely accepted as meaning he was dry. The next day, a close
friend, who had worked with him in the drafting of the
address, called in reporters representing wet newspapers, and
solely for "local consumption" gave them a wet "slant" on
the President's remarks. These papers used this interpretation
in his behalf throughout his Presidential campaign.

The day following his expression on the Wickersham Report
select correspondents were called to the White House and
there given a distinct wet interpretation of the declaration.

On the power issue the President's course has been even
more tortuous and reactionary. He is wedded to private,
monopolistic ownership and control of this great and vital
industry. Yet, during the whole of his 1928 Presidential campaign he was grimly silent on this major problem—with one
local exception.

When he spoke at Elizabethton, Tennessee, he made a veiled
reference to government operation under certain conditions.
Muscle Shoals is a matter of greatest moment to this section.

The editor of a nearby Scripps-Howard newspaper, speaking to him privately, asked him if he had Muscle Shoals in mind as one of these exceptions.

"You may say that means Muscle Shoals," the President told him. The Scripps-Howard papers, supporting him, published it widely.

Press associations and newspapermen, upon his return to his campaign headquarters in Washington, inquired as to the accuracy of the story. After several hours of conferences with political and campaign advisors, the President issued a statement in which he declared that "there is no question of government ownership (of Muscle Shoals) as the government already owns both the power and nitrate plants."

Not a word was to be found in the statement about government operation, which was the question raised, and not ownership. The tenor and implication of the statement, however, indicated approval of government operation of Muscle Shoals. The message was so accepted by the public and the press and not denied by Hoover.

Yet, from then on, he covertly fought and opposed every effort to enact a sound government-operation program for the great plant. Through his control of the House of the Seventy-first Congress he obstructed and sabotaged such legislation as long as he could, and when, finally, after months of laborious negotiation, powerfully assisted by the defeat for reëlection of his spokesman in the House on the question, an acceptable measure was enacted, he vetoed it in a message filled with misstatements and misrepresentations.

His course on governmental regulation of utilities has been equally devious.

Addressing the annual convention in 1925 of the National Electric Light Association, the trade organization of the utility industry, he insisted that there had been outrageous exaggeration concerning the need for control of public utilities. Such supervision in "purely local affairs," he contended, would prove a menace to individual initiative.

This anti-Federal regulation pronouncement in 1925 was a reversal of views he expressed when he addressed the Association Conventions in 1922 and 1924. Then he saw a hopeful rôle for the national government in coördinating and strengthening the regulations of power developments that were outside the jurisdiction of the individual states.

Between his 1925 speech and 1929, he maintained a tight silence on the question of regulation. Not even his Presidential race could force him to speak out on so important a subject. Lacking any other information, it was generally taken for granted during these years that his views were unchanged and that he was against Federal regulation.

But in his message to Congress in 1929, he again turned a hand-spring, this time going back to his more liberal ideas of 1922 and 1924. He conceded that there were instances of inter-state character that were beyond the control of the states and recommended to Congress that it extend the authority of the Federal Power Commission.

Having reversed his reversal, the President promptly shifted his policy once again. This time he did it covertly and by indirection.

Through a member of his Cabinet he attacked the idea of Federal regulation while personally, by means of weak appointments, he stultified the effectiveness of the Federal Power Commission, whose creation he had recommended to Congress for the purpose of strengthening governmental control.

Secretary of Interior Wilbur, President-on-leave of Leland Stanford University, which has large water power investments, attacked Federal regulation in the last annual report of the old Federal Power Commission, of which he was the dominant member, and advocated state supervision as the sound and wise way to deal with this stupendous problem.

Attorney General Mitchell coöperated in this undercover drive by rendering an astounding legal opinion in which he undertook by interpretation to repeal practically every portion of the Federal Water Power Act set up by Congress over two decades ago for the protection of the public.

This amazing attack on a statute he was sworn to safeguard and defend by the highest legal representative of the government raised such a storm of protest that the old Power Commission did not dare proceed on it as Wilbur had intended.

Judge George W. Woodruff, Solicitor for the Department of Interior under President Roosevelt and one of the authors of the Water Power Act, declared that if the opinion was allowed to go unchallenged it would sweep away twenty-five years of effort to protect the interests of the present and future generations in vast water power rights.

"The public stewards," he said, "become the friends of the exploiters of public property. The crisis is very grave indeed."

President Hoover never repudiated or made any statement regarding either Wilbur's or Mitchell's action.

*

In the long and tragic travail of the economic depression, the most tragic thing was the President's fear of admitting that a great disaster had befallen the country. For months, while gloom, unemployment, and deflation settled on the land, he refused to admit their reality or do anything fundamental about the situation. His approach to the problem was wholly that of the boomer, the bull-market operator, concerned only with his own political interests and willing to resort to any device or misrepresentation to further them.

Facts, statistics, plan, organization—there have been none, and when proposed by others have been rejected and stifled, secretly when possible, openly when that was impossible.

One policy alone has dominated his course: not to do or say anything that would reveal the truth about the great catastrophe. Suppression and inaction have been his unshaken rule.

The detailed record of this effort tells the story eloquently:

On December 14, 1929, Mr. Hoover declared that the volume of shopping reported to him indicated that the business of the country was "back to normal." That was some six weeks after the stock market crash.

Early in January, 1930, Secretary of the Treasury Mellon, under pressure from Hoover, announced, "I see nothing in the present situation that is either menacing or warrants pessimism. I have every confidence that there will be a revival of activity in the spring." These ebullient assurances were greeted with a drop in stock market prices to new low levels.

A year and five months later Mr. Mellon, addressing a group of international bankers in Washington, and apparently free for the moment from White House restraint, frankly admitted: "I have no means of knowing when or how we shall emerge from the valley in which we are now traveling."

On January 22, the President personally expressed the view that the "trend" of employment had changed upward and then Secretary of Labor Davis, carrying out the refrain, gave it on his word that "every major industry was showing increases and that we can expect a great deal of business in 1930."

In February and early March, Secretary of Commerce Lamont, acting on White House orders, took up the burden and on three occasions solemnly gave assurance that "there is nothing in the situation to be disturbed about."

All this time, according to the most reliable labor statistics available in the United States at present, those of the New York State Labor Bureau, factories were closing down in increasing numbers and the unemployment line was steadily lengthening.

On March 8, 1930, the President himself again entered the lists with his now famous prediction that the crisis would be over in "sixty days." (See May 2 statement below.)

On March 16, Julius H. Barnes, close personal friend and under-cover agent for the President, as Chairman of the President's National Business Survey Conference, declared "that the spring of 1930 marks the end of a period of grave concern." Barnes failed to add however that others would follow of even greater gravity.

On May 2, the President, with the expiration of his "sixty days," trimmed his sails very sharply. In a lengthy pronouncement he conceded that things were rather disturbed, but was still irrepressibly optimistic. "We have been passing through one of those great economic storms which periodically bring hardships and suffering to our people," he admitted. "While the crisis took place only six months ago, I am convinced we have passed the worst and with continued unity of effort we shall rapidly recover."

Two months later, in the privacy of his office and under strict and repeated admonitions of secrecy, he petulantly told Amos Pinchot and a group of important business men who had called to urge him to do something drastic to relieve unemployment: "Gentlemen, you are six weeks too late. The crisis is over."

Three months later, with bread lines longer than ever before and facing state and congressional elections, he set up, amid much fanfare, a national unemployment committee to "coördinate" employment activities.

In January, 1931, Colonel Arthur Woods, director of the committee, summoned before a Senate committee to tell about his work, estimated unemployment as around 5,000,000 and informed the Senators that his organization was preparing to disseminate pamphlets on how to stimulate relief. A week later the President issued a proclamation asking the public to contribute $10,000,000 to the Red Cross for food relief.

Three months later the Census Bureau announced that a special unemployment survey it had made showed an estimated 6,050,000 out of work.

The President's actions leading up to his signing the Smoot-Hawley Tariff Act probably were the most vacillating of his entire career. Three days before he announced he would approve it, one of his secretaries categorically informed reporters that the President had not made up his mind about the measure and would make no decision until it had come to him from Congress and he had sent it to the various departments and received their formal views on the matter.

This story was printed far and wide. Seventy-two hours later, while the Act was still unfinished legislation in Congress, the President let it be known that he would approve it. The reasons he gave for bowing before a tariff act every one knew he bitterly resented were thus characterized by Senator Pat Harrison on the floor of the Senate:

"This statement is unworthy of the President. It is one of

the most intellectually dishonest statements ever to come from the White House."

The final story of Herbert Hoover is yet to be told. Only time will make available the mass of secret documents and the details of his business career, now so zealously guarded, by which the complete picture can be filled in. Only time also will tell the final story of how Herbert Hoover was pushed into a plan to postpone German reparations and Allied debt payments; a plan which Owen D. Young had worked out and which Henry L. Stimson, coöperating with the British government, had urged upon his chief in the White House; a plan which was finally put over on Herbert Hoover through the combined efforts of Charles G. Dawes, Dwight W. Morrow and Andrew W. Mellon plus a dozen New York bankers who clamored at him in person and by long distance telephone for nearly a month. Finally, his confidence restored by a trip to the hospitable Middle West, Mr. Hoover adopted the plan and was never more surprised in his life when it was heralded as his master stroke.

Whether it will carry him on to reëlection, only time can tell. But time long after that will tell the story of one of the super-promoters of the age.

It will be the story of a paradox. A man who, despite the handicap of a fundamental timorousness, was able by a consummate sense of publicity to create the illusion of heroism and greatness and to attain for a time world acclaim.

It will be the story of a man who had the genius to create a great rôle, but lacked the essential requisites of character to enact it. It will be the story of a success which failed because it succeeded too well.

Had Herbert Hoover never gained the Presidency, he might well have remained a shimmering hero. The illusion he so skilfully wove never would have been shattered. But before the ruthless realities and the merciless tests of that office his fundamental inadequacy of character undid him and he stands to-day stripped of all his carefully conjured glories.

CHAPTER FOUR

EGG CHARLEY

OR a third of a century, in the House and in the Senate, Charley Curtis, of Kansas, drew his salary and mileage, spread abroad in unrestrained generosity the garden seeds and moral documents paid for by the Treasury, planted his share of patronage where it served him best, upheld loyally the hand of the President—if he was a Republican—and in all other ways was a steady, dependable, unquestioning Party plug, dull, regular, and conforming, no worse than the rest of the pack and in some ways a lot better.

By political standards, he was a pretty square shooter. He didn't pose as a sage or a superman; he didn't steal; he never went Red hunting; and if he waved the flag and occasionally declaimed sonorously about home and mother he was at least not of the smug type of Senator David Reed of Pennsylvania, the Mellon political and legal bodyguard, nor of the buffoon ilk of Senator Tom Heflin.

Coming from Kansas, he was a voting dry, of course. But he made no secret of the fact that he was fond of a good game of draw poker, and nothing gave him greater pleasure than to take a $1.25 pot from Senator "Jim" Couzens of Michigan, who, despite his $40,000,000 Ford-made fortune, would always howl in anguish.

Charley didn't profess to be a regular church-goer. His

skill in profanity was widely recognized and he was an enthusiastic and regular patron of the ponies.

Of course, no one ever accused him of being a Progressive.
But the feminists, nevertheless, called him friend, and it is one
of the proudest of his claims that he led the Senate fight for
the Nineteenth Amendment and was the author of a bill
protecting the rights of American women sufficiently affluent
to hire foreigners to marry them and of another creating a
series of select Federal women's prisons for ladies tangled up
with the law. Finally, his vote was recorded for the Child
Labor Amendment—and whether the fact that Kansas has no
mills had anything to do with it is perhaps beside the question.

In those carefree congressional days Charley liked nothing
better than to chin with the boys in mocking manner about
the social game in Washington, about which he troubled himself not at all and in which he felt like a fish out of water.
The pushing and climbing of some of his colleagues and of
the other strutters in the official arena were a source of much
amusement to him, and his comments thereon were tart and
devastating.

Altogether, he was personally a decent enough fellow—for
an Old Guard Senator.

He played the political game in a smooth, efficient manner,
and not too offensively, and thus for thirty-three years he
served Kansas and the Republican Party. He made no speeches
if he could help it, and when, in the closing years of his congressional career, he became Republican floor leader of the
Senate and would rise from his seat and bring endless hours
of hokum to a close with "Mr. President, I move we adjourn,"
his name was called blessed by all.

This daily motion was his sole contribution to statecraft
during his years as majority leader. His name is not written
on any legislation of importance, either good or bad, but who
is there who will not grant that Charley also served?

But while on the surface he was always a placid, humble,

unchanging, decent fellow, his long years in Washington finally left their mark on him.

In his old age he was stricken with soaring ambitions and they began to plague him. His humility turned to gall.

A life-long inferiority complex, arising out of his Kaw Indian descent, began to be complicated by the recurrence of a childhood fairy story that every American may hope to be President.

This fixation took hold of him as his physical powers declined, and in a short time it had flamed into an irrepressible libido.

The idea of aspiring to the Presidency came to him quite suddenly. Mediocrity in the Presidency had become the fashion and he was not only mediocrity incarnate, but, as politicians go, more or less honest—a combination far from common, and one, just then, urgently needed by the Republican Party.

If Harding and Coolidge could reach for the purple, why not he?

He was not—at least, not then—a man given to thumping his chest in self-righteousness, but his comfortable little paunch and his soft, round, copper-brown jowls covered a dogged heart and a determined jaw. Once the fatal aspiration to imperial grandeur was implanted in his psyche, it possessed him completely.

The idea of a Red man, even though only a half-breed, sitting in the White House made him sweat and pant with wonder and delight. He saw himself in the stirring rôle of uplifter of a broken race. And in no time at all there were plenty of sycophants about him to help the idea along.

It didn't take Charley long to get started and once under way the illusion grew by leaps and bounds. A first-hand knowledge of the putrid deal that resulted in Harding's nomination and an intimate acquaintance with what took place during the several years of his Presidency enormously strengthened Charley's determination to run.

When, in 1924, scme one proposed that he be made Cool-

idge's running-mate, the new complex burst into full and fiery
bloom. He became a definite candidate—first for the Presidency, and then, if that turned out to be impossible, for the
noble desuetude of Vice President. Coolidge's petulant rejection
of his name, because Charley had opposed him, as had most
of the other Republican Senators, on the Soldiers' Bonus handout, only increased the pressure in his gauges.

In a quiet, skilful way he set about restoring himself in the
favor of the White House. When, after the 1924 election, it
became apparent that Coolidge and Dawes loved each other
like a pair of strange cats, Charley utilized to the full the
advantage the place as Senate floor leader gave him and set
about making himself solid. No painted warrior on the trail
ever trod a more wary and skilful path than he in the puerile
wrangling between the Senate and the little Yankee carpet-
bagger.

When the Equalization Fee fight was on he voted for both
the bill itself and to sustain Coolidge's veto of it, all the time
braying into the skies about the trials and burdens of the
befuddled farmer.

When, early in 1927, he became ill, he brooded darkly over
the possibility that death might intervene between him and
his goal. He doctored grimly, and despite the call of a trying
legislative situation, dropped everything and hustled off to
Florida to nurse himself back to health.

From then on he adhered carefully to a strict regimen,
taking long walks, eating with caution, and abandoning all-
night poker sessions.

All this time Charley was still keeping within the bounds
of reason. The Presidency he thought of only as a wistful
possibility. His real and immediate goal was the Vice Presidency.

But when Coolidge outsmarted himself with his famous "I
do not choose to run" statement and the bewildered Republican zealots took his words for what they appeared to say and

the race for the 1928 nomination was thrown open, Charley's final efflorescence rapidly set in.

One by one such appalling candidates as Jim Watson, Willis of Ohio, and the egregious Goff solemnly strutted forward and set up their claims. It is not, therefore, to be wondered at that Charley, observing their gall, suddenly ran amok—and promptly passed from reality altogether.

His madness, to be sure, was not altogether without its logic. With Coolidge out, and such men as Watson, Willis, and Goff accepted as serious contenders, he reasoned, there was a real chance for him, too.

Wasn't there every likelihood that history would repeat itself? Might not the leaders, Hoover, Lowden, Dawes, kill one another off and deadlock?

And might not the oil and high tariff bosses, turning to the second-stringers, cast their eyes upon the Indian Brave from Kansas?

Was he not from the Corn Belt, supposedly deeply disaffected? Wasn't he a friend of the farmer, and yet a party man of unimpeachable regularity and conservatism?

And finally, wasn't there a chance that, if the worst came to the worst, a good strong grab for the Presidency would make him a sure shot for second place.

Thus he reasoned—at first. But as the fight developed, ambition soared and raged within him. His walk may be the waddle of a fat old squaw, but brave warrior blood of the Red man of the plains courses in his veins.

Charley, in the hectic days of the spring of '28, actually came to believe that he would be President. Watson, Goff and Dawes might secretly consider themselves outside long-shots, but not Charley. He knew that he was a man of destiny.

So Charley set about to hack, hammer and wangle his way to the White House. He wrote thousands of letters enthusiastically extolling his virtues and proclaiming his availability. He opened headquarters in various States. He formally joined the anti-Hoover forces and metamorphosed a casual contempt for his opponent into a bitter Indian-like hatred.

To nominate Hoover, he said, publicly and privately, would be to place a hopeless burden upon an already overladen party. Hoover was intolerable, unspeakable, unthinkable.

That Hoover finally beat him he has never forgiven—and never will now that every day of Hoover's administration brings further proof to Charley that everything he said about him in the nomination campaign has been more than realized since he took office.

To this day Charley believes that he was double-crossed on the nomination. Those who know him well say he is sure that if Mellon and the Pennsylvania gang had played him square he would be in the White House to-day. They assert that he had promises from the Pennsylvania bosses, who distrusted Hoover, that he would get their backing.

Indeed, if they had gone over to him at the right moment at Kansas City, he might well have been chosen. Stranger things have happened at Republican conventions

Many reasons give Charley cause to believe that way. To begin with, Hoover was a minority candidate when the delegates assembled at the convention. Outside of the paid Negro cohorts from the South, carefully garnered by the sly C. Bascom Slemp and the mysterious Claudius Huston, and closely guarded after a Lowden kidnapping raid the day before the convention opened, he had only a few States actually pledged to him.

New York, dominated by Charles D. Hilles, and Pennsylvania, presumably controlled by Mellon and Joseph R. Grundy, wanted Coolidge, or anybody but Hoover. Lowden was obviously out of it. Thus, if these two big Eastern delegations had been thrown to Charley, as he was assured they would be, they might very well have swung the anti-Hoover majority to him.

Then, after a few ballots with Hoover losing ground,

Charley would have captured the rail on the home stretch and clattered in the winner.

But Coolidge's duplicity left his henchmen, William M. Butler, of Massachusetts, Hilles, and Mellon, completely up in the air—his autobiographical explanations, to the contrary notwithstanding. Thus a situation arose which the Hoover organization was quick to take full advantage of, with its powerful propaganda machine, servile press support and limitless financial resources.

The mass of delegates, standing around open-mouthed, waited for a push in some direction. William S. Vare (Philadelphia boss), with a hopeful eye to the Senate contest over his disputed seat and to the chance of giving the greatest Secretary of the Treasury since Hamilton a good swift boot, put over a fast one and came out for Hoover. Mellon and his muscle-man, Senator David Reed, bewildered and groggy over Vare's lightning play, found themselves trotting dejectedly with the Hoover herd.

The rest was simple—to Charley's heart-rending anguish.

His outburst the day before the convention, in which he had fervently declared that Hoover could not be nominated because "we don't want a candidate we will have to apologize for," while commendably frank, almost lost him the Vice Presidency.

In fact, if Coolidge had not put over a final bluff on the Hoover crowd, in a message to the effect that if Dawes, whom they really wanted, was nominated, he would consider it a personal affront, Charley, instead of being where he can give full play to his grandeur libido would be a sad and disillusioned Indian to-day.

With Dawes out, there was no one else at the moment, and so he got the break, thanks to Borah.

Goff and Watson, the Hoover people would not stand for. Fuller of Massachusetts dripped too freshly with Sacco-Vanzetti gore. Teddy Roosevelt, Jr., and Representative Tilson,

House leader, who panted and groveled for the place, couldn't even muster their own delegations.

So, after a night of futile searching, conferring and dickering, made notable by the pursuit by the reporters of blundering old "Doc" Hubert Work, Hoover's Campaign Manager, as he tried to sneak up and down the stairs of the Muehlbach Hotel in an effort to evade them, Hoover and the convention bosses threw up their hands and turned to Charley—as a last resort.

Next morning Borah piously mounted the rostrum and nominated him, to a pathetic scattering of applause.

And then Charley, like the true party wheel-horse that he is, swallowed his bitter words of a day or so before, and began the bleat he mouthed so dolorously all through the campaign: "And now I want to tell you about a man whose heart beats for the woman and the child, a man who, blah, blah, blah ... Herbert Hoover ... I thank you."

But in realization came also frustration and therein is to be found the clew to the strange mood that came over Charley when he assumed the Vice Presidency.

Believing, as he does, that but for a foul deal of fate he might have been nominated President, and that even to-day there stands between him and his consuming ambition only a fat, harried, and miserably inadequate man, Charley in his heart of hearts always sees himself in the White House.

In his improved raiment, his measured whispering, his determined reserve, his rabid clamor for full official honors upon any and all occasions, he has but one thought—the Presidency.

That is the secret of Charley as he is to-day. If the White House portals should ever actually open to him, he would be the most presidential President in the history of the land.

As has already been indicated, Charley is really a pleasant, homey enough sort of fellow. The world has guffawed at his outcries in defense of his deep-bosomed sister-hostess' social status, but little it knows the high ideals and lofty sentiments that prompted this hazardous crusade.

First of all, there is Sister Dolly herself—no small item.

Sister Dolly is a most determined and ambitious lady. By blood a half-sister—the Indian half missing—she, too, like Charley, has risen from the lowliest beginnings.

The wash tub and the kitchen range are not unknown to Dolly. The delicate nuances of society are of little moment to her. What Dolly wants she wants, and with Brother Charley as Vice President the esoteric superiorities of Senate ladies, Cabinet ladies, and Diplomatic dames awe her not at all.

Dolly, well over two hundred pounds and arrayed like Solomon when in all his kingly glory, is determined to have her rightful place and there is no squeamishness about her as to how she gets it.

And if she and Charley should by chance ever take up residence at 1600 Pennsylvania Avenue, with what relish would they both pay off scores! Many a society matron would pay dearly for the cutting jibes and smarting flippancies they now so gayly hurl at the pair.

There lopes about Washington a story that Charley's Indian name, literally translated, means Man-afraid-of-his-sister. No doubt that is wholly apocryphal, but what is true is that there is a real and strong bond of affection between brother and half-sister. Some years ago, when Mrs. Curtis was a helpless invalid, Dolly voluntarily took up the care and management of Charley's household, and this kindness over trying years has naturally not lessened his affection for her.

But it is not alone brotherly love and gratitude that inspired Charley to make his crusade for a due and proper recognition of the eminence, importance and dignity of the Vice Presidency. Deeper and profounder motives set him off.

No one knew better than he how useless and utterly ornamental the office really is. His years in the Senate and as a floor leader had left him no doubt on that score.

Also, as a Senator and floor leader, he had countenanced no change of the Vice President's lowly status. But once in the rôle himself, he saw things in a different light.

As Vice President, Charley approached the office from the angle of his Presidential fixation.

The Vice Presidency at best is a gamble. Its incumbents live only to fill a dead man's place. A few win; most don't. But the percentage is encouraging enough for the politician to take a chance, idle and utterly inconsequential as the life is.

Some of the Vice Presidents, such as Tom Marshall, fill the place with a philosophical detachment and amusement. Others, like Dawes, play a deeply-hidden but nevertheless potent rôle in legislative affairs. Both courses are impossible to Charley; the first, because he isn't detached or philosophical and has lost all sense of humor; and the second, because the political situation is against him.

He might be willing enough to dabble in the undercurrent, but the Hoover machine won't stand for any such meddling without a fight, and Charley never had a stomach for insurgency. The only time he covertly intruded he still remembers the chilly and tight-lipped hostility with which he was greeted about the White House when he came for the bi-weekly Cabinet conferences.

And as it was such a petty thing it required no imagination to picture what the Hooverian outrage would be should he really do something important.

Charley had merely loaned his official car to a group of Senate malcontents who called on Hoover to inquire how he stood on the Debenture Plan. To be asked to state his position, bluntly and unequivocally, was shock enough to the President. To learn that this outrage had been conveyed in Charley's official car was well nigh unforgivable.

Anyway, the indignation displayed by the President and his staff was enough to cure Charley. That little flyer in conspiracy was all he wanted of that sort of stuff.

But being a man who for many years had been in the midst of the political stew, Charley just had to do something—especially with those tireless complexes gnawing in him. If he couldn't be a philosopher, humorist, or conspirator, he could

at least be a stern and unbending disciplinarian in the Senate
and a defiant defender of Vice-Presidential rank and precedence there and elsewhere, particularly at social dinner tables.

It is easy to smile, and Charley's friends and former Senate
colleagues have been gleefully doing that since he assumed
his lofty rôle, but a heart-to-heart chat with him will prove
that it is really no laughing matter.

He is profoundly and earnesly distressed at the condition in
which he found the Vice Presidency, and until he goes up or
out—the former preferably, of course—he intends devoting
his time and strength advancing its fallen and sadly neglected
estate.

If, by God's will, he must be content with the Vice Presidency, this labor of love and patriotism will be his self-sacrific-
ing and lofty contribution to his native land. Laughter and
raillery will daunt him not.

He proposes to force the Senate to decorum if he has to
shatter gavels as fast as they can be made, and official society
will bow to the majesty of his rank if he has to embarrass a
thousand Secretaries of State.

"Might as well settle this thing once and for all," it is related
he told a friend in a confidential moment. "You can never tell
what will happen, and we might as well get this thing straightened out now."

It is what the psychologists call a defense mechanism, of
course. But, as Charley might well say if he knew about such
things, who is there without one? He is Vice President, and
wants to be President. The odds are against him, for he is
sixty-nine and Hoover is only fifty-five.

It is true that Hoover is fat, flaccid and worried and a dismal
failure. But he has as yet never been seriously ill and Charley
is not only fat but much older. Further, if the 1932 Republican
nomination is worth anything, Hoover will get it. If it is not
worth having, Charley doesn't want it.

So he has to content himself with day-dreaming about the
Presidency—and meanwhile he tries to make the Vice Presi-

dency as awe-inspiring and important as he knows how, even to the point of tossing aside the usual rules of courtesy between the two branches of Congress and encouraging the forthright and insurgent Norris, despite the shocked protest of that paragon of rigid immobility, Fess of Ohio, to speak bluntly and fittingly about the Republican crew of political mercenaries in the House.

To the social Old Guard of Washington, Charley and Dolly may be a riotous joke. But for the Vice President and his hefty and militant sister the others are a pack of snooty, strutting swells, who faze them not at all and with whom they are prepared to exchange blow for blow regardless of the shrieks of merriment from the onlookers and the outraged scowls of the stiff-backed Hoovers.

Principle is principle, and Alice Longworth and her crowd will take place after Charley and Dolly or, by God, they won't take place at all. In the Senate, Charley harries the chamber, demanding silence and order with a zeal and clamor that frightens the galleries and enrages the Senators, and in the evening, accompanied by the redoubtable Dolly, he raids and ravages dinner tables to satisfy their craving for precedence.

What matter if the world chortles in derision? By his vigor of conduct and the magnificence and array of his residences and office establishments shall they know him.

Charley's offices in the capital are to-day one of the most astounding sights of Washington. They are a cross between a giant tribal wickiup and a Sultan's seraglio. A section of one of the corridors of the Senate Office Building was blocked off to accommodate them. The corridor was converted into a lofty outer reception room and filled up with massive and glistening desks and chairs.

To the left are the chambers of his secretarial staff, of a number befitting so exalted a dignitary. These offices and ante-rooms are also equipped with new and lavish furnishings. To the right of the reception-room is Charley's official salon and the crowning glory of Capitol Hill.

It is impressively indicated by a chaste sign of three-inch gold lettering on a cherry background, reading "The Vice President." The room itself is the size of a manorial hall. A multitude of overstuffed chairs and lounges serve only to outline its vastness.

At the head of the cavern is a vast table of blockhouse dimensions, cherry red, as is all the rest of the furniture. What is probably one of the most curious throne chairs in the world faces it.

Its back is almost six feet in height, and is of carved and filigreed wood. At the top, in gilt letters, are the words, "The Chief." In the center is a plaque of carving. Around the rim of this piece of artistry is inscribed, also in gold lettering, the fact that the chair is the gift of the Original Curtis Boys and Matthew Quay Glaser.

Within are the mysterious words: KO-TNA-U-CA-SHE-THI-CE-XTSI-MO-KO-ONTHIA-ETTO-N, apparently some secret code, understood only by Charley and his brother tribesmen.

One wall is practically taken up by a ponderous book cabinet, the size of a corn-crib, with long panels of glass, all closely curtained. No sign of a book is visible.

Festooning the walls are numerous pen and ink cartoons of Charley, all complimentary, of course, the gifts of humble newspaper artists. A four-foot panorama of a great wheat field, a photograph of his log-cabin birthplace, so he claims, another of his former Topeka home and one of his present Topeka residence, and a picture of an Indian head are interspersed among the sketches. Indian moccasins, heavily beaded, and a miniature tepee are strewn about the huge marble mantelpiece.

In several corners stand banners. One, Charley explains, is the national standard that flew over the capitol the day he was inaugurated Vice President. The other is the Vice President's flag, the second ever made. The first, he relates, was made for Dawes and was taken away by him when he retired. Along one wall is a great over-stuffed leather couch, easily ten feet in length. Everything is as shiny as a mirror, twice as large as normal size, and as gaudy and ornate as a movie palace.

Charley takes a deep and stirring pride in the establishment. The interested caller is carefully shown all its wonders, and he modestly explains that it was all his own idea. Other Vice Presidents have had luxurious quarters, but it was he who conceived the idea of blocking up a whole corridor to make a throne room and of fitting it out with regal magnificence.

For years, as a member of Congress, Charley resided in an unostentatious dwelling in a modest residential section in Washington, but, elected to the Vice Presidency, he found it shabby and too meager.

Nothing less than the imperial suite of the fashionable Mayflower Hotel would do for him and the Ganns, meaning Dolly. There is a Mr. Gann, of course, but officially he is wholly inconsequential.

There is a good deal of mystery about this ten-room hotel apartment. For a while the story about town was that Charley got it rent free. When his social-precedence crusade was in its first bloom, reporters made inquiries of the management about the matter.

The hotel people were reluctant to discuss it, but persistent interrogation elicited certain details. It was learned that the regular rent of the apartment is $25,000 a year, but that since royalty comes to the capital only rarely, it had been used but infrequently.

From information obtained as to the number of days in the average year it had been occupied, the reporters calculated that it brought in about $7,500 annually. Taking Charley's and the manager's word that he really did pay rent, it was concluded that this figure was approximately what he got the suite for.

But the estimate is only a guess. Whatever the rental, the hotel apparently considers the difference between what it gets and what the place is listed for as fully compensated by the fact that the Vice President of the United States is one of its resident guests.

In fact, so satisfied is the management with the arrangement, that it is understood to have offered Charley and Dolly a private elevator. That is, when they entered one of the lifts it would go up or down to their destination without stopping for other calls. But Charley, ever the man of the people, declined this undue ostentation.

For him, only the simpler ways. He has no fear of brushing elbows with his fellow-man.

When the reporters approached Charley about the question of rent he went straight up in the air.

"It's nobody's —damned business what I pay," he roared at them. "They made me a proposition and I accepted it. What that is, is strictly between them and me."

Charley also strongly intimated that he knew the source of all these malicious tales. And nothing would give him greater pleasure, he added, than to break their necks.

The Vice Presidency, despite its endless social demands and opportunities—and Dolly takes full advantage of them, thus necessitating Charley's presence to safeguard her precedence—has made a lonely man of him.

His days may be taken up with vigorous gavel wielding and every night of the season filled with a dinner engagement, but these are empty satisfactions to a man of his habits and instincts. Even under ordinary circumstances to be relegated to the Vice Presidency would be a hardship to a man who, for a third of a century, was an active participant in the political mêlée.

But his social crusading has withdrawn him still further from the fellowship of his former senatorial colleagues. By the very nature of this ruckus, he has been forced to assume a certain standoffishness, and the cloak-room joking about this, and even more about Dolly's pranks, of which he is fully aware, has raised a wall between him and his one-time Senate colleagues.

When the Senate ladies haughtily refused to make Dolly, as she demanded, the president of their exclusive luncheon club, friendly relations between Charley and a number of husband-Senators naturally did not flourish.

The Indian in him just can't help cropping out when a chance arises to hammer them out of order and curtly command them to take their places and keep quiet. The Senators in turn resent the rebuke, with the result that a below-the-surface but nevertheless most active feud rages between them and the Vice President.

As floor leader, Charley was constantly called upon by the reporters. Every day a score or more of them would seek him for information about plans, line-ups and dope. He liked to growl and grumble about their "starting things," but he enjoyed the contact thoroughly, and the pressmen considered him a pretty good scout.

But as Vice President the press gallery pays no attention to him, except to josh his social-gunning. The loss of his press relations distresses Charley deeply. He is bitter about old reporter friends who have written jokingly about his social activities, and if he should ever take up his residence in the White House many a newspaper home will languish in gloom waiting a bid to the sacred dinner-table.

Charley may not be a great engineer or humanitarian, he has not fed the children of Belgium nor did he put an end to an anarchistic uprising of Boston police, but in his way he, too, has an active sense of the spectacular. Witness his ten-room hotel suite in all its oriental-rug magnificence, to say nothing of silks and satins and numerous tinted-tiled bathrooms, and the regal opulence of his offices.

But it was during his campaigning that he really showed his stuff as an impresario of the dramatic. The travelling show he put on was one of the drollest staged in a Presidential race in a long time. The glamor of the big-top act that Al Smith produced caused Charley's carnival to be overlooked, but in its way it was a gem.

As a speaker, Charley was a total loss, but what he lacked in oratory or logic, he more than made up in showmanship. He didn't miss a trick, and, with the aid of the accommodating reporters acompanying him, he now and then got quite a play in the papers.

There was the time he pinched a few fingers in the door of an automobile and then bandaged his whole hand, hung it in a sling from around his neck and heroically announced that though stricken low nothing could keep him from his onslaught upon the foe. That play was worth quite a spread, with pictures.

Then there was the time he underwent a disconcerting heckling from a farmer who insisted on asking particularly obnoxious questions about Charley's and the Republican Party's record on fulfilling pledges to render aid and succor to agriculture. Angered by the effectiveness of the quizzing, Charley roared out that there was no use answering, as the interrogator was "too damned dumb to understand."

The Republican press made much of this incident, but no mention was ever made of the aftermath. The Smithites in the rural districts took to appearing at Charley's meetings with signs reading, "Farmers, you are too damned dumb to understand." Charley didn't like that at all.

When he first took to the stump he traveled in an ordinary Pullman car. But Sister Dolly waxed indignant at this, and one day hied herself over to "Doc" Work's office, where she bitterly berated the apologetic campaign director for the indignity that was being heaped upon Charley.

The campaign, she declared, was a Hoover-*Curtis* campaign, and don't you forget it. Hoover might be a great and good man, but so was Charley. He was just as good-looking as Hoover and they had better begin using his picture.

So Charley was given a private car, a press agent, a barker —introducer, was his official designation—and an Indian Princess.

Also his visage, with his scraggly mustache carefully and

neatly trimmed by this time, was plastered up by the side of Hoover's on all the official posters. Press associations were invited to send staff men on the car, and thus equipped, Charley finished out the campagin.

One of his missions was to line up the Indian vote. From Iroquois to Sioux and from Winnebago to Pueblo, they all took him into the fold, and presumably he won them all for the Republican ticket.

Charley had two neat acts for his appearances, depending on what kind of stop was made. At short back-platform turn-outs the barker and the Indian Princess did their stuff.

The spieler would appear at the rear of the car and in vigorous tones bark up the crowd. He would then present the Princess, who would warble a sad Indian melody that made ado over "Hi-o-hi-o-hi-o." The lady finished, Charley's broad smile would put in an appearance.

Sometimes there would be a few words from him, but whether he spoke or not there was always much handshaking. As the train pulled out, the Princess would wave farewell with a pretty flag. It was all simple, sweet and unaffected.

At the big evening meetings, held indoors, Charley had another effective gag. After the introductions, he stepped forward to speak; the band in the hall—primed in advance for the stunt—would break into "The Star-Spangled Banner."

Charley would instantly stiffen to attention and, of course, the mob would have to get out of its seats. When the music ceased, Charley would then pull a line that never failed to get a big hand.

"I want to thank the musicians," he would say, "for playing our glorious national anthem. I would far rather start my speeches to the strains of 'The Star-Spangled Banner' than to those of 'The Sidewalks of New York.'"

The campaign was the cause of Charley's being invested by reporters with the curious title of Egg Charley.

Since then some of the Washington correspondents have

debased the designation to other purposes, and it has now come to mean among them a certain state of alcoholic exuberation. Charley, it should be stated in all fairness, is in no way associated with this later development.

In the beginning, applied to him, the nickname arose out of a sort of satirical affection for him among the reporters who covered his Vice-Presidential medicine show. Being a staunch and unswerving Republican, he is naturally a high-tariff zealot. In all his speeches, he made much of the great benefits that have come to one and all from this great boon to mankind.

Getting down to particulars, he would relate in detail the important part he played from time to time in making possible its manifold blessings. There was the instance, he would tell, when the farmers came to him and begged him piteously to protect them from the ruinous inroads of oriental dried and frozen eggs. He was, it appeared, deeply moved by their pleas and indignation flamed in his breast against this subtle yellow peril.

He rose heroically to the occasion and through his indefatigable efforts a high impost was plastered upon the perfidious foreign products. But if Charley thought the fight was over he was mistaken.

After a time sinister interests approached him and with devious wiles attempted to play upon him to have the duty removed. The farmers, they said, no longer needed the protection.

But Charley was not to be taken in.

"You have come to the wrong Sen-a-toah," he would relate he had roared at them.

And they, taken aback, slunk back into the dark realms from which they had come. American eggs had been saved, and Charley rested modestly content with the great victory.

Always he would begin the recital of this saga with a fierce shout: "And what about eggs ... ?"

The effect of the outcry was always encouraging.

The by-this-time drowsing audience would be startled out of its dozing and with a fresh start Charley would tear into the gory details of his egg battle.

The reporters, amused at the antic, evolved the Egg Charley appellation, and it promptly spread far and wide, particularly in political circles. Naturally, it soon reached Charley's outraged ears.

After thinking it over he finally decided to drop the egg story. But every now and then he would forget, and casting about for something with which to bestir his drooping listeners, he would inadvertently yell at the point in his speech where formerly he would begin his egg tale:

"And what about...?"

He always caught himself in time and would veer off to something else.

Before he went on the stump, Charley had made few speeches in his life. In his twenty-odd years in the Senate he had not made over a half-dozen, if that many. In his campaigning in Kansas, his electioneering was almost entirely glad-hand and personal-contact work.

On his feet he is awkward and unhappy. When he took to the hustings he fixed up a speech and kept closely to it. He was one of the dullest of the campaign orators.

But what he lacked in eloquence he more than made up in sudden outbursts. It was as if he would get peeved with himself and bored with the crowd and take it out in an outbreak of roaring.

His address had a large number of references to the "flag we all love and revere" and there was much about home, mother, womanhood and that sort of thing. The publicity agents of the National Republican Committee got up press releases that gave so-called extracts from his daily speeches.

These briefs ranged the entire scope of the campaign issues —that is, the ones that were talked about by the Republican candidates. Charley would make sufficient reference to the released press-matter to protect the reporters and then carry on with his regular harangue.

*

THERE was a bit of Jacksonian touch to his beginnings, but he didn't live up to the promise of his early youth. He was a regular from the start. On his mother's side his ancestry goes back to White Plume, Chief of the Kaw tribe of Kansas Indians, to Pawhuska, a famous fighting Chief of the Osage tribe, and to a French trader, one Louis Pappan.

His father was the adventurous scion of a New England family who rose to a Captaincy in the Civil War. His mother died when he was three years old, and he was taken by his Grandmother Pappan, who lived on an Indian reservation, sixty miles west of Topeka.

There is a legend that while he was a boy on the reservation, the peaceful tribe heard that the Cheyennes had gone on the warpath, and that Charley was sent to summon aid. It is his sole martial adventure.

Later, he became a jockey and his love for horses remains one of his happiest traits. All his life he has been a frequenter of race-tracks, and be it said for him that this is one habit he has not changed since becoming Vice President.

Charley's fondness for the race-track was responsible for a really unfair accusation against him during the 1928 campaign. Senator Bruce of Maryland, an ardent wet, openly charged that he knew of an instance when Charley had pulled a flask from his hip and invited some friends with him to partake.

Bruce named names, and the fight was on. Charley vehemently denounced the accusation as a canard. The men mentioned were interviewed and they too denied the story. Charley really is not a drinking man. After his illness several years ago he was advised by his doctors to take a small drink daily as a tonic, and he did so, but only as a medicine. He does not care for liquor and he has never toted a flask.

In his personal life he has been as regular as in his political affairs. His one vice is a fondness for watching the thoroughbreds run. He never bets.

Charley got into politics soon after putting out his shingle as a lawyer. Topeka, though dry, had a hundred flourishing and wide-open saloons. The good folk grumbled loudly thereat and threatened a reform ticket.

The local bosses and saloon-keepers, casting about for a safe candidate who would at the same time mollify the respectable element, hit upon the youthful and ambitious Charley. They knew him for a good fellow, quiet and modest but no fanatic, and they felt they could safely entrust things in his hands.

So, backed by the wets and the drys, Charley was elected. He promised to enforce the law, which didn't disturb the politicians and satisfied the drys.

In office, with his eye on the congressional seat, and considerably, it is related, to the politicians' disgust, he proceeded to make good his pledges. He closed the saloons and went to Congress—again enthusiastically supported by both sides, the drys to reward him and the wets to get him out of the county.

He served in Congress, with the exception of a two-year period when the Populists defeated him, continuously from 1893 until his election to the Vice Presidency in 1928. He came to the Senate in 1907.

As Republican leader, following the death of Henry Cabot Lodge, Charley came to be known as the greatest whisperer in the history of Congress. Whenever he took his favorite pose, with a short fat arm coiled around another Senator's shoulders, the Press Gallery got busy. It was a sure sign that something was doing.

As floor leader he adhered to his dislike for speeches. "Talk, talk, talk," he would complain to the reporters about the endless Senate deliberations. He was one of the originators and most persistent sponsors of the cloture rule permitting a limit on Senate debate by means of a two-thirds vote.

It is his firm belief, borne out by extensive experience, that everything can be fixed by friendly and confidential getting together. As, of course, it usually is—despite the seas of words.

As a fixer Charley was one of the best in the business. He isn't much to look at—a little, fat, saffron-skinned man, with a round seal-like visage—and there is no affectation of culture or learning about him, but he was worth a dozen austere and disdainful Lodges in fixing things up.

Charley, as floor leader, had no illusions about his colleagues, but as long as he was one of them he didn't high-hat them. He got along agreeably with Republicans, Democrats and Insurgents.

Norris once said of him that "Charley Curtis' word is as good as gold."

From the very start of his congressional career he was a resourceful fixer. Czar Reed was boss and Speaker of the House when Charley was a beginner there. One day Charley dropped into Reed's office to see about some patronage matter and found a caucus of the leaders in progress.

He started to leave, but Reed called to him, "Indian, what do you know about this?" The gang was trying to frame a gold-standard bill and couldn't get together on a scheme.

Charley didn't know anything about the gold standard but he was fast on figuring out ways to fix things up. He suggested that the job be taken out of the hands of the crowd and turned over to a select and trusted committee.

The suggestion took well and was promptly acted upon, and thereafter Charley was recognized as a young man of promise.

Of course, he voted for the War, and like all the other regulars, said nothing about the Harding Administration's scandals. He followed Lodge in fighting the League of Nations, and Coolidge a few years later in voting adherence to the World Court—with reservations.

He didn't have any strong convictions either way about either question. Whatever the Party did he was for. As a matter of fact, he has never had any deep convictions about any issue. He isn't built that way.

He believes unquestioningly in the Republican Party, a high tariff, the flag, home, mother and the irresistible efficacy of small favors to constituents. Since his elevation to the Vice Presidency he has added slightly to this store of beliefs by becoming convinced of the social eminence of the office.

Charley knows more people in Kansas by their first names than any one else in the State, which is why he stayed in Congress for thirty-three years. William Allen White, likewise round and soft of belly and jowl, and like Charley a kindly man, once said of him, "For thirty-five years Charley Curtis had been depositing favors in the political bank and today he is drawing checks on them."

All his life, indeed, Charley has devoted himself to doing favors for good Kansas Republicans. His appeal has always been personal. In that capacity he is an affable, efficient, useful man, and as long as Kansas was his field and Congress his goal he could handle the situation.

But once smitten by ambition and racked by suppressed desires Charley lost his equilibrium. With the robes of purple dangling teasingly before him, he has trimmed his straggling hairs and scraggly lip-furze, keeps a pretty regular crease in his pants, and knots his neckties with care. He has taken up a permanent relation with a stiff topper. His good-natured and friendly growls have given way to an affected pronunciation and if he whispers it is only in his sleep.

Of late, a new cause for alarm has stricken him. A strong suspicion has arisen in his mind that if Hoover is renominated, he may not be his running mate.

The Hoover faction have made no secret of their disapproval of Dolly's social ambitions and Charley's outcries about precedence. Charley was only a makeshift in 1928 and, with time to prepare for the 1932 convention, they might well shelve him, if they can safely do so.

Charley is too clever a politician not to know what is going on in the Hoover camp. Neither he nor the President has any affection for each other. The whole matter rests on whether it profits Hoover more to keep or to drop Charley. Should he decide on some one else, Charley would have to go.

The realization of this situation adds no happiness to Charley's days. He can hope only that Hoover finds himself so beleaguered that he can't take any chances and will have to hold on to him.

But Charley is taking no chances. In this racking dilemma he is preparing for the worst by refreshing his wide Kansas contacts. Should he lose out on the Vice Presidency, Charley is determined not to languish but to seek his old Senate seat. A Democrat holds that now, but Charley is not discouraged. The seeds, the handshakes, the scores of favors of the past he is sure will not be forgotten.

In the meantime, he is carrying on unabated his labor of love of trying to make the Vice Presidency a potent and re-spected estate.

"Good-night," said Mrs. Ruth Hanna McCormick, and an old friend of Charley's, one evening in response to his thanks for a pleasant visit at her home. "Come again, Charley."

"Say," was the outraged rejoinder, "where do you get that Charley stuff? Don't you know I am Vice President now?"

CHAPTER FIVE

WRONG-HORSE HARRY

AFTER Herbert Hoover had spent two months of rather cramped and sometimes seasick life aboard a battleship for the purpose of wooing Latin America, he came back to the United States and appointed, as the member of his Cabinet responsible for continuing this courtship, the one man whose name more than any other was anathema to all Latin America.

It was not that Latin Americans knew anything at all about Henry Lewis Stimson. They did not know whether he was liberal or conservative, whether he had brains or was the world's worst dumb-bell, whether he parted his hair in the middle or was bald-headed. They only knew that he had represented President Coolidge in Nicaragua, and Nicaragua to them was the symbol of all that was ill-smelling about North American relations with Latin America. It did not make any difference what Henry L. Stimson had done in Nicaragua; it only mattered that he was there.

The day the news leaked out that Henry L. Stimson had been appointed Secretary of State, the press associations which feed the great newspapers of Buenos Aires, Santiago and Rio de Janeiro with some three thousand words of North-American news daily, devoted exactly that number of words to direct quotes from Henry L. Stimson's book on Nicaragua. The book was written as propaganda for the State Department in order to whitewash its maladroitness in that country, and was intended only for consumption in the United States. It did not go down well below the Rio Grande.

Probably there are few Secretaries of State who have got off to a less propitious start than Henry L. Stimson. In the first place, he was late arriving in Washington. After winding up his work as Governor General of the Philippines and after a slow trip across the Pacific, he found the Hoover Administration already four weeks in office with the State Department machinery, which Frank B. Kellogg, after two years of travail, had whipped into comparatively efficient shape, going at top speed. A revolution was ramping up and down Mexico. Europe was in the throes of formulating the Young Plan. Elihu Root had been in Europe drawing up a protocol by which the United States might slip quietly into the World Court; the League was preparing to convene its Preparatory Commission on Disarmament and the Coast Guard had just sunk the Canadian rum-runner, *I'm Alone,* two hundred and fifteen miles off the Louisiana Coast, in a manner which promised to make prohibition history.

Into all this, Henry L. Stimson, accustomed to working five-hour days, a multitude of servants and the leisurely ways of the tropics, was suddenly plunked. The result had to be either complete stoppage of the fast-whirling machinery of foreign affairs, or else the spectacle of Henry L. Stimson bumping along over the cogs trying to keep pace with the wheels.

What happened was a combination of both. The revolution in Mexico, the formulation of the Young Plan and the indignation of the Canadian people at the sinking of the *I'm Alone* could not be slowed up despite Mr. Stimson's inexperience, and so, in these cases, Mr. Stimson went bumping along on the cogs of the machinery of foreign affairs, trying to keep up with the outside world. Regarding matters of lesser importance or those over which the United States had some power of initiation or control, Mr. Stimson pretty effectively applied the brakes.

One of the first obsessions he acquired after arriving in Washington was that certain people, more particularly the press and the bureau of press relations, were lying awake nights planning to knife him when his back was turned. As a result he issued an order that no news could be released to the press without his approval. And such fear did the new Secretary of State inspire in his subordinates that in one case such routine handouts as a birthday message to the President of Uruguay and an announcement of American participation in a Pan-American Infant Hygiene Conference were held up two days awaiting Mr. Stimson's return from a week-end.

Week-ends of the British variety, which begin early Friday and do not end until Tuesday morning, were Mr. Stimson's regular diversion during his first summer in Washington, and they contrasted rather disastrously with Frank B. Kellogg's habit of fretting and fuming at his desk literally day and night without vacation for four years.

Despite this, it was Mr. Stimson's constant but good-natured complaint that Mr. Hoover was working him too hard. Mrs. Stimson was not so good-natured about it. She told her friends that Mr. Hoover was a slave driver. Comparatively speaking, he was. The gentleman who sat in the White House across the street had become accustomed, as a big corporation head, to prodigious effort and he expected it of others. Mr. Stimson's long week-ends got no Presidential sympathy.

Nor did they get much sympathy from any one else. On one particular Saturday morning when important news regarding revision of German War payments to the United States had been received at the State Department, Mr. Stimson informed the press that he could not meet with them at the scheduled hour because he was engaged in "work for the President." Half an hour later, he appeared on the White House tennis court clad in immaculate flannels. The President was not there.

Next morning the newspapers published a detailed account of the importance which Mr. Stimson attached to his membership in the "Tennis Cabinet"; how he had hired, at State Department expense, an extra Negro messenger whose job it was to bring his tennis clothes down to the Department in the afternoon and lay them out in the dressing room adjoining his office, and how the Secretary, after donning them, put himself at the head of the "Tennis Parade"—Regnier his aide, Keatley, his personal stenographer, and Roach, his valet,— while guards saluted and salaamed.

For two years Mr. Stimson never missed another press conference without valid excuse.

Finding that things were happening all around him, about which he knew nothing, Secretary Stimson issued an order that each political division of the State Department should report to him daily on the work it had accomplished. Non-political divisions, such as the Passport Bureau, the Visa Office, the Personnel Office, that of the Solicitor, he required to report twice a week. The result was that on Wednesdays and Saturdays almost every one in the State Department was so busy writing reports to the Secretary that nothing much else was accomplished. The stenographic division was swamped, and Mr. Stimson himself carried home with him a stack of reports which every one surmised were thrown in the waste basket like so many uncorrected examination papers.

All of which did not add materially to the efficiency of the State Department and created the general impression among his subordinates that Henry L. Stimson was a high-handed executive with military ideas and a propensity for giving orders which he had inherited from his days as Secretary of War.

This, of course, was a "spot" impression, created at that very unfair period when Mr. Stimson was green and when the State Department was dealing with some of the most important matters before it in years.

*

Two years have passed since that hectic period. The State Department functions much more serenely now. Its personnel have more confidence in their chief and chafe less at his whims and eccentricities. But even to-day, Henry Lewis Stimson remains an enigma to most of those around him. He favors universal military conscription, yet was the most hard-hitting enemy the militarists had when they opposed a naval reduction treaty. He paid $800,000 for a palatial estate in fashionable Northwest Washington, yet he believes in the redistribution of wealth and advocates increased income taxes for the wealthy. He is cold, aloof, criticized as being snobbish, but does the most generous and thoughtful things for those around him. He is a strange mixture of conservatism and liberalism, of pacificism and militarism, of gentility and democracy.

The secret of this contradiction is Stimson's family. He has never been able to forget the proud part it played in the founding of these United States. He tries to forget; he tries to mix with his fellow-men; but never has he been able completely to divorce himself from the inherent instinct that he is of a race born to rule.

This instinct was first planted when John Stimson, fifth great-grandfather of Henry Lewis Stimson, born in England in 1605, came to America in the *Truelove,* settling at Watertown Farms. His son, George Stimson, having moved to Ipswich, Massachusetts, took down his rifle and powder horn to fight the Indians in King Philip's War. The latter's grandson, also named George, served as a Captain in the French and Indian and in the Revolutionary Wars, later returning to Windham, New York, in which State the Stimsons ever since have dabbled in politics, made money and been proud to live.

The first Henry Stimson, great-grandfather of Henry Lewis, born 1772, was one of the few Stimsons who has not been a fighting man. However, Stimson's father, Lewis Atterbury, made up for it by serving as a Captain and aide-de-camp in the Civil War.

By this time the family had accumulated a considerable fortune. Henry Clark Stimson, grandfather of Henry Lewis, born 1813, had become a wealthy banker and railroad president just at the period when the Morgans, the Harrimans and the Hills were making railroad history in the United States. Stimson's father, therefore, was under no compulsion to earn a living. He studied medicine, became Professor of Surgery at the Cornell Medical School and eventually built up a lucrative practice among New York's Four Hundred. He was known as New York's most fashionable physician and was as popular for his yacht racing as he was for his prescriptions. Few were the summers when he did not enter his yacht in the Trans-Atlantic race. For a while he held the record for this contest.

Young Henry Lewis Stimson was born into a stultifying world of wealth and luxury. He had no particular reason for worrying about the problem of making a living, and his early youth was not calculated to inspire such worry. While an undergraduate at Yale, he spent his vacations in what is an expensive luxury even for the sons of Eli—big-game hunting. He made annual excursions to the Rockies or to Canada and later gained some reputation for himself as the first white man to climb "The Chief" in the Glacier National Park. He interspersed these hunting trips with vacations in New Brunswick, Quebec and Switzerland, where he climbed the Matterhorn and the Rothhorn. Graduated from Yale in 1888, Stimson was, with two exceptions, like any other rich man's son who has a pipe-line to his father's purse and a desire to satisfy his curiosity.

These two exceptions were: family pride and an uncle.

Family pride has been the outstanding characteristic of all Stimsons since John Stimson crossed from England in the *Truelove*. Next to the pride they have taken in their family they have been proud of their country and their State. The State of New York they have considered a community corporation in which every Stimson must play his part. The United States they have considered only slightly less so. There-fore, it was incumbent upon young Henry Lewis to uphold the tradition of the Stimsons by upholding its pride in the Nation and the State.

Henry Albert Stimson, now ninety years old, and uncle of Henry Lewis, had felt this way. But instead of giving his life to the healing of the sick and the racing of yachts, as did Henry Lewis's father, he had dedicated it to the work of the Lord. He raised seven children, preached from pulpits in Minneapolis, St. Louis and New York, and became the out-standing and most liberal Congregationalist divine of his day.

In the life of Henry Lewis Stimson, his namesake, the Reverend Doctor Stimson played a great part—probably the most important part any individual has played. Young Henry Lewis took his problems to his uncle. They saw much of each other. Even to-day, when the present Secretary of State makes hurried business trips to New York, he seldom fails to spend an evening with the aged divine, and his uncle in turn never hesitates to sign his name to lengthy petitions urging the Secretary of State to take certain steps in international relations which other members of the State Department con-sider rank heresy.

From his uncle, therefore, Henry Lewis Stimson got a cer-tain humanitarian and idealistic slant on life which, together with his family pride and his luxurious youth, made his character, even in its formative period, a combination of weird contradictions.

Dominant in his character was the inbred belief that being a Stimson, blessed with the privileges of wealth and prestige, he was born to rule. This rule, however, thanks to the teach-ings of a kindly uncle, was to be beneficent and for the good of the people. Mixed up with this were all the characteristics which ordinarily accrue from a life of luxury. Stimson was mentally and physically lazy. He had never been compelled to work. He was surrounded by conservative friends and conservative influences. Yet despite this environment, and partly because of his uncle, young Henry Lewis was able to keep a liberal and detached view on life such as most wealthy young men lost before they were graduated from knee breeches.

With this groundwork of character, Henry Lewis Stimson started out on a life that was to make him more renowned and more criticized than any of his distinguished ancestors.

*

WHEN Stimson, Governor General of the Philippines, was summoned to Washington to become Secretary of State, a friend wrote of him in the New York *Times*:

" 'The stern Daughter of the Voice of God' has stood ever at his elbow, laying on him the compulsions that she laid on men of old. * * * You saw him bow his head when the call came and sail away like a Roman proconsul. * * * It is as if some one out of the Good Book had put his hand on Stimson's shoulder with the familiar words, 'Well done, good and faithful servant.' "

Those words convey most accurately the impression which Mr. Stimson gives to the casual observer. On his face is the look of bored martyrdom. He, a Stimson, has been summoned to accept the responsibilities of his patriotism and his position, and he is not one to spurn the challenge....

The facts, however, belie both the look on Stimson's face and his friend's description quoted above.

Mr. Stimson became Secretary of State not at the command of the "Stern Daughter of the Voice of God," nor at the urging of some one out of the Good Book, but because his law partner, Elihu Root, and his old friend, William Howard Taft, were back in Washington pulling the wires for his appointment.

In fact, it has been the "Stern Daughter of the Voice of God" in the person of Elihu Root that has got for Mr. Stimson many of those important positions which, to the initiated, appear to be the reward of great merit plus the discernment of God. It was Elihu Root, a former Secretary of War, who recommended young Mr. Stimson for that post in 1911. It was Elihu Root who suggested him to Theodore Roosevelt as District Attorney for Southern New York in 1906, and, probably most important of all, it was Elihu Root who gave young Stimson his first job.

Also from an old and distinguished New York family, Root believes that old and distinguished New York families should stick together, and when Henry Lewis was 26 years old, a graduate of Yale and of Harvard Law School, Root took him into his law firm. Root's solicitude permitted young Stimson to marry Mabel Wellington White, who can trace her ancestry back even further than Stimson's to the first voyage of the *Mayflower*. Stimson did not particularly need to work to support a wife, but it was considered the more respectable thing to do. As soon as Stimson entered Root's firm, therefore, the marriage took place.

The cases which came across Stimson's desk as a member of the firm of Root and Clarke were the usual routine work of championing big business upon which most New York law firms fatten, and there was no indication during this period that young Mr. Stimson was any less conservative or more idealistic than the average scion of wealth and aristocracy.

After twelve years of private law practice, however, Theodore Roosevelt, himself a scion of wealth and aristocracy, believing as Root did, that such scions should stick together, appointed Stimson, still in his thirties, District Attorney for Southern New York. For the first time, Stimson showed flashes of the liberal background his uncle had helped instill in him. It was in the heyday of Roosevelt's trust-busting boom and Stimson, inspired by all the righteous wrath of his Puritan soul, went for the Sugar Trust. Having made a name for himself on this, he prosecuted Charles W. Morse, accused of misappropriating funds from the National Bank of America.

For a politician, it was a heaven-sent opportunity. Whether Stimson realized this or not, his prosecution of Morse won for him the Republican nomination for the governorship of his State.

There is some difference of opinion as to whether picking Stimson for this fight was a real act of friendship on Roosevelt's part. John A. Dix, experienced Democrat, was running as the Tammany candidate and was sure of election. However, some one had to run against him, and Stimson was picked as the goat. Only forty-three years old and a comparative babe as far as politics were concerned, he never had a chance. However, family pride, the inherent feeling that a Stimson is born to serve his country and rule it well, urged him on.

The result would have been laughable had it not been so tragic. Here was a wealthy young aristocrat never having felt the pinch of hunger, never having soiled his hands with manual labor, never having mingled with his fellow-men, pitted against a rough-and-tumble political fighter in an election whose success depended upon winning the toughest elements of Brooklyn and East-Side New York. His cultured accent, his uneasy platform presence, his cold personality, almost every detail of his manner betrayed his birth and breeding, gave his electorate an impression of a young aristocrat who condescends to rule, and who, though he may be a good ruler, condescends.

The opposition press called him the "human icicle." Then, after a half-dozen speeches, during which Stimson never varied his theme of "I stand squarely behind the policies of Theodore Roosevelt," and after Roosevelt had referred to him endearingly as "his" candidate, the nickname was changed to "Our Harry."

Stimson's failure as a glad-hander, brought to light so glaringly during the New York gubernatorial campaign, has remained a real handicap throughout his life. He is naturally cold and aloof, but not nearly so much so as he appears. At times he tries desperately to overcome this handicap. As Secretary of State he is constantly inviting people out to his colonial residence to chat and get acquainted. On these occasions he tries with almost visible effort to pull himself out of his shell, to radiate charm and personality. But he is a slow and diffident conversationalist, would rather sit in front of a fire with Mrs. Stimson and a book, and, on the whole, he fails. In Washington, the Diplomatic Corps, the State Department personnel, his Cabinet friends, all respect him and like him in a mild sort of way, but there is no enthusiasm. The inescapable fact is that Henry L. Stimson was born an aristocrat, and despite a kindly democratic soul, he never has been nor ever will be able to escape from perpetually giving the appearance of an aristocrat.

Although Stimson's personality plus his political ineptitude caused a Democratic landslide for John A. Dix, his efforts were not unrewarded. Theodore Roosevelt never forgot his friends, and a few months after his political defeat, Roosevelt and Root persuaded Taft to appoint Stimson Secretary of War. He was one of the youngest men ever to fill that office.

Although Stimson served for only two years as Secretary of War, he probably enjoyed it more than any other office he has held. The army at that time had not reached the impressive peace-time proportions that it has since the "war to end war," and the Department to a considerable extent ran itself. Something which he may have inherited from the ancestors who fought in the early wars of the nation has always endeared the pomp and ceremony of military life to Henry L. Stimson, and in the War Department he felt very much at home. Also, he liked the high-ranking Generals who surrounded him. He considered them extremely capable and let them run his Department pretty much as they pleased.

Mr. Stimson, therefore, had time to enjoy some of the luxuries he had indulged in during his early youth. He rode in Rock Creek Park every morning, frequently wearing his riding boots to his office after the custom of young aristocrats in those days. It was at that time that he won the nickname, "Light-Horse Harry," and one of the most striking pictures which graces the ante-room of the Secretary of War to-day is a full-length portrait of Henry Lewis Stimson, breeches, boots, crop and all.

After the disruption of the Taft-Roosevelt honeymoon had thrown Mr. Taft out of the White House in 1913, Mr. Stimson went back to New York, and with the exception of some help which he gave Al Smith in reforming the State Constitution in 1915, applied himself rather assiduously to his law practice and to building up a fortune. He acquired Highold, an expansive estate on Long Island. He went in for fox-hunting. He ruled over his little suburban world like any twelfth-century feudal lord.

After fifteen years of this, the fortune was built, the practice was thriving and Mr. Stimson had sunk rather successfully out of the public eye. So far had he sunk that when he came back with a reverberation which put his name on the cables to all parts of the world, every newspaperman handling the story had to scratch his head and run to *Who's Who* to find out just who Henry Lewis Stimson was.

The reverberation occurred in 1927, when the Coolidge Administration had got itself into more trouble in one small country than had any other administration in years, and needed a man to straighten out the mess. Colonel Stimson, as he was then called, was drafted as President Coolidge's personal representative in Nicaragua.

Just how he happened to be drafted, Mr. Stimson himself does not know. Most people suspect Root and Taft. Stimson was in the middle of an important law case, when the "Stern Daughter of the Voice of God" called up in the form of Frank B. Kellogg and asked him to come to Washington. Stimson protested. At that particular time he was getting a little tired of the martyr complex. Partly because it was a call from the President, however, partly because his curiosity was aroused, Stimson came.

Calvin Coolidge gave him laconic instructions to go to Nicaragua and straighten out the mess Kellogg had got into.

Stimson demurred. But he did not demur very vigorously. At heart he was flattered that the long list of services which the Stimsons had rendered their country was to be made longer. So he made only one condition with the President, namely, that he, Stimson, should have complete authority to do whatever he found necessary once he arrived in Nicaragua. Coolidge agreed.

Mr. Kellogg, however, was not so amenable. While Stimson was on the high seas, Mr. Kellogg began to fidget. He began to conjure up all kinds of mistakes which the Special Representative of the President might make when confronted with the pitfalls of Nicaraguan jungles and politics. Finally, fidgety Mr. Kellogg sent a telegram to head off Mr. Stimson at Managua. The telegram surrounded him with buts, ifs, whereases and warnings against the further use of American armed force in Nicaragua and against any pledge to guarantee Nicaraguan elections. Mr. Stimson, however, completely ignored this. He sent a telegram to the White House saying that he still assumed full authority to do whatever he considered expedient, and once again Calvin Coolidge replied in the affirmative.

Stimson took this literally. At one time he pledged, in effect, the entire military and naval force of the United States to make Jose M. Moncada, Nicaraguan rebel leader, lay down his arms. He did exactly what Mr. Kellogg did not want him to do. He promised that American marines would remain in Nicaragua and that they would guarantee a free and fair election.

Whether Mr. Stimson was wise in using this force and in making this pledge is for historians to decide. There is no question, however, that he substituted a definite policy for one of Kellogg vacillation and there is no question, also, that Calvin Coolidge was pleased. It was because Mr. Coolidge was pleased that he sent Mr. Stimson to the Philippines, where a somewhat similar mess needed to be straightened out.

*

No situation could have been better ordered to the kindly despotism of the Stimson family than that which existed in the Philippines at that time. For six years the Philippines had been handled with the mailed and military fist of General Leonard B. Wood. Wood had been abrupt and peremptory. He had vetoed the bills of the Philippine legislature on a wholesale scale and almost without explanation. He had surrounded himself with the famous "Cavalry Cabinet"—military men who had become so biased against any human being with a brown skin that their advice was impossible. They believed that the way to keep a native in his place was to apply the tip of the toe to the seat of his pants. They drew a strict color line even to the point of prohibiting football matches between Filipinos and white service teams, for fear white prestige would lose "face" by defeat. Filipino political leaders—even the President of the Senate and the Speaker of the House—were considered too lowly to attend Government House receptions. They had so many mistresses, it was explained, that it was socially impossible to decide upon the correct wife to invite.

Into this situation walked a man whose ancestral lineage was so secure that he could afford to mingle with people far below him and who believed it his duty to mingle, a man who had been reared with the idea that he was born to rule but that his rule must be kindly, considerate and fair.

Mr. Stimson started from the premise that the Philippine Islands existed chiefly for the benefit of the Filipino people, not for the benefit of American business, not for the purpose of giving the United States a naval base in Pacific waters, and not for the aggrandizement and glory of the American empire. Once the Filipino politicos appreciated that premise, they were with him one hundred per cent. Mr. Stimson initiated a régime of full and frank discussion. His aim was to secure what he wanted by persuasion and coöperation rather than by force. On the whole he was successful. But at heart always the aristocratic despot, he never relinquished his final whip hand. If, after discussion, argument and persuasion, he could not get what he wanted, the army and navy of the United States were always at his command.

His first act was to fire the Cavalry Cabinet. His second was to invite Filipinos and their wives to Government House. The American colony never forgave him, and any Governor who offends the American colony can be rated, *ipso facto,* as having independence, courage and the interests of the Philippine people fundamentally at heart.

So there grew up between Stimson and the Philippine leaders a genuine affection, which continued long after the Governor-General relinquished his palace at Malaccan and came to Washington. Even as Secretary of State he made special trips to Congress to fight the sugar tariff and once caused deep resentment in the Diplomatic Corps by entertaining a Filipino delegation before he condescended to invite any foreign diplomat to his table.

When he finally sailed away from Manila in the spring of 1929, there was no question that Henry Lewis Stimson left behind him one of the best jobs he had ever done.

*

AFTER Secretary Stimson had weathered a rather severe initiation during his first few months in the State Department, the weird mixture of liberalism and conservatism, of pacifism and militarism, which makes up his character, began to crop out.

His first important step was the appointment of the late Joseph P. Cotton as Under-Secretary of State. Cotton was a thorough liberal. Where Stimson's liberalness balked, when it got too far away from the home base of conservative birth and wealthy environment, Cotton never stopped at anything. He was a man who not only would have been glad to have defended Rosika Schwimmer in her citizenship fight before the Supreme Court, but publicly boasted of it. Furthermore, Cotton was gifted with rare executive ability, and Stimson, wise enough to realize this and himself inherently a little lazy, let him run the Department.

The two men worked in closest harmony. Whether Stimson or Cotton was responsible for turning over many of the old precedents, set up as sacred under the Kellogg-Hughes régimes, it is difficult to say; but at any rate, between Cotton's restless energy and Stimson's placid liberalness, they were knocked down one by one.

The first to go was the ban against the dread Count Karolyi, whom the nervous Frank B. Kellogg had barred from the United States as a red menace. The wisdom of the Stimson move was promptly demonstrated by the pathetic way in which the poor Count proved a complete flop except at the tea tables of earnest old ladies and other innocuous worshippers of foreign titles.

Later Stimson did not bat an eye when the patrons of patriotism threw up their hands in horror because he had given a passport to Dorothy Detzer, militant pacifist, despite the fact that she declined to take an oath swearing to defend the Constitution with traditional rifle and pitchfork.

When it became apparent that descendants of American Negroes who founded the Republic of Liberia as a haven of freedom were selling their black brothers at $15 a head for the plantations of King Alfonso, Stimson pushed an investigation of it, and later sent the President of the Black Republic the most scathing diplomatic rebuke which the United States has sent any nation since it declared war on Germany. Later through Cotton's foresight, he headed off another slave scandal in Abyssinia by getting advance guarantees from the J. G. White Corporation that no slave labor would be used in the construction of the Lake Tsana dam at the mouth of the Blue Nile.

One of the most surprising things about Stimson was the way he meticulously refrained from following his predecessors' practice of raining a steady stream of pokes and punches at Soviet Russia. He had ample provocation. Maxim Litvinoff's

scathing chastisement of his attempt to prevent war in Manchuria gave Stimson ample excuse to hit back.

Furthermore, he did not join in the chorus when the Pope
broadcast his castigation of Russia, nor did he approve the
suggestion of the man he worships most, Elihu Root, that the
United States create an agency to guard against Soviet propaganda. Finally it became apparent that Mr. Stimson had certain sympathies with Soviet Russia; that while he did not
condone the communist system, he did believe that somewhere in between the extremes of Russian communism and
American capitalism there might be a happier utopia; that
while he did not approve Russia's forcible confiscation of
property, he did believe that the tremendous concentration of
wealth in the hands of a few was a decided handicap to the
welfare of the United States and that a more equable distribution of wealth was absolutely necessary.

It was these ideas which led him to order a thorough research and study of everything Russian—a study to be made
not by the career diplomats who for years had been manu-
facturing Bolshevist bogies for Frank B. Kellogg, but by out-
siders who had not lost their vision and perspective.

Finally, Stimson has constantly kept a weather eye on the
wealthy social clique which long has dominated the foreign
service. Before he took office, his liberal friends warned him of
the pitfalls these gentlemen could place in his path, and he
has been suspicious of the Butler Wrights, the Joe Grews, the
Hugh Wilsons and all the others ever since. Almost immediately he assumed office, he gave them one of the most subtle
but position-putting pieces of punishment ever meted out to
the career service.

It occurred at the first diplomatic tea held at Woodley. It is
the usual custom at these functions for the wives of the various
Assistant Secretaries to assist the wife of the Secretary of State
in pouring. These ladies are Mrs. Wilbur Carr, Mrs. William
R. Castle, Jr., and Mrs. Frances White—all charming, acquainted with the Diplomatic Corps, and socially secure. Mr.

Stimson, however, had heard that the career service was coming to view these functions as their own, so he reversed the process. He selected Mrs. Ruth B. Shipley, Miss Margaret M. Hanna, and one or two other equally efficient but none-too-social ladies who had worked their way up from clerkships to the rank of bureau chiefs, and he put them behind the tea-pots.

A lot of things happened that aren't supposed to happen at the usual well-oiled diplomatic tea. For one thing, Captain Regnier, Stimson's young and precocious military aide, did the announcing and got the Minister of Bolivia mixed up with the Minister of Sweden, which was no compliment to the latter. And when the Italian Ambassadress wanted her car she had to wait thirty minutes for it. But for the most part, the party delighted a great number of people who do not usually experience much delight at diplomatic receptions and it performed the wholesome function of putting the career corps decidedly in its place.

*

WHILE Henry Lewis Stimson was being labeled revolutionary and radical by the career corps in regard to Count Karolyi, Liberia and Russia, he was being bull-headed, militaristic and inept in handling a score of other things, including Brazil, Fascism and Major-General Smedley Butler.

Fundamentally, Mr. Stimson is as honest as he tries to be fair. He has two definite handicaps, however. One is an exceedingly bad memory. The other is a temper. On occasion, Mr. Stimson has completely lost control of the latter. He has sputtered, fumed and issued red-hot statements which focused public attention upon his difficulties. Very few people in the United States ever would have heard of the Washington *Post's* insult to Prince de Ligne, the Belgian Ambassador, had not Stimson publicly denounced it. Nor would any one have cared a tinker's dam whether he was properly consulting with the Secretary of the Navy during the Japanese naval negotiations, had not Stimson, grim-lipped and white-faced, bitterly denounced a Washington *Post* editorial saying that he was neglecting the navy.

Like his temper, Mr. Stimson's memory is constantly playing him tricks. Once he announced that he had sent a telegram instructing the American Ambassador in Havana to take up with the Cuban Government the long controverted claims of Joseph E. Barlow. After the newspapers had featured this on their front pages, Mr. Stimson had to announce next day that he had made a mistake, that no telegram had been sent to Havana, and that he had been thinking of a telegram he sent to Berlin in regard to the Orloff case, in which Russian forgers had linked Senator Borah with Soviet conspirators.

It was not a faulty memory, however, that has sometimes caused Mr. Stimson, his back to the wall, to issue what is referred to in polite circles as a diplomatic denial, but which among the more hard-fisted is known as an ordinary variety of cheap garden lie.

Every foreign office in Europe issues them—on the average of two or three times a week. But American diplomacy has so boasted of its own chastity and Mr. Stimson has been given such a character of aristocratic saintliness, that it surprised some of his friends to hear Rear-Admiral Hilary P. Jones inform a Senate committee under oath that he had told Mr. Stimson he would not go to London, whereas Mr. Stimson had previously told the press that Admiral Jones had told him no such thing. Again it jarred some of those not conversant with the wiles of diplomacy to hear Mr. Stimson say that the Canadian Minister, Vincent Massey, had never expressed alarm over American tariff increases, whereas Senators Borah and Watson said that Mr. Stimson had told them quite a contrary story.

It was neither faulty memory nor entirely a desire to deceive, however, which led Mr. Stimson into his imbroglio in regard to Brazil. It was just plain bull-headedness. The Solicitors of the State Department—having devoted entire lives to studying international law—had informed their Secretary of State that there was no provision under international law requiring him to declare an arms embargo against Brazilian revolutionaries. After receiving this advice, Mr. Stimson stepped into the next room and informed the press that he was placing an embargo on arms shipments to Brazil. He maintained that international law required this.

Unfortunately, Mr. Stimson was right but didn't know it. The United States and Brazil both had ratified a multi-lateral treaty some four months before making such an embargo obligatory, but Mr. Stimson didn't know it existed and the bright young men who advise him had forgotten about it.

Forty-eight hours after declaring this embargo, the Brazilian Government, which Mr. Stimson had sought to keep in power, was overthrown.

Thereafter, Stimson's old nickname was changed to "Wrong-Horse Harry."

He has been trying to explain his Brazilian mistake ever since. During the course of one of these explanations, before the Council of Foreign Relations, Mr. Stimson cited the arms treaty as justification for his embargo, but failed to mention the rather relevant point that he did not know of its existence at the time.

It was also bull-headedness that got Secretary Stimson into such a mess with those two poles of personality, Benito Mussolini and Smedley Butler. Stimson had supported Hoover in his demand that the stormy petrel of the Marine Corps be court-martialed instead of merely reprimanded as punishment for calling the Premier of Italy a hit-and-run driver.

After the court martial had been ordered and there had been ample time to gauge the nation-wide abuse which it was heaping on the Hoover Administration, an emissary of General Butler's approached Stimson suggesting the court martial be abandoned. He found the Secretary of State in a mood reminiscent of the days when he was Secretary of War—of the days when his great-grandfathers had taken down their rifles to fight in King Philip's War, the French and Indian War, the Revolutionary War and the Civil War. Mr. Stimson pounded on the table. He puffed out his chest. He swore that General Butler was a soldier and would have to take a soldier's medicine.

He did not then know how much he was to regret that moment of militarist indignation!

A day or two later the Italian Ambassador himself came to ask that the court martial be abandoned and it was Stimson's turn to send an emissary to General Butler. He found the General's attorney, Major Henry Leonard, the coolest poker player he had ever encountered.

Stimson made his first move—a proposal that instead of a court martial, Butler be reprimanded, removed from his command and placed on the list awaiting orders. Leonard laughed in the emissary's face.

Stimson made his second move—a proposal that Butler be reprimanded, removed from his command and sent to Guam instead of being put on the list awaiting orders. Leonard laughed again.

Stimson made his third move—a proposal that Butler be reprimanded, continue his command, but write a letter of apology to the Italian Government. Leonard refused. Then he played his trump card. He sent word to Stimson that enough time had been wasted, that Butler had witnesses whom he had to subpoena from Italy, and that he would give Stimson only twelve hours more in which to offer a suitable compromise.

Stimson then made his last move. He asked what terms Butler wanted. The reply was: "Butler gets off with a mild reprimand, and he writes it himself."

The terms were accepted.

This was the second time Mr. Stimson had gone wrong where Mussolini was concerned. At the height of his clean-up of Kellogg's moth-eaten imperialistic policies, Mr. Stimson's attention was called to the fact that Mussolini's Ambassador in the United States, together with his consuls, had been promoting a reign of terror among Italo-Americans. Mussolini's envoys had been endeavoring to collect taxes from them. They had tried to prevent their naturalization as American citizens. They had spread Fascist propaganda among American schools, in one case causing the dismissal of a school teacher who refused to use the propaganda supplied her. And they had insisted that all Italians join and contribute to the Fascist League of North America.

Stimson ordered an investigation. But it was carried out under the direction of William R. Castle, Jr., then Assistant Secretary, whose best friend is Ambassador Martino and who gives to Fascism the same respectful reverence that his missionary ancestors divided between the Bible and the acquisition of land from Hawaiian natives.

The result was a white-wash of both Mussolini and his representatives in the United States. Mr. Stimson could not help knowing that Castle's investigation was violently partisan. But as a result of his birth and background, Mr. Stimson has a certain respect for established order, especially when it is in the form of a high-powered and successful dictatorship with which he is trying to negotiate a naval agreement. So he saved for Liberia and Nicaragua the invective which Mussolini justly had coming to him, and accepted the Castle report.

*

THERE is nothing more confusing about Henry Lewis Stimson than the fact that despite his naïve and tenacious worship of the folderol of militarism, he is a devout disciple of peace. A constant struggle goes on within him between reverence for the military exploits of his ancestors and the pacifist ideals implanted by his benign uncle. The former found expression in his youth when he became an enthusiastic member of the crack cavalry regiment of the New York National Guard. It found expression again when war was declared. Stimson had attended Plattsburg, got a commission as a First Lieu-

tenant and was one of the first to enlist. But to have a former
Secretary of War rank no higher than a Lieutenant was most
embarrassing, and Pershing very soon assigned him to the
305th Field Artillery with the rank of Colonel. Like all
Stimsons, he served faithfully, though not brilliantly, saw real
service in France and won the respect and devotion of his
men.

After the War was over, after he had become Secretary of
State, even after he had participated in ceremonies com-
memorating a Pact Renouncing War, Stimson showed how
deeply implanted is his devotion to the military by declaring
his views on compulsory military training unchanged—that
now, as before the War, every young man in the United
States should be compelled to spend several precious months
carrying a rifle around a dusty parade-ground for the honor,
glory and defense of his country.

Despite all this, Mr. Stimson considers himself a devout
disciple of peace. He makes this declaration so often that he
gives the impression he is chiefly trying to convince himself
of his own pacifism. And while Henry Lewis Stimson would
become an outright pacifist only if he, himself, could perpetually dictate the terms of peace, he does have very genuine
but poorly managed impulses in that direction.

The two outstanding examples are his effort to uphold the
Kellogg Treaty in Manchuria and the London Naval Conference.

Stimson's attack on naval disarmament had been painstakingly planned. He stumbled into the Manchurian row by
accident. Although it is not generally appreciated, Stimson
probably did a better job in Manchuria than at London.

In dealing with the crisis in Manchuria, Stimson showed
more nerve than he has displayed in tackling any other
problem. Although the slap which he got from Litvinoff for
his pains resounded with such a whack that it drowned the
real effect of his work, actually Stimson ended a near war in

the Far East and a slap in the face is not an exorbitant price to pay for that.

Possibly if Mr. Stimson had known the Senate in those earlier days as he does now, he would have been more cautious. The principle of what he did went diametrically against the grain of what a majority of the Senate has stood for during a century of isolation. Manchuria was some 6,000 miles away. Only about $12,000,000 worth of American property and a score of Jewish-American fur-buyers are located in the entire area and they were nowhere near the scene of the dispute.

There was no material reason why the United States should have been interested in a war in Manchuria except this:

The United States had taken the initiative in negotiating a treaty for the outlawry of war. The last nation had ratified the pact, and President Hoover had invited its author, Frank B. Kellogg, and all the diplomatic representatives of the nations which had signed it, to attend a gala ceremony at the White House, formally declaring the Pact in effect and war outlawed throughout the world.

And just on the eve of this ceremony, Russian and Chinese troops mobilized on the Manchu-Siberian frontier.

Mr. Stimson had the alternative of acting vigorously or seeing the Kellogg Pact and the White House ceremony become the laughing stock of the world. He was not, however, goaded into action by ridicule alone. Essentially slow-moving and lazy, ridicule supplied the kick-off, but when Henry Lewis Stimson got going, he went all the way. He made it clear that his action in throwing the entire weight of the United States against war was a precedent, and that thereafter the United States intended to set itself up as the protector of the Pact of Paris and the guardian of the peace of the world.

The brilliant audacity of Stimson's move left the Senate a little breathless. Few Senators will attack a man who is both belligerent and successful, and even those who had howled the loudest at Woodrow Wilson's entangling alliances now sat silent and approved. They did, that is, until Litvinoff slapped Stimson in the face. Then like all small boys who love a fight, they guffawed.

Litvinoff's slap could have been avoided. In the first place Stimson's battle had been pretty well won before Litvinoff retaliated. In the second place, although few people knew it, Stimson had been fighting on Litvinoff's side.

All during the controversy Mr. Stimson had championed the Russian cause. The chief bone of contention was whether China should return the Chinese Eastern Railroad before the dispute was arbitrated. Russia contended that the railroad had been seized illegally and that its future ownership could not be arbitrated fairly while it remained in the possession of China. Stimson backed Russia in this contention and he backed her to the limit. He summoned the meek little Chinese Minister, C. C. Wu, to his office, pounded on the desk and demanded that the railroad be turned back to Russia. His eyes snapped and his words rasped. When Stimson starts one of his pounding scenes he can be an awesome individual.

But after going to bat for Russia in a big way, Mr. Stimson, true to the habits he had formed as a rich man's son, went off to his Long Island estate for a Thanksgiving week-end.

When he left, Russian troops, having waited to take advantage of frozen ground, had advanced some eighty miles into Chinese territory. Mr. Stimson was absent for five days. During those five days the Russians completely evacuated Chinese soil. Mr. Stimson, when he returned, did not bother to read the telegrams the State Department had received reporting this evacuation and sent two sharply worded notes drawn up during his vacation, to China and Russia.

Litvinoff was in a position to reply that no Russian troops were on Chinese soil, and, with all the genius a Russian has for sarcasm and invective, he made the most of his opportunity.

Mr. Stimson probably regrets the time element in regard to his last note, but he has never regretted the stand he took to uphold the Kellogg Pact. Nor has he nursed any particular grudge against Litvinoff for the way he clouded an issue which otherwise would have stood out as the most courageous work Mr. Stimson performed during the first two years of his tumultuous State Department administration.

*

Mr. Stimson has confided to his friends that his greatest ambition before he became Secretary of State was to end the back-biting rivalry between Great Britain and the United States which reached its climax after the abortive Geneva Naval Conference, when France and Britain negotiated a secret agreement of their own and Mr. Coolidge, in retaliation, instructed Frank B. Kellogg to snub the British by sailing only within nose-thumbing distance of their shores while en route to Ireland in the summer of 1928. Mr. Stimson's hope was to negotiate, as the foundation for a new Anglo-American friendship, a new naval treaty.

Sincere as this ambition was, Mr. Stimson, as in most things, was pushed into it. Even before he became Secretary of State and was *en route* from the Philippines to Washington, the Japanese, worried about increased cruiser construction, got Stimson ashore at Tokyo, wined and dined him and emphasized the importance of holding a naval conference as soon as possible.

A day or two after his arrival in Washington, Stimson was called into a conference between President Hoover and Hugh Gibson, perpetual plenipotentiary for the United States at all disarmament conferences. These two had been planning some surprises for the French and British at the session of the Preparatory Commission on Disarmament opening in Geneva two weeks hence, and Stimson's capacity at that first conference was merely to listen and nod approval.

During all of those early naval negotiations through the summer of 1929, it was Hoover who did the pushing and

Stimson who scrambled to keep up. Along toward mid-summer, however, with the embarrassing sinking of the *I'm Alone* out of the way, the Vice President's wrath over the seating of his half-sister, Dolly Gann, appeased, and the volatile Dawes playing to the galleries with hit-and-run trips between London and Scotland, Stimson actually began to sink his teeth into naval negotiations. From that time until the Senate confirmed his treaty during a sweltering extra session, exactly twelve months later, Stimson never took his teeth out.

Unquestionably in this case tenacity was a virtue. But with Stimson naval negotiations monopolized his time almost to the exclusion of everything else. During November and December, prior to the departure of the American delegation in January, Mr. Stimson spent practically all of his time in his study at Woodley. There, rather than at the State Department, he held conferences with the admirals, the experts and the members of the delegation who were to accompany him. There he held long sessions with the Japanese Delegation when it passed through Washington. There the details of the American program were meticulously worked out. Rarely did Mr. Stimson set foot within the State Department, and the foreign affairs of the United States, other than those pertaining to the navy, were left entirely in the hands of Mr. Joseph P. Cotton.

At the end of this period of preparation, Mr. Stimson remarked to one of his fellow-delegates that no other delegation could possibly be as well-prepared as the American. This was true—in so far as it pertained to the American delegation. Mr. Stimson knew just exactly what he wanted, and had worked it out in detail down to the last ton and the last gun caliber. He also knew what the British wanted and had worked out a plan by which both could, and later did, agree. And he knew what the Japanese wanted and had some ideas as to how their demands might be met or mollified.

But despite his advance concentration on naval affairs, despite the months of detachment at Woodley, Mr. Stimson failed completely to take into consideration the same factor which had upset Woodrow Wilson at Versailles. And it was the jealousies of continental Europe with their demand for political concessions from the United States that harassed Mr. Stimson at London as it had Mr. Wilson at Paris, and which, exactly one year afterwards, was exacting from Mr. Stimson countless cable tolls, trans-Atlantic telephone conversations and loss of sleep trying to complete his London Naval Treaty.

After Mr. Stimson had just about finished his advance labors at Woodley and was about to sail for London, a Democrat, Norman Davis, suggested to him that perhaps too much emphasis on Anglo-American friendship was alienating the French, and that to counterbalance this, Aristide Briand should be invited to Washington.

Stimson had to admit that he had forgotten all about this until it was too late. At London he had ample time to regret his mistake.

The problem Mr. Stimson faced at London was far different from anything he had tackled before in his entire life. In Nicaragua and the Philippines he was dealing with primitive peoples and had the army and navy of the United States at his back. His word was law. He could engage in the most generous discussions with them, but if they did not agree in the end they had to yield.

At London, however, Mr. Stimson was not dealing with subject peoples. All four nations sitting around the conference table with him had armies larger than the United States. One nation had a vastly superior navy and another had a navy almost as big. Mr. Stimson faced equals. The army and navy of the United States meant nothing. What counted at London was Mr. Stimson's ability to think fast and on his feet.

In this emergency he fell down. He fell down with the press at the start. He fell down with his fellow-delegates on the straight-away. He fell down with the American public on the home stretch.

The London Conference was his supreme moment. His

ambition had been to put an end to naval competition and to begin a new era of Anglo-American friendship. All eyes were on him.

And he muffed the ball.

His chief fault lay in the fact that he knew this was his supreme moment. He knew that all eyes were on him. He knew that responsibility for success or failure rested entirely on his shoulders. So he accepted every infinitesimal and unimportant responsibility there was to accept. He delegated little to others. He was surrounded by six American delegates, all touted by the Hoover Administration as headliners. Of these, four at least, deserved their reputations. Ambassador Dawes had been able to make a recalcitrant Europe accept a revision of reparations. Dwight W. Morrow had come out on top of a score of difficult negotiations in the Allied shipping controversy, to say nothing of the collapse of Cuba and the oil and religious controversies in Mexico. Senators Reed and Robinson were tried and trusted warriors who had been able to wheedle and jockey agreements out of difficult political alignments.

A good executive would have used these men. Stimson did not. To Reed and Morrow he delegated certain negotiations with the Japanese and the French. The other negotiations he kept chiefly in his own hands. And he worried over them. He fretted with detail. He became nervous and confused, until, sometimes at meetings of all seven delegates, six would be in unanimous agreement and an extra hour was necessary to bring the chief delegate—Mr. Stimson—into line.

Four factors contributed to Stimson's downfall at London:

Poor executive ability; the fact that at the State Department and during most of his life he has been surrounded with "yes" men, whereas at London he was surrounded by equals;

A slow-moving mind accustomed to taking days and even weeks to thresh out decisions;

The habit of relying on the whip hand he held in the

War Department, in Nicaragua and in the Philippines, and which was lacking in London;

Nervous fatigue.

The latter contributed to the delays and difficulties of the London Naval Conference more than any one outside the intimate circle of the American delegation has ever known.

There appears to be a lack of resilience in Stimson's physique, a lack of hardening to long hours of worrisome wear and tear. Perhaps this is the secret behind the long week-ends of exercise which he has insisted upon all his life. Or perhaps, on the other hand, the fact that he has always had this exercise proves to be his undoing when he is without it.

Stimson suffers from only one physical complaint. On a big-game hunting trip as a young man, a rifle back-fired and a piece of steel penetrated one eye. At times since then he has feared that he might lose the sight of that eye.

Whether this or something else was responsible, Stimson was perpetually worn out in London; and despite the fact that the fall of the French Cabinet gave him three weeks' breathing spell, despite the fact that he had two weeks on the high seas coming from and going to London, he took two months' rest in the Adirondacks immediately the treaty was ratified.

Probably the secret of his fatigue was the fact that Stimson was a country squire transplanted from his broad acres at Woodley and Highold, set down in a cramped London hotel and given the job of running a naval conference. After half a day of strenuous negotiations, Stimson was fagged out and literally gasped for a breath of his moors.

Knowing his own weakness for the wide open spaces, Stimson fortunately had provided himself with a country estate just outside of London, and in it he took refuge when the prospects of agreement looked blackest. So all the American delegation blessed Stanmore and there were those who said that without it no treaty would have been signed at all.

Next to his fatigue, which he could not prevent and which

therefore might be termed an act of God, no man-conceived problem so bedeviled Mr. Stimson as the now famous "consultative pact." This was largely Mr. Stimson's own fault. He arrived in London with a bland and vague idea in the back of his head that sometime when he got round to it he would have to give a little attention to some form of political concession to Europe.

And as with a great many other things which have mattered much in his life, he was rushed into a situation before he knew what it was all about.

The day the French delegation arrived in London forty-eight hours before the Conference had convened, Tardieu issued a diplomatic warning through the press that in return for a naval agreement he expected the United States to agree to consult with Europe in case war threatened in the Mediterranean. A few days later, when the Baltimore *Sun* and the New York *World* followed an account of a luncheon between Morrow, Reed, Briand and Tardieu with a report that the American delegation favored a consultative pact, Mr. Stimson authorized a vehement denial. During the next two weeks, the American delegation did nothing about a political concession to Europe and let a score of American journalists speculate daily as to whether the United States would or would not agree to consult with Europe in case of war.

Finally, when Secretary Stimson, at a journalistic luncheon, let drop the fact that he favored a consultative pact, American public opinion had been so see-sawed back and forth, so juggled up and down, for and against a consultative pact, that ratification in the Senate appeared unlikely and President Hoover finally cabled Stimson to drop it.

An impasse followed. It became clear that France was not going to sign the treaty unless she got some political concession from the United States, some pledge that the United States would not use her greatly augmented navy to break up any concerted boycott which the League of Nations might impose against an aggressor nation. That is, this became clear to almost every one except Mr. Stimson. Finally, Mr. Morrow undertook to bring his chief around to this point of view.

On Saturday, March 22, he hied himself to Stanmore, where he spent the day trying to persuade Mr. Stimson that the consultative pact was the key to the entire treaty situation; that if the United States would agree to consult, Great Britain would agree to the French naval figures, and France in turn would make concessions to Italy. Finally Mr. Morrow succeeded. Mr. Stimson told him he could go back to London and notify the other members of the American delegation.

Having done this, Mr. Morrow waited for Mr. Stimson to send a cable notifying the White House of the new move. Most of Sunday passed and no cable was sent. Finally Mr. Morrow motored back to Stanmore, trailed Mr. Stimson around the golf course, finally caught up with him and got him to send a cable to the President. The cable, however, was vague and poorly phrased. It failed to set forth the reasons which prompted Mr. Stimson to make his extraordinary move.

The next day, Monday, Mr. Morrow drafted his own cable, got Mr. Stimson's signature and sent it to the President.

But it was too late. Mr. Hoover, irritated by press reports that the consultative pact had been revived, and unconvinced by Stimson's first explanatory wire, issued a statement to the press condemning the consultative pact. Simultaneously Mr. Stimson in London was issuing a statement to the press explaining the terms on which the United States would accept a consultative pact.

The difference between those two gentlemen on this subject has never been reconciled.

*

ELIHU ROOT is fond of telling a story on his young protégé, Henry Lewis Stimson, when the latter, then District Attorney for Southern New York, was riding one of his favorite horses in Rock Creek Park and met Theodore Roosevelt, then President, accompanied by Mr. Root, then Secretary of War. The creek was between them. Roosevelt, who knew Stimson, but did not recognize him at a distance, asked Root who the soldierly-looking horseman was.

"Lieutenant Stimson, of the New York National Guard," replied Root. And then, calling across the creek, he ordered:

"Lieutenant Stimson! The Secretary of War orders you to report to your Commander-in-Chief."

Stimson turned his horse and spurred him into the creek. The water was flooded and the horse at times went over his head. Stimson rode up the bank on the other side, reined in his mount and saluted.

The incident is illustrative of one of the most important points in Stimson's make-up. He is a fighter, but first of all he is a soldier. He obeys orders. He has courage, both moral and physical. He has guts and he has nerve. He will not retreat—except under one condition—if ordered.

As Secretary of State he has now got to the point where he encourages in his subordinates a great deal of discussion. He is liberal to the extent of listening to their views and usually accepting them. On occasion he gives orders. And when he gives them, he expects them to be obeyed.

There is only one man from whom Mr. Stimson, himself, takes orders. When he receives them, being a good soldier, he obeys.

Therefore when the President of the United States tells Mr. Stimson he is opposed to a consultative pact, when he tells him that he will not under any circumstances recognize Russia, when he tells him that he is opposed to too much American participation in the General Disarmament Conference at Geneva, Mr. Stimson obeys.

Mr. Stimson now has more definitely than ever made up his mind in favor of a consultative pact. He believes the Kellogg Treaty should be strengthened by providing some machinery to check war when it threatens. But the President is opposed to this; and Mr. Stimson, the good soldier, does not argue.

Mr. Stimson is sympathetically inclined toward Soviet Russia. Mr. Hoover has lost money in Russia, has had unfortunate food-relief experiences with Russia, is unalterably opposed to having the remotest possible contact with Russia. Mr. Stimson does not argue.

Mr. Stimson believes that a serious situation confronts Europe. He believes that unless Europe can show some really tangible reduction of armament, the seeds of another war are as good as sprouted. Mr. Hoover points out that too much American participation in European affairs will react against his reëlection in 1932. Mr. Stimson, always the good soldier, obeys orders.

Henry Lewis Stimson has come to be a much more effective and efficient Secretary of State. His memory is still bad but he controls his temper. He has surrounded himself, on the whole, with good men. He has won their loyalty. Most difficult of all, he now gets along even with the newspapermen and the Senate.

Mr. Stimson is a home-loving man. One of the tragedies in his life is the fact that he has no children. He has surrounded himself with pets and has all but adopted Captain Eugene Regnier, his military aide, not because he needs an aide, but because down deep in his heart he needs a son. Regnier, naïve, charming and with a streak of fundamental good sense, comes nearer being that than he does anything else.

So Mr. Stimson, always the country squire, each day lives in anticipation of the early afternoon when he can leave the routine of the State Department and go out to see his dogs and his parrot and wander over his expansive acres at Woodley.

There, before an open fireplace in the late afternoon or early morning, Mr. Stimson is at peace with the world.

CHAPTER SIX

PINK PEPPERMINTS AND PROTOCOL

ONCE one penetrates the massive pile of dirty gray pillars which an act of Congress has finally decreed must give way to the capital's beautification program, the Department of State is not an unattractive place. Its high ceilings, wide corridors and walls three feet thick make it cooler than any Maryland or Virginia country club during Washington's sweltering summers. Its southeastern rooms overlook prim Presidential lawns; across the street, green stretches of Potomac Park and the broad Potomac itself reaching out toward Alexandria, the Chesapeake and the sea. Its swinging lattice doors, its wide marble mantelpieces, the carefully polished copper fixtures in its wash-rooms—all create an atmosphere of antiquity, solidarity and imperialism characteristic of the hand at the helm of American foreign affairs.

Languid Negro messengers doze or work cross-word puzzles at little tables in the corridors. One of them has served the Secretary of State ever since the administration, fifty years ago, of Hamilton Fish, grandfather of the Red-baiting Congressman. Another was Theodore Roosevelt's coachman and still another is a lawyer, who receives Negro clients at his table in the corridor and discusses divorces, debts and disorderly conduct quite oblivious to worried young diplomats who rush downstairs clutching cables from London and Paris.

137

Everything about the Department, from its deep fireplaces to its portraits of stern and ancient Secretaries of State creates the impression that not a single thing, not even a colored messenger, has been changed for a hundred years.

This is a delusion. The State Department has changed. There was a day when Thomas Jefferson, the first Secretary of State, moved into his new quarters in Philadelphia, with a staff consisting of four clerks and one French interpreter, plus three ministers and sixteen consuls stationed abroad. There was a day when letters to ministers and consuls were laboriously copied in the American Letter Book, when these notes required four to six weeks to reach their destination and sometimes were written in invisible ink with a notation on the outside: "To be sunk in case of danger from the enemy."

To-day State Department telegraph operators working day and night, send and receive cablegrams costing $200,000 a year. The messages are coded or decoded by trusted experts sitting in a room to themselves, mimeographed, and placed on the desks of the Secretary and his assistants twenty minutes after their arrival. About 3,400 letters are mailed from the Department daily, while fifty diplomatic pouches of mail are taken off steamers in New York harbor every morning by special Department representatives and rushed to Washington several hours ahead of ordinary mail. These fifty pouches contain the reports of the 4,000 representatives which the State Department maintains at some 425 foreign posts, and these reports in turn are circulated among the 600 officers and clerks of the Department by a system which despite the age and decrepitude of its messengers cleans out the file boxes in each office every twenty minutes.

Not only has the State Department changed, but despite its pleasant atmosphere of antiquity, its machinery, at least, is now about as efficient as that of most government departments. This is rather a back-handed compliment, when the top-heavy and cumbersome organization of some Depart-

ments, especially the army and navy, is taken into consideration. However, despite the fact that the State Department is
no worse than any of the others, its reputation is just the
opposite. In Washington it is called the most inefficient, dilatory, procrastinating and red-tape-bound bureaucracy in the
government service. Outside of Washington, businessmen
compare it unfavorably with the Department of Commerce,
while editors leap at opportunities to pooh-pooh the slightest
tendency toward white-spats and namby-pambyism on the
part of its officers.

The State Department has played all the trump cards in
its hand in order to live down this reputation. The Secretary
of State has made speeches, the Under-Secretary has gone on
a barn-storming trip, and the Bureau of Current Information
has inspired articles—all to no avail. The fact remains that
most people in the United States, who have ever heard of the
State Department at all, have heard of it as a social club whose
members are selected from blue-stocking Bostonians, wield
their forks with their left hands, and are no more representative of American life than the Redskins whom their ancestors
pushed west.

Broadly speaking, this is not true. There is just enough
truth in it, however, to make the picture persist. Out of the
four thousand-odd diplomats, consuls, clerks, and stenographers, who represent the State Department both at home
and abroad, only a few hundred honestly deserve the epithets
they get. However, these few not only are completely impossible, but also happen to be placed in strategic places where
they constantly and consistently act as a cinder in the public
eye.

There are two other concrete reasons why the State Department's unenviable reputation continues to persist.

First, there is a sense of self-importance inspired by association with monarchs and their ambassadors which turns the
heads of almost every young man, even though he comes
from Kalamazoo or Keokuk and arrives for his first State

Department examination with the back of his neck shaved and a nasal twang that sends cold shivers down the spine of the chief officer of protocol.

Second, the career men of the State Department were given their chance in 1925, failed to grasp it, and have never been able to live down that failure.

How great their opportunity and how disastrous their failure, few people who did not witness it realize.

*

AFTER years of effort to take the Diplomatic and Consular Services out of politics, the career men in 1924 succeeded in pushing the Rogers Act through Congress. This amalgamated the two services on the same salary basis, boosted pay all around, provided that all career men begin at the bottom of the ladder and climb up, gave them the opportunity to become Ministers and Ambassadors and, in general, took the foreign service out of politics.

The Rogers Act also drew a sharp caste line between the foreign service, or career men, on the one hand, and the drafting officers on the other. Drafting officers are permanently appointed to serve in the State Department and never go abroad to serve in legations and embassies. Men of more brains than means, they frequently write the orders which the Ambassador in the field must carry out. The career, or foreign service, officers, on the other hand, are supposed to spend practically all of their time abroad, being allowed to come back to Washington occasionally for short periods of service in the State Department. Their salaries are higher than those of the drafting officers, and they also receive small allowances for rent, teas, dinners, receptions, wreaths, birthday gifts and other means by which a diplomat justifies his retention in a foreign capital.

Within the foreign service itself, the Rogers Act failed to eradicate a second caste line, not so sharply drawn, however, between the consuls and the diplomats. In theory, the two branches of the service are one, and a man may transfer back and forth between them. Actually, however, the diplomats look down upon the consuls, who have to keep regular office hours and bother with such plebeian routine as bills of lading, clearance papers, reporting trade opportunities and sending home the clothes of dead seamen. The diplomatic branch requires money, a broad Bostonian A, and the knack of handling a tea-cup. There are about one hundred career diplomats and over four hundred career consuls in the service.

The Rogers Act put this diplomatic group of career men on top of the State Department. They could get anything they wanted and their appetites were insatiable. Frank B. Kellogg, nervous, inexperienced, had just come back from the Court of St. James. Qualified to become Secretary of State only because he was one of the very few Senators who had chatted occasionally with Calvin Coolidge, then a very much snubbed Vice President, Kellogg relied on the career men.

He found as his Under-Secretary, Joseph Clark Grew, wealthy descendant of the Boston Cabots, and related by marriage to the House of Morgan. Not knowing what else to do with his time or his money, Grew decided that the Diplomatic Service was as pleasant and patriotic a career as any and had prepared for it by tiger shooting in Manchuria, elephant hunting in India, and a clerkship in the American consulate in Cairo at the age of twenty-four. In the twenty years which followed, he had made an excellent record for himself and attained the rank of Minister. As Under-Secretary of State, however, Grew was in constant hot water. The administration of a legation abroad with a staff of three or four, he discovered, was far different from the problem of running a high-powered machine employing six hundred people which grinds out American foreign policy for every part of the world.

With Grew, in the inner sanctuary of the State Department, were J. Butler Wright, arbiter of protocol and diplomatic dress; Leland Harrison, scion of a wealthy New York family; and Hugh Robert Wilson, heir of the Chicago shirt manufacturer. These men ran the State Department. They appointed themselves and their own tried and trusted friends as members of the Personnel Board to pass upon promotions. They picked their friends for the best foreign posts and saw to it that the amenable Mr. Kellogg got them approved at the White House. Every time such an appointment came back from the White House bearing the initials "C. C.," Hugh Wilson, in charge of press relations, called in the newspapermen and whispered "most confidentially" that a certain appointment was about to be announced, that it was to be a great triumph for the principle of a career service and that the newspapers would do well to play it up as such.

The career diplomats had the wheel and they drove the Department at a to-hell-with-every-one-else clip straight down their own narrow road.

That road led to the famous State Department smash of 1927. During that smash everything that possibly could break against the controlling career clique did break. The Senate Foreign Relations Committee launched an investigation of the career service. Mrs. Edith Nourse Rogers, widow of the author of the Rogers Act, introduced a bill aimed to patch up the holes which the clique was taking advantage of. Senator Moses succeeded in getting a similar bill passed by the Senate. The late Representative Steve Porter, Chairman of the House Foreign Affairs Committee, introduced a bill calculated to do the same thing. Representative Edwards of Georgia introduced a resolution exposing the fact that the wealthier and more favored diplomats had been promoted at a far faster rate than the less wealthy and less favored consuls. Lawrence Dennis, Chargé d'Affaires of the American Legation in Nicaragua, resigned after writing a scathing rebuke of the favoritism displayed by the career clique. Tracy Lay, American Consul General at Buenos Aires and one of the authors of the Rogers Act, followed him. John Gray, Secretary at the American Legation in Panama, did the same. Every newspaper in the country carried articles and editorials denouncing the self-promotion plan of the career men. And worst of all, big business, the god whom the State Department strives chiefly to serve, joined in the denunciation. Victor M. Cutter, President of the United Fruit Company and who ought to know diplomats, made a speech before the high moguls of big business gathered at the annual meeting of the United States Chamber of Commerce, denouncing the career men as lounge lizards and displayers of the white spat; while *The Magazine of Wall Street* published a scathing article, illustrated with sketches of a high hat, stick, gloves, spats and all the accouterments of the career service.

As result of all this, the career clique's bubble burst with tremendous reverberations and the following consequences:

1. The ring-leaders of the inner circle, Joe Grew, J. Butler Wright, Leland Harrison, Hugh Wilson, having seen the hand-writing on the wall, appointed themselves as Ambassador to Turkey, Minister to Hungary, Minister to Sweden and Minister to Switzerland, respectively, just before the smash occurred.

2. Frank B. Kellogg was forced to come out with an acknowledgment that Representative Edwards' criticism of favoritism toward diplomats as against consuls was valid, and he, Kellogg, proceeded to correct the injustice by promoting a long list of consuls.

3. Henry L. Stimson entered the office of Secretary of State one year and a half later, nursing a profound distrust of career diplomats.

The career scandals of 1927-28 have not yet been lived down. Nor will they be. The glaring favoritism and high-handed snobbery practised by the clique in those days is no more, but enough of it still exists to make the State Department, and especially the career service, a most vulnerable target.

The men who steered the service in the old days of its rampant glory have been dispersed but are still functioning.

Their creed is snobbery, favoritism, self-protection, ultra-conservatism, and assiduity in pleasing the Secretary of State.

Illustrative of their frame of mind is Robert Wood Bliss, now exiled to Argentina as American Ambassador and a high priest of the career men. His training in exclusiveness began at an early age when his father, manager of the firm which manufactures "Castoria—Children Cry For It," took as his second wife, Mrs. Anna Blakeley Barnes, owner of the firm. Young Bliss then married his step-mother's daughter, Mildred. The marriage has been a most happy one and has the added advantage of keeping in the family the tremendous fortune rolled up by "Castoria," a product which Washington children cry for in vain because Ambassador Bliss's desire to live down his plebeian ancestry has caused him to rule that his father's and step-mother's medicine shall not be advertised in the District of Columbia.

Herbert Hoover, after watching Bliss work at Buenos Aires during the Presidential good-will trip, decided to appoint a new Ambassador to Argentina, but came home to find that Bliss had been a heavy contributor to the Republican campaign fund. In order to take no chances, Bliss usually contributed to the campaign funds of both parties. His rise has been rapid.

Before Bliss became an Ambassador, however, and while he was merely an Assistant Secretary of State, he once pulled a *pièce de résistance* of snobbery which used to be typical of the career clique and which still is typical of their mental attitude. Bliss was giving two receptions for the State Department at his beautiful Georgetown mansion, inhabited only by a caretaker seven-eighths of the time, and had invited to the first reception all of the members of the career service. To the second reception, he had invited the clerks, stenographers and lesser lights, together with the drafting officers, many of whom outranked the career men.

Harry Dwight, Chief of the Near Eastern Division, author of "Stamboul Nights," a high-ranking person but a drafting officer, had received an invitation to the first reception for the career service. Discovering this fact, Bliss recalled the invitation and asked Dwight to come to the second reception for the common people.

There was nothing unusual about Bliss's social snobbery. It is rather common in the State Department. The social line drawn between the foreign service officer of the select career service and the drafting officer who sometimes rises from a clerkship used to be as strict as the distinction between Brahmin and untouchable. To some it still is. Joshua Butler Wright is of the old school. He does not appear to be. He once punched cattle on a Wyoming ranch and still labors under the delusion that he can mix with "folks." His old job as Assistant Secretary of State did not give him much time for this, however. He was the State Department's glad-hander and took pride in his work. Every ticket-puncher and porter at the Union Station knew him. There was even a rumor that some of them called him "Butsy." The sight of Joshua Butler Wright, attired in Bond Street topper, cutaway, tailored in Saville Row, cream-colored gloves and malacca stick, strolling down to Gate Number 18 was the cue to every employee in the Union Station that a new Ambassador was arriving in town.

Despite the fact, however, that Butsy may have been "Butsy" to the hired help at the Union Station, he took his social P's and Q's just as seriously as does Dolly Curtis Gann; so that on one occasion when the German Embassy was giving a dinner and Prentiss Gilbert, then a mere drafting officer, was invited, Assistant Secretary of State Wright informed Mr. Gilbert that there must have been some mistake.

Those were the halcyon days when the State Department was a rich man's club and no one was afraid to admit it. Its members took this for granted. In fact, many of them opposed the Rogers Bill boosting salaries because they sincerely believed that high salaries would open the gates of diplomacy to *hoi polloi* and that the responsibility for representing the U.S.A. abroad should fall only on the shoulders of the wealthy few.

No one is very brazen about admitting such a thing these days, but, occasionally, in shadowy corners of the Metropolitan Club one hears whispers that the career service is not what it was in the good old days when a substantial private fortune was necessary in order to become a Third Secretary of Legation.

As a matter of fact, it still takes nothing short of a miracle for a man to get transferred from the consular to the diplomatic branch of the service unless he has a private income, at least a small one. This is one of the factors which tends to make the career service so unpopular with the general public.

The general public, traveling in Europe for the first time in the person of a school teacher from Wichita or a banker from Pueblo, drops in at the American Embassy in Paris or Madrid with the feeling that he is helping to pay for the upkeep of the place and might possibly run across some of the folks from home. However, he meets there a young man with glasses who has spent all of his life since graduation in the rarefied atmosphere of pink teas, protocol and diplomacy, who knows nothing of the United States outside of Cambridge, New York, Bar Harbor and Washington, who has soiled his hands at no manual labor more arduous than bridge, and the result is a clash which not only does not enhance the prestige of the foreign service back in Kansas and Colorado but which makes the young man feel that his country is populated with hicks who don't deserve to have their interests protected.

The result of all this is that the career service has never been known to sympathize with any point of view other than that of entrenched wealth. Its members are ideally qualified to protect the interests of those who contribute to the Coolidge and Hoover Administrations. Most of them have spent their lives hanging on to what their fathers made. The business man who has made money on his own initiative is rare in their midst, and as a result, their approach to every problem is negative rather than positive. Their motto is that which hangs in Pullman car vestibules after ten o'clock: "Quiet is requested for the benefit of those who have retired."

So warped is their vision, so ultra-conservative their outlook on life that Dorsey Richardson, one-time Assistant Chief of the Western European Division, cautioned a colleague against mentioning the fact that he had lunched with Senator LaFollette. Similarly Noel Field, a studious and naïve idealist just entered the Department, was considered too radical to be assigned to duty abroad because he had written a pamphlet on international conciliation published by the Carnegie Foundation.

Another man who was temporarily detained from going to the field was Eugene Macfarlane Hinkle, but for entirely different reasons. Gene was a nice boy and socially successful. But although he had squeezed through the State Department examinations, he still didn't know what it was all about. Even after he had remained in the Department for the usual training period of one year, his knowledge was still confined to such rudimentary ideas as the fact that Russia is Red and Latin-American relations are difficult. Therefore, it was decided that Hinkle's only salvation was a year's service in the Division of Current Information where he would have to answer a half-hundred newspaper queries a day on everything from the width of the Suez Canal to the make-up of the French Cabinet. The newspapermen were patient—at first. Hinkle took hours to answer queries. He wound himself up in red-tape. Finally, the press protested. After several protests they took their case to the Secretary of State—to no avail. Hinkle had a friend at court. He was a relative of Joseph Clark Grew, then Under-Secretary.

For a year Hinkle strove valiantly to answer the queries which the newspapermen could not avoid giving him, and then having become something of a man of the world, he went to Cape Town as Vice-Consul. It is the advertised custom of the foreign service to keep a fledgling diplomat in the consular branch of the service for an apprenticeship of about five years. Some of them never get out at all. But this rule did not hold with Hinkle. After two years at Cape Town, he was transferred to Constantinople where he became a Secretary of Embassy under the watchful eye of his relative, Ambassador Grew.

The cardinal principle of the career service is that fresh blood shall never be admitted unless it starts at the bottom of the ladder. It makes no difference whether a man has made a reputation at law or in business. If he then decides that he has acquired certain experience which makes him valuable to his country and if he decides to serve his country as Diplomat or Consul, he is then given an opportunity to throw in his lot with a bevy of college boys who have boned up for the examination, and if he works brilliantly and consistently, he may, before he reaches the age of sixty, have been promoted from a salary of $2,500 a year to $6,000 or $7,000.

This principle of self-protection is the first rule of the service. So sacred is it that one Frederick Dagonet Kellogg LeClercq was able to continue in the service long after his value to the State Department had ceased. Freddie also was a nice boy. He had wit and the old ladies liked him. His rise was rapid. As Secretary of Embassy in London his duties were light. He persuaded his Ambassador to let him spend his time studying at Oxford. This, Freddie argued, would better prepare him to serve his country. Freddie was graduated from Oxford and went to Tokyo, where he used to create sensations by strolling around the lobbies of the Imperial Hotel in his pajamas. Arrested on a Japanese train for gambling, he was foolish enough to escape by pleading diplomatic immunity, much to the disgust of his Ambassador. Returned to Washington shortly after this incident, Freddie worked only part time in the State Department, using the balance to study law at George Washington University, again arguing that this, also, would prepare him for the service of his country. Freddie's colleagues realized his weaknesses but protected him.

Thanks to the protective code of the foreign service, Freddie led a charmed life. He had his stay in Washington extended beyond the usual term in order to get his law degree. Finally, however, with the sheepskin a month from his grasp, Freddie fell. Charges were preferred against him by a group of high school girls he had met in a bus.

The protective code of the foreign service had stood for a great deal but it could not quite swallow that.

Unless one is as reckless in his amours as Freddie LeClercq, or unless one as flagrantly misbehaves as the inebriated diplomatic secretary who told President King of Liberia that the United States was god damn tired of its mandate over his Republic, practically no one is ever thrown out of the career service. That is one of its greatest faults.

It even permitted Hugh D. Auchincloss to remain in the State Department and a bond house at one and the same time, until newspaper protests forced his resignation. State Department rules require that all officials shall sever their connections with private business, but "Hughey" hailed from one of New York's wealthiest and socially prominent families. He thought he could get by.

To throw a man out is to admit publicly the weakness of the service, so its members argue. The result is—deadwood may drift on forever.

A great many people quit, but usually they are wealthy, fed-up, or feel their service has not been properly appreciated at home. For instance, William Phillips resigned as Minister to Canada ostensibly because he wanted to educate his children in the United States, but actually because he was peeved at not being made Ambassador to Rome. Leland Harrison resigned as Minister to Uruguay partly because the flies were bad and his children sick, but chiefly because he was piqued at not getting Billy Phillips' post in Ottawa and felt that he was being shunted off to a post much below his dignity. Fortunately for Harrison, Henry P. Fletcher had resigned as Ambassador to Rome with the idea of becoming either Secretary of State or Senator from Pennsylvania and, having failed at both, had to content himself with the thankless and insignificant chairmanship of the Tariff Commission. So he took Harrison on his staff. Franklin Mott Gunther, whom the foreign service frowns upon because he got Senator Swanson to push his appointment as Minister to Egypt, resigned because he was offered nothing more important than a ministership to Ecuador. Failing even the luck of a berth on the Tariff Commission and not wanting to degrade himself with his father's fur trade, Gunther has taken up archeology.

With the passing of these and the many others who for years dominated the career service, the State Department has lost officers with charm and some ability. But their passing has sealed completely the fate of the inner clique which once ran the foreign affairs of the United States as tyrannically as the Comintern rules Russia. Wealth still dominates. Personal favoritism still influences promotions and transfers. But these are now transfused generally throughout the service instead of being concentrated in the hands of a few.

The State Department to-day, although subject to all the stops and starts, the faltering and failing, the prejudice and pettiness of any great bureaucracy, is now functioning more efficiently than at any time in its history. In view of the past, this is meager praise. Furthermore, it does not apply to the foreign service outside the State Department.

But on paper, at least, the State Department's machinery is perfect. The Department is divided up into divisions, There is the Western European Division which handles the countries of Western Europe with their colonies, watches every political move made in that area, writes instructions to American diplomats in Western Europe and advises the Secretary of State in regard to Western European problems. The same is true for Eastern Europe, the Near East, the Far East, Mexico and Latin America.

There are other divisions—for passports, visas, protocol, historical data, law, foreign buildings, personnel, treaties, economics, accounts, publicity and archives—all of which looks excellent on paper. However, it is the men who run the divisions, not the way they appear on an Efficiency Bureau chart, who really count, and in the State Department there is a vast difference between paper and people.

The administrators of this conglomeration of divisions are three Assistant Secretaries of State. The oldest in point of service is Wilbur John Carr, the only man in the State Department who has worked his way up from a menial clerkship to a position of major importance. For nineteen years he supported an invalid wife on an infinitesimal salary and rose from Clerk to Chief Clerk, then to Director of the Consular Bureau. His wife died, and seven years later he married again, this time to a lady of wealth. Wealth is the first requisite of success in the State Department and from that time on Carr was made. Carr had not only wealth but experience and a reasonable amount of brains. The result is that he runs most of the administrative bureaus of the State Department and runs them fairly well. He is slow, meticulous to the last T, and has the habit of getting his desk piled so high with papers that the Under-Secretary of State once ordered him to clean them off. He is cursed from every side. It is Carr here and Carr there, and Carr's to blame for anything happening anywhere, but if he passed out of the picture the State Department would look years before it could replace him.

Next to Carr in time of service is William R. Castle, Jr., who could be, if he would, the most effective man in the Department. Castle has most of the qualifications necessary for a successful diplomat. His family supplied him with money, and thanks to the fact that his missionary ancestors knew how to secure Hawaiian pineapple fields as well as convert the heathen, he is supplied most liberally. He also has great charm, a sense of humor and a keen mind. On two points only does Castle miss out in being a really effective man. He completely lacks breadth of vision and he is what the French call a *bon fou homme*.

His narrow-mindedness frequently has resulted in embarrassing diplomatic mistakes. It was he more than any one else who championed Mussolini's flagrant persecution of Italians in the United States who became Americanized instead of joining Fascist organizations. It was Castle who pooh-poohed the idea of outlawing war until he saw it had become an obsession with Frank B. Kellogg, after which he found it expedient to become discreetly enthusiastic. Finally, it is Castle who is behind almost every reactionary move in the Department of State.

This is not at all surprising. Castle's background certainly is not conducive to communistic tendencies. His grandfather, settling in Hawaii in 1837, was one of two missionaries about whom Queen Liliuokalani complained so bitterly as having come to preach the gospel but stayed to corner the wealth of the islands. Castle's father was one of the American planters who overthrew Queen Liliuokalani, after which he headed a delegation to Washington to ask for annexation to the United States. For two years he remained in Washington as Minister, lobbying for annexation. Having achieved it, together with the abolition of all tariff restrictions, Hawaii entered a period of unprecedented prosperity, and Castle wealth entered a period of unprecedented control of the islands.

The Castles imported cheap labor from Japan and the Philippines, paid it little, and sold its products to the vast and tariffless market in the United States. They even made a profit on transporting this labor to and from the Orient, on selling it the fundamentals of life, and on transmitting its savings back across the Pacific. So that to-day when you visit Hawaii you will find Castle's father head of the Honolulu Gas Company, his uncle president of the Honolulu Street Car Company, and his family owners of the Hawaiian Commercial Sugar Plantations, the Oahu Railway and Land Company, the Ewa Plantations, the Lewers and Cooke Lumber Company, the Honolulu Telephone Company and the chief express company of the islands, all of which have averaged around one hundred per cent profits.

In traveling to Hawaii or shipping goods to any of its ports you can use the Matson Line or the Oceanic and Oriental Steamship Company, both of which are owned chiefly by the Castle family and operated by Castle's cousin. If you stop at a hotel in Honolulu you may select the Royal Hawaiian, operated by Castle's cousin, the Moana, also operated by Castle's cousin, or the Seaside, owned by Castle and Cooke. If you cash a check, the chances are that you will use a Castle bank, since out of the $97,000,000 of assets in all the banks of the Islands, $82,000,000 are in those controlled by the Castle-Cooke families. Finally if you read a newspaper you may choose between the Honolulu *Star Bulletin,* owned by the Castles, or the *Advertiser,* owned by a fellow-missionary, also turned businessman, and entirely dependent upon Castle advertising.

In view of all this, Castle's conservatism could be forgiven on the grounds of conviction were any one convinced that Castle has any real convictions. Long ago, however, his friends ceased to have any illusions on that point. His worst enemy is his own tongue. He can be as polite, suave and complimentary as an Oriental, and behind your back as vindictive, as unfair, as destructive as a police court lawyer.

Stimson was shrewd enough to size up Castle at the very start. Castle had pulled every wire there was to be pulled to get himself appointed Under-Secretary of State. He had gone to the Kansas City convention under the pretext of marshaling votes for Herbert Hoover. He had dug up old passports in the State Department to prove that Hoover had retained his citizenship during the period he was abroad. He had made every kind and degree of obeisance before the Republican candidate's altar.

In return Hoover sent Castle's name to Stimson as a possible Under-Secretary of State, but he coupled it with so many others that Mr. Stimson felt under no obligations to appoint him, which he not only did not do but was decidedly put out over the way Castle brought pressure upon him to secure the appointment.

Castle had another opportunity after the death of Joseph P. Cotton. This time he could not afford to fail. Already he had been passed over three times, once by Stimson and twice by Kellogg. To be passed over the fourth time would mean resignation, or so he told his friends.

So Castle rolled up all his big guns, the most important of which was David Aiken Reed, astute Senator from Pennsylvania and Castle's neighbor on S Street. Reed went to another neighbor on S Street—Herbert Hoover—and demanded Castle's appointment. Reed had battled Hoover's and Stimson's London Naval Treaty through the Senate. He had upheld the President's hand against the Democrats on Arkansas food relief and a dozen other things. Hoover was in no position to refuse. Furthermore, he liked Castle.

Stimson, however, did not. During the two years he had been Secretary of State he had never worked with him. Important questions were deliberately routed around Castle's desk and he found out about them only by accident. Moreover, some gossip which Castle had circulated about Cotton, while the latter was virtually on his death bed, had reached Stimson's ears and increased his prejudice. However, Stimson was no more in a position to refuse a request from Reed than was Hoover. Furthermore, he needed Reed's help on the ratification of the World Court. Castle was appointed.

A few weeks later, Reed announced his support of American entrance into the Court.

Francis White, Assistant Secretary of State in charge of Latin-American Affairs, is one of those persons who couples a remarkably effective brain with a rather ineffective personality. He has that asset of looking dumb but being just the opposite. After one knows White all his virtues burst into full bloom, but he takes eons of knowing.

Like almost every other man who has risen to high rank in the State Department he was born with a silver spoon in his mouth. He comes from one of the old aristocratic, horse-and-hound families of the Maryland Green Spring Valley, as does also his wife; and her buoyancy and charm fully compensate for the initial lack of charm of her husband. Latin Americans wonder how he won her.

Despite his background of wealth, however, White's advice to the various Secretaries of State he has served usually has been dispassionate and devoid of favoritism toward American vested interests in Latin America. He has been tireless in his efforts to smooth out a dozen or so boundary disputes between Latin-American countries—disputes which cause constant rankling and ill will, and in which the peacemakers receive more criticism than thanks.

White got the blame for one serious slip-up which Secretary Stimson made when he slapped an embargo on arms shipments to Brazilian rebels just a day before those rebels overthrew the government which Stimson was endeavoring to keep in power. Stimson justified his embargo on the ground that it was required by international law—a contention which was directly contrary to the opinion of his legal experts. Had Francis White been diligent in digging up the facts, however, Mr. Stimson would have been able to justify his embargo by a treaty to which Brazil and the United States were both parties, proclaimed by President Hoover only four months before, and which bound both countries to declare arms embargoes in favor of the other in case of revolution. No one in the State Department seemed to know about the treaty until Drew Pearson published it in the Baltimore *Sun* several days later, which caused Secretary Stimson to wax exceeding wroth at his Assistant Secretary in charge of Latin-American relations.

White speaks perfect Spanish with a strong British accent. One of his greatest assets is his ability to wait, and this made him the Latin-American bumper for Frank B. Kellogg. Kellogg wanted immediate action and would drive full force into Francis White. White would recoil and then gradually ease Kellogg down to a full stop.

White's chief handicap is his lack of executive ability. He puts in longer hours than any one else in the State Department, due, first, to the fact that he has not built up a strong Latin-American Division to support him, and second, to the fact that he does not know how to delegate responsibility even if he had. In view of the emphasis which the Hoover and Coolidge Administrations placed upon Latin-American good will and the economic empire to the south, this division should be the strongest in the Department. It is not. Its chief, Walter Clarence Thurston, is a polite and timid figurehead who secured his appointment because he stands in with the remnant of the old State Department clique. Transferred to the Consular Service a few years ago, he showed himself so incapable of handling the affairs of the Consulate in Sao Paulo, that he had to be relieved. Under him Thurston has some excellent men, but they are switched back and forth to the field so rapidly that they hardly have time to get acquainted with their new work. Two of the ablest men in the division, William R. Manning and Joseph Whitla Stinson, economic advisors, Thurston ignores because they do not happen to be career men. The Division's weakness accrues from the fact that the average career diplomat would rather kiss the hands of royalty and spend two or three hours a day at an overstaffed embassy in Europe, than battle the heat, the flies and malaria in a Latin-American capital where United States interests are on the firing line every minute. As a result, career diplomats who really know Latin America are as scarce as white spats in the State Department ever since the newspapers started ragging the career service about them.

The absolute antithesis of the stodginess and formality of the career service is James Grafton Rogers, whom Mr. Stimson, after a year of dilatory and haphazard search, finally appointed as his Third Assistant Secretary of State.

Rogers is a yodeling lawyer who comes out of the west. He writes plays of western romance, of the mining days, of wild Indians and wilder buffalo—plays which are produced by the

Cactus Club, high up in the mountain amphitheater near Denver, where Rogers lived. Coupled with this bizarre artistry, Rogers has a regard for the legal profession second only to that held by Stimson himself. The law to him is a sacred thing, and as Dean of the University of Colorado Law School, he made it his duty to impress that sacredness upon the minds of others. Coupled with this worship of the law is a streak of radicalism, which prompted him to champion Sacco and Vanzetti when all other good lawyers were proclaiming their guilt. He is complex, ambitious, jazzy and loves conviviality. How Stimson happened to pick him, few people know, but the secret is the same channel through which he selected his Under-Secretary, the late Joe Cotton. That channel is Felix Frankfurter of the Harvard Law School.

Of the different political divisions responsible for directing at least the detail of American foreign policy, probably the most efficient are the Near Eastern and the Far Eastern. This is due to the fact that a devoted group of consular officers have been willing to spend their entire lives in the isolated interior of China and the steaming cities of the Levant, studying the language and the people, working without interpreters and performing all the burdensome routine, from reports to revolutions, expected of an American consul.

In Nelson T. Johnson, now Minister to China, Willys R. Peck, Consul-General in Nanking, George C. Hanson, Consul-General in Harbin, and a score of other "China hands," the State Department has some of the outstanding men in the service who have been responsible for the high regard which the United States holds among the 400,000,000 people who crowd China's borders.

Nelson Johnson is one of the few men in the career service who has reached the top without having his path plentifully lubricated with money. Johnson lives only on his salary, which is meager. Probably that is why he has never married. He has spent some twenty years among the Chinese but unlike most people who have lived close to the yellow race, he has not soured on them. While still Assistant Secretary of State and just before his departure to China, Lyle Wilson of the United Press showed Johnson a toy paper airplane which looped-the-loop, dipped and circled automatically. Johnson was as pleased as a small boy. A few days later Wilson went back to the store to get another plane, but the dealer was sold out. He explained that the new Minister to China had purchased his entire stock.

Johnson appreciated the Chinese sense of humor. He was preparing for his new job.

In the Near East the State Department is almost as fortunate. Gardiner Howland Shaw, George Wadsworth, Paul Knabenshue and Paul H. Alling know their Turkey, Egypt, Syria and Arabia far better than they know the United States. Shaw, frequent target of the Ku Klux Klan, because he once studied for the Jesuit priesthood, is one of the ablest members of the foreign service. A man of great wealth, he leads the life of a recluse, poring over tomes on Turkish politics, the Arabic language and Persian art. Wallace Smith Murray, despite an ingrained and incurable streak of imperialism, stands above the rank and file in intelligence and has boosted himself to be Chief of the Near Eastern Division.

Despite the fact that he is surrounded by able and brilliant men, Ambassador Grew also is surprisingly successful in the Near East. The secret of this is the fact that Grew is an excellent diplomat when stationed abroad but a poor executive when administering the State Department. He now has set up an ambassadorial record in Constantinople of having saved two Turks who, on different occasions, were about to drown. He is the most popular foreigner in Turkey.

The Mexican and Eastern European Divisions are small and comparatively unimportant—the former because of the high caliber of the two latest American Ambassadors to Mexico, the latter because of the lack of importance which Latvia, Lithuania, Esthonia, and Eastern Europe generally play in the foreign relations of the United States. This division would be essential were the United States carrying on relations with

Soviet Russia, but at present most people in the State Department forget its existence. Robert F. Kelley, Chief of the Division, is the high priest of the fanatic little clique which believes that nothing good can come out of Russia, not even the Moscow Art Players. He, together with Bill Castle, was responsible more than any one else for the bitterly anti-Russian policy adopted by Charles Evans Hughes and Frank B. Kellogg. Kelley has never been in Russia. He knows nothing of the Russian people. Except for a few months spent in Calcutta as Vice-Consul, all his service for the State Department has been within the narrow walls of his own office. Yet from that office the Russian policy of the United States has been dictated for the past eight years.

Since the day when Dwight W. Morrow became Ambassador, American policy in regard to Mexico has been run from Mexico City and the Mexican Division has become a mere rubber stamp. With Joshua Reuben Clark succeeding Mr. Morrow, this is still true. Clark was partly responsible for Morrow's success. Trained in the State Department's legal department, Clark is an outstanding authority on international law and held the office of Under-Secretary of State prior to Cotton's appointment. Clark could have remained in that office, had it not been for two facts. First, he had no love for Herbert Hoover. Second, he was drawing a salary of only $10,000. Ambassador Dwight Morrow offered him much more.

Both Hoover and Clark swallowed their dislike of each other later when Morrow read them an ultimatum to the effect that his work in Mexico would have to be carried on and that Clark was the only man who could do it. Even then there was some doubt as to whether or not Clark, because of his modest circumstances, would take the appointment. His wife, however, soon settled that. Asked by newspapermen at her home in Salt Lake City whether Reuben had enough money to swing an ambassadorial job, she answered:

"Of course he has. You can say that he will take it."

Mr. Clark is a Mormon but he has only one wife.

Under William R. Castle, the Western-European Division ranked next to the Latin-American Division as the weakest in the Department. To-day, under James Theodore Marriner, it is one of the strongest. This is not Marriner's fault, however. He is not an administrator. His health is not good and he is so fond of basking in the admiration of doting old ladies and pretty young things that he can never say no to a dinner invitation, with the result that his health does not improve. Marriner is witty, brilliant and keen. He is in Mr. Stimson's complete confidence and is his most trusted expert on disarmament. Although Castle is supposed to be Marriner's superior, the latter is given far more responsibility by the Secretary. On the whole, Marriner is an excellent advisor, though like so many career men his tendency is to anticipate what the Secretary wants and serve it up to him on a silver tray, pre-digested.

Marriner has under him two assistants who, except for specialties in which their chief is interested, practically run his division for him. They are John Crawford Hickerson and Pierre de Lagarde Boal. Hickerson is the specialist on Canadian affairs and one of the soundest thinkers in the Department. Boal, born in France of American parents, married a French wife and served in the French air service. He is a conscientious and able expert on French affairs and disarmament. Outstanding among others in the Western-European Division are Robert Green, a former Princeton professor, Paul Culbertson, brother of the Ambassador to Chile, and John Carter, former editorial writer for the New York *Times,* who suffered agonies trying to make his journalese conform to the stodgy style of diplomatic notes when he first entered the Department. He still keeps his pen pointed by writing inaccurate but amusing articles under a pseudonym.

These six political divisions are constantly on the State Department's firing line. It is through them that instructions to American ambassadors regarding the most important events taking place abroad are constantly sent. And it is the political divisions, if any trouble occurs, which get the brunt of the blame.

There are a dozen additional divisions in the State Department but they are behind the firing line. There is the Solicitor's Office, probably the most important section in the whole machinery of foreign affairs, but like a munitions plant in the rear, it grinds out legal opinions—ammunition for the political divisions. And it grinds thoroughly and slowly. At its head is Green H. Hackworth, jovial, ponderous, able, and hemmed in by so many of Mr. Stimson's legal friends in the persons of Allen Trafford Klots and James Grafton Rogers that his style is severely cramped.

There is also the Division of Current Information, directed by Michael McDermott, an amiable Irishman, naïve and idealistic enough to believe that the hand of God guides the Secretary of State, which makes him suffer inward agonies in dealing with agnostic newspaper men.

There is also the Office of the Historical Advisor, built up to be one of the most valuable in the Department by Tyler Dennett, who finally rebelled at the obstacles put in his path by the career clique and took leave of absence until such time as Secretary Stimson could make up his mind whether he did or did not want to continue the policy inaugurated by Abraham Lincoln of publishing without censorship the past diplomatic correspondence of the United States.

These there are and many more, all of them managing, despite petty personalities and ill-concealed jealousies, to turn the great machinery of foreign affairs with a slow, cumbersome motion supposed to resemble efficiency.

Away from the stern eye of Henry L. Stimson and the searching spot light of the press, however, havens of escape and refuge are dotted all over the world where career diplomats, unhampered, can practise at their trade. In one of them Edwin V. Morgan, oldest of career ambassadors, is free to rule his little roost in Rio de Janeiro as any Twelfth Century tyrant, refusing to let his assistants have the key to his dispatch box and permitting no man to be stationed with him of higher rank than a Third Secretary. In this rarefied atmosphere also lives Hugh S. Gibson, sent to Brussels as Ambassador, despite the fact that his Belgian wife has never quite clicked with the Leopolds and the Alberts, and who is perpetually charged with disarmament negotiations despite the fact that he is the most disarmament-discouraged diplomat in Europe. It is an atmosphere in which David K. E. Bruce, son-in-law of Andrew W. Mellon, could get nine months' leave of absence out of the first twelve months of his service, and in which Alan Winslow, son-in-law of William R. Castle, could get three promotions in twelve months, until exposure of that fact plus his wife's generosity in presenting him with twins, caused him to resign for the more lucrative bond business.

Many things may happen in these havens of career refuge which the State Department at home seldom hears and certainly never lets leak if it does. It is a nice tight little diplomatic world, with a premium on pink peppermints and protocol, and into which entrance for the uninitiated is as difficult as for a camel to pass through the eye of a needle.

CHAPTER SEVEN

THE MAN WHO STAYED TOO LONG

ANDREW WILLIAM MELLON will go down in history as the man who did not know when to quit.

For eight years he dominated the national capital. For eight years his word was law with every banker throughout the land. For eight years Presidents served under him. So powerful was his influence, so great his prestige that he told them what to do and his judgment was final.

In Congress his name was spoken in hushed tones. By the press he was referred to only with profound obeisance. When he rewrote the taxation system of the United States, the entire nation echoed his praise. When he relieved the wealthy of their taxes, when he took billions out of the Treasury in the form of tax refunds and returned them to already over-prosperous corporations, only a handful of Senators raised their voices against him.

His awesome presence squelched a damning senatorial investigation whose report later disclosed that he and his corporations had been the biggest gainers through tax refunds. When another Senate Committee, examining the Continental Corporation phase of the Teapot Dome oil lease scandal, asked him to explain a secret $25,000 contribution to the Harding campaign deficit, even so stern a prosecutor as Senator Thomas J. Walsh of Montana treated him with gentleness and deference.

Small, emaciated, shy, giving the impression of being timid, but always surrounded by an army of assistants and servitors, Andrew Mellon became a figure of might and power. To his simply furnished office in the barred and guarded Treasury Building, politicians, social leaders, diplomats and the barons of big business came to bow before him.

For eight years he was reverenced in high places. For eight years his wisdom was hailed as sublime. For eight years his views were acclaimed as enduring philosophy, his achievements labeled historic. Far and wide he was heralded as Great.

He was King Andrew, the Mighty, ruler of the taxes, the surpluses, the finances, the prosperity of the United States. He was the monarch who sat on an intangible throne of prestige more powerful than that in the White House. He wielded a golden scepter of colossal wealth. His sway was all-powerful.

But to-day, like so many monarchs, who, having failed to gauge the pulse of popular rebellion against their rule, King Andrew is no more.

Gone are his magic surpluses. Gone are his promises of tax reduction. Gone are the hallowed days of prosperity. Gone is the time when the White House accepted his word as law.

Fame, throne, scepter, halo, all have been torn from him.

They disappeared the day Herbert Hoover persuaded him to remain in office. For Herbert Hoover he had neither regard nor affection. But he had listened to the adulation of the multitude. He had heard his name on the lips of the people. He liked it. And he stayed on.

So now he speaks when it suits the White House, and he says what the White House wants him to say. If the White House wants an announcement that there will be no deficit, Mr. Mellon announces that there will be no deficit. If the White House says there is to be continued tax reduction, Mr. Mellon reverses his original statement and says there is to be continued tax reduction.

And behind Mr. Mellon's back the world titters.

Calvin Coolidge, a lesser but wiser man, refused to tempt

fate. But King Andrew could not tear himself away. He stayed to maintain the prestige of another fictitious character, and they both went down together.

Had King Andrew, in the fullness of his glory, retired on March 4, 1929, he would be doubly revered to-day. In retrospect, his era of golden surpluses, contrasted with the present dismal days of Treasury deficits, would have made him appear more than ever the legendary hero he had been hailed.

Press and magnate would have sighed for him and recalled his financial wizardry. His successor, even had he been the mighty Alexander Hamilton himself, would have received the blame. King Andrew's scepter would have been put aside but his glory would have gone marching on.

Every month since March 4, 1929, King Andrew has sunk in public esteem. His calculations and estimates have been mocked and derided. His tax policies have been denounced and condemned. The Senate has flaunted him and the House of Representatives has booed his name.

In the closing session of the Seventy-first Congress as the House prepared to enact the increased soldier bonus over the protests of the White House and Treasury, Representative Treadway of Massachusetts arose on behalf of Mr. Mellon to make a last appeal against the bill.

"The greatest Secretary of the Treasury since Alexander Hamilton," Congressman Treadway boomed, confident that this, at least, would get across.

The House leaned back and roared in derision.

King Andrew had stayed too long.

*

ANDREW W. MELLON became the third or fourth richest man in the United States chiefly through a series of fortuitous circumstances over which he had little control. Of course, Mr. Mellon did nothing to stem the tide of fate which carried him on to wealth and power, and, in fact, materially aided it. But

Mellon was born rich, and would have been a millionaire to-day had he done nothing more energetic than spend his life on the front porch of a nursing home.

His father migrated to the United States from County Tyrone, North Ireland, early in the last century, landed at Baltimore, went overland to Pittsburgh and having the usual Irish aptitude for politics, became Judge of the Court of Common Pleas of Allegheny County. The position was one conducive to both prestige and wealth, and eventually Thomas Mellon retired to establish the private banking firm of T. Mellon and Sons, later to be known as the Mellon National Bank.

Andrew Mellon is fond of telling the story of how as a boy he sat under the Judge's bench, where no one but his father could see him, and listened to cases being tried in Court. On one of these occasions news came that Lee had surrendered at Appomattox. Such an uproar followed that Thomas Mellon adjourned court, and the crowd having piled into the streets, the Judge and his son left the court room together, Thomas Mellon stopping on the way to wind the clock.

From his father Andrew Mellon inherited a certain business shrewdness, an aptitude for juggling figures, and a large portion of his private fortune, plus a precise and orderly process of thought such as that which prompted him to wind clocks in moments of great stress.

Long before his father's death, however, Andrew Mellon had come to play an important part in the latter's bank. Early in their teens, young Mellon and his brothers—Richard and James—had been taken into the bank and given the responsibility of passing upon loans.

Like any common parasite, the Mellon fortune was built on the back of Pittsburgh industry—steel, coal, glass and power companies. The bank took slight risks and got a three-fifths interest in most of the business. The *entrepreneur* got two-fifths. As he prospered, the Mellons prospered.

Thus the Mellons loaned to one Henry C. Frick, then a

clerk in the Overholt Distillery, the sum of $20,000. Frick had the vision of building ovens at Connellsville, Pennsylvania, to turn coal into coke. The Mellon bank took a mortgage on the plant and an interest in the business. It loaned Frick an additional $40,000 and then another $50,000. And as Mr. Frick, later head of the Carnegie Steel Corporation, increased his profits, so also increased the profits of the Mellon family.

The work of the young Mellon brothers in passing on loans took them out into the industrial field. It was their job to spend several weeks studying the factory which applied for the loan, making a survey of its production, its markets and its balance sheets. Young Andrew showed unusual ability at this, and at the age of 25 he was practically in charge of his father's bank. Five years later, Thomas Mellon retired, leaving Andrew in control of his entire estate.

Mellon's banking career was not one of great genius. It was conservative and sound, but without initiative. The two exceptions to this were when he broke Standard Oil in Pennsylvania by building a rival pipe line from the western oil region to the Delaware River, and when he foresaw the great use to which aluminum was going to be put and cornered the bauxite deposits of the United States.

Aside from this, however, Mellon millions have come from the process of advancing the money and reaping the profits from the initiative of others; and through this, Mellon influence has reached its tentacles into steel, linseed oil, railways, water power, construction, plate glass, traction, locomotives, insurance, shipping, engines, bridges, motor trucks, steel cars and gun carriages.

As a banker, Andrew Mellon was relatively unknown outside of Pittsburgh. He lived a secluded, sheltered life, surrounded by friends and relatives. Up until the time he came to Washington, not only had he never been interviewed by the press, but he quailed before the thought of such sordid contact with the every-day world. Despite this he knew something about politics, in fact had built up the powerful Mellon machine which occasionally defeated the Vare organization for the control of Pennsylvania patronage.

How this rather shrinking individual happened to land in the very middle of the Washington political maelstrom is something which never has been satisfactorily explained. It appears, however, that Mellon, timid as he was, modest as he pretended to be when it came to the political limelight, had begun to get a little tired of the monotonus routine of walking back and forth between his home, his club and his bank, had begun to be bored with donating money to hospitals, with buying rare portraits, and with seeing everything he touched turn to gold. He yearned for new worlds to conquer. So it was not mere accident that found him at the top of the list of heavy contributors to the $7,000,000 Republican campaign fund raised by men who expected to realize far more than six percent on their investment by putting Warren G. Harding in the White House.

Andrew Mellon was one of the first to cash in on his investment. As Secretary of the Treasury he later paid himself a tax refund of $400,000, the largest awarded to any single individual.

*

THE first time Andrew Mellon came to Washington, then a boy of 16, the Washington Monument was not yet completed. It had been built up to the point where the marble now ends, and young Andrew had the distinction of climbing up the scaffolding of the monument that far.

Mellon did not visit the White House on his first trip to Washington. In fact, he did not visit the White House at all until the day he entered it as a member in the ill-fated Cabinet of President Harding. Since then he has been going in and out of the White House, always by the rear entrance, like the swinging to and fro of a saloon door.

With these frequent goings and comings he became the mystery man of the Coolidge Administration, about whom was built up a myth—the myth that placed in his hand the scepter of power, and that made him King Andrew, the Mighty, the monarch who stayed too long.

While still a member of the Coolidge Cabinet there was no man in public life who so captured the public's imagination. Much of the basis for this Mellon myth rested upon his personality. A thin, half-frightened individual, Mr. Mellon looks so esthetic, so almost spiritual, that the natural impulse of the press and even of congressional investigating committees was to protect him.

When he first came to Washington, he made so pathetic an appearance that his under-secretary always stood at his side at press conferences and bore the brunt of the questioning from congressional committees.

Now, Mr. Mellon has become much more assured and self-confident. He has an air of composure and detachment—the worn, fragile face of a poet and dreamer. If one did not know that he was among the half-dozen richest men in the world, the expression of his face almost could be compared with the aloofness and spiritual composure on that of Mahatma Gandhi.

Mellon's fingers are long and tapering like those of an artist, and in them he nervously twists a cigar, the size of a cigarette. The fingers do not belie Mr. Mellon's character, for his art collection, although not large, is exceptionally rare, and reveals the soul of an artist.

Nor do Mr. Mellon's fine features belie his character. Through it runs the quality of instinctive courtesy combined with loyalty, decision and generosity, all of which endear him to his friends and contribute materially to the Mellon myth.

The myth, however, extends far beyond the small circle of friends who have the privilege of personally knowing some of Mr. Mellon's admirable qualities. In fact the myth, as far as the general public is concerned, rests solely upon three factors:

First, Mr. Mellon has established himself as the great sorcerer who waved his wand and brought taxes tumbling from their war-time peak to almost nothing.

Second, Mr. Mellon is the wonder-worker who entered the Treasury, then "running amuck under wasteful and ignorant Democrats," balanced the budget, and out of his magic hat began pulling surpluses.

Finally, Mr. Mellon is the stern realist who made the dilatory war debtors of Europe reach down in their jeans and cough up the billions they had been owing Uncle Sam.

The net total of all these illusions in the public mind created the super-illusion that Andrew William Mellon was the crafty old wonder-worker to whom the public was really indebted for eight years of so-called Coolidge prosperity.

To what extent Mr. Mellon actually was responsible for turning Treasury deficits into surpluses, he is his own best witness. The credit given him for this has been the result of the clever publicity promoters of the Republican National Committee, for he himself repeatedly has said that he was merely carrying out the sound policies worked out for the reduction of public expenditure after the war by his Democratic predecessors, Carter Glass and David F. Houston.

Mr. Mellon was lucky enough to take over the Treasury when it was the easiest and most popular job any man had held in a generation. All he had to do was sit still and watch the sinking fund reduce the public debt. With this reduction he could bring about a simultaneous reduction in taxes—and get all the credit for it.

War-time expenditures would have been reduced no matter who was Secretary of the Treasury. When a nation is paying out billions of dollars to feed an army of 5,000,000 men, to buy tons of ammunition and to build fleets of ships, and when that expenditure suddenly becomes unnecessary, it requires no particular genius to bring about Treasury surpluses and tax reduction.

One of the first things Mr. Mellon did to endear him in the hearts of his banking colleagues was to refund the public debt. A total of $7,000,000,000 was due to be repaid or refunded within two years, and for every percent of reduction in interest rates, American taxpayers would save $70,000,000 annually. Interest rates had dropped after the War, and Mr. Mellon, taking advantage of this drop, was able to save them this much and more.

He was hailed as a wonder-worker.

Compared with the refunding operations of the Treasury after the Civil War, however, his was no miracle at all. At that time Benjamin H. Bristow, faced with comparatively as heavy a debt, refunded it with a reduction just as great as that achieved by Mellon, despite the fact that he was in the middle of the post-Civil War financial panic with interest rates much higher than those after the World War.

Mr. Mellon and his miracle deserved the sober praise extended by the *Journal of Commerce*—"a good Secretary of the Treasury, faithful, businesslike and efficient"—and that was about all.

The Mellon settlement of the Allied War debts was easy. Europe not only could not repay the United States what she owed for carrying on the war to end war but she needed to borrow more money with which to build up her shattered industries, construct new fleets and maintain armies even larger than those which were ready to be mobilized when the fatal bomb struck the Archduke Franz Ferdinand at Sarajevo in 1914.

The State Department, however, ruled that this new money could not be borrowed until the old debts had been settled. One by one, therefore, and very reluctantly, the Allies sent their delegations to Washington to receive the terms Mr. Mellon was willing to give them. On their way home, they stopped in New York and borrowed from Wall Street more than enough to pay Mr. Mellon—as Calvin Coolidge so eloquently testified in his 1928 Armistice Day speech. Mr. Mellon's debt-funding operation, therefore, merely consisted of shifting the burden of the war debts from the Federal Treasury to the American buyer of European bonds.

Mr. Mellon's idea of tax reduction was first conceived by a New York bank and worked out by that very capable individual, Parker Gilbert. The great contribution which the Secretary of the Treasury gave to the plan was publicity. On every possible and conceivable occasion he hammered home the idea that tax reduction would release funds for investment and bring about prosperity. The idea got across big. Every small business concern, every bank, every newspaper in the country rallied behind it.

Only the elder La Follette and the Democrats stood out against him. Still remembering the war days when the country had been taught to believe that wealth should bear a greater sacrifice than the poor, they blocked the Mellon move to reduce the tax on large incomes from forty to only twenty-five percent. But later, when La Follette, the chief obstructionist, died, the Democrats yielded to popular pressure and permitted a reduction down even to twenty percent.

By this cut, Mr. Mellon, chief sponsor of the reduction, lopped about $1,500,000 off his own income tax.

All this, of course, was lost in the general pæan of praise and prosperity which followed Mr. Mellon's so-called masterstroke. The oil scandals were forgotten. The machinations of the Ohio Gang, the trivialities of Calvin Coolidge, the petty politics of Warren Harding—all were obscured in the rejoicing over tax reduction. That tax reduction was inevitable, was just as certain as the fact that the War had ended. And in the face of the tax-reduction "wizardry" of Andrew W. Mellon, no scandal conceivable by the hand of man could have prevented the reëlection of Calvin Coolidge in 1924.

*

MR. MELLON is a man of such great personal magnetism, such apparent sincerity that it is difficult to reconcile these with two qualities of character which, the record of his life shows, must exist. One is vindictiveness, which Mr. Mellon has given vent to so bitterly, both in the treatment of his wife and in his case against Senator Couzens. The other is carelessness in accepting large favors, both for himself and his firms, from the Federal Government.

His record in the latter respect is astonishing and with men of less standing would be called dishonesty.

Mr. Mellon, of course, is a good enough executive not to fret himself about every tax refund made by his Department, and therefore it is only fair to absolve him from any knowledge regarding the action of his subordinates in illegally refunding to the Mellon banks the sum of $91,472, supposedly for surplus taxes which the Democrats had collected in 1917. However, it does seem that after this refund became a public incident, Mr. Mellon might at least have protected his old friend and senatorial office boy, David Aiken Reed.

As it turned out, Senator Reed, whose law firm protects Mr. Mellon in Pittsburgh, and who considers it his duty to extend that protection also to Washington, immediately rushed to Mr. Mellon's support on the floor of the United States Senate. He said that the sum of $91,472 could not be returned to the Treasury since the case was now definitely closed; following which the Treasury inconsiderately acknowledged Mr. Mellon's critics to be right and David Aiken Reed to be wrong.

Mr. Mellon also may have been completely ignorant of the action of his subordinates in refunding taxes to various firms which the Mellon family owns, but the record is not one of which the other great Secretary of the Treasury, Alexander Hamilton, would be proud. More than one million dollars was refunded to each of forty organizations and people, among them the Gulf Oil Company, the Aluminum Company and its subsidiaries, and the Standard Steel Car Company, all three largely owned and completely controlled by Mr. Mellon.

It may also be true, but it is scarcely conceivable, that Mr.

Mellon was ignorant of the favoritism shown to certain newspapers which supported the Administration. He may not have known, for instance, that whereas the excess profits tax for forty-five representative newspapers was about twenty percent, some of them who had stood by the Grand Old Party had theirs scaled down to around two percent. He may not have known also that William Randolph Hearst's Star Publishing Company, a staunch supporter of the Administration, got reductions in tax liabilities for three years totaling $1,737,007.

It seems incredible, however, that Mr. Mellon was able to maintain the same convenient ignorance regarding some of the moves Congress and Coolidge made on behalf of his own interests.

Mr. Mellon's aluminum company has a monopoly control of aluminum production, and the Republican-written Fordney-McCumber Tariff made its hold on the domestic market doubly certain by increasing the duties on aluminum 250 percent. Shortly after this, the Tariff Commision pointed out that the duty on linseed oil of about 25 cents a gallon was too high and recommended that it be decreased. Mr. Mellon owns two of the eight large linseed crushers in the United States, and President Coolidge, not ignorant of this fact, pigeon-holed the Commission's report. The tariff on linseed oil never was reduced.

Most of these items in the record of King Andrew, the Mighty, would be gathering dust in the archives of the Treasury Department had it not been for Senator Jim Couzens of Michigan. Single-handed except for the support of a handful of Progressives, Senator Couzens forced an investigation of the Mellon myth.

The Democrats, frequently more servile to wealth than their Republican confrères—because they so seldom come in contact with it—stood on the side-lines. They did not even give platonic support. Mr. Mellon was too rich, had too powerful support from wealthy newspapers and was too popular with the banking interests because of his tax reduction.

Besides, even a Democratic Senator must frequently appeal to the Bureau of Internal Revenue on behalf of some wealthy constituent in order to get his taxes reduced, and if you have been a critic of the Secretary of the Treasury, who heads the Bureau, your chances of tax reduction are slim.

"Give me control of the Internal Revenue Bureau and I will run the politics of the whole darn country," Senator Couzens once said.

And so he fought alone.

Frank Kent tells the story of how both Mellon and Senator Couzens were invited to dine at the White House through the mistake of a social secretary. For several hours Mrs. Coolidge suffered exquisite agonies. However, when Mr. Mellon, always the perfect gentleman, arrived, he saw Senator and Mrs. Couzens across the room, and took his daughter Ailsa over to meet them.

If this story is true, Mr. Mellon has the ability to draw a line of demarcation between social and political hates which he has not evidenced in many other things and for which few people have given him credit. Bankers who have opposed Mr. Mellon in business have discovered to their regret that he was a good hater.

Senator Couzens also discovered this when Mellon started a counter-attack on him by reopening an old suit in which the Treasury demanded a $10,000,000 additional tax payment on the sale of Couzens' stock in the Ford Motor Company— a suit which Couzens won and which made King Andrew look ridiculous.

The most vindictive chapter of Mr. Mellon's life, however, is that dealing with his marriage.

Nora McMullen was the grand-daughter of old Peter Guinness, famous as the manufacturer of Ireland's best-advertised stout. It was not Mr. Mellon's ownership of the Overholt Distillery which brought them together, as is sometimes supposed, but a tourist party which visited the United States in 1897. The party was entertained at the Mellon home in Pittsburgh, and Miss McMullen was a member. She was vivacious, rosy-cheeked and twenty years old. Mellon was forty-five. He fell in love. He visited her again in England, wooed her ardently and after three years of persuasion, she consented.

They were married in 1900, and went back to live in Mellon's palatial Pittsburgh residence in an atmosphere of iron, steel and hard work as foreign to the green moors of England and Ireland as anything ever could be.

The cards were stacked against a happy marriage from the start. Mellon slid back into the groove into which he had fitted as a hard-working bachelor for forty-eight years. He had the same friends, the same long office hours, the same devotion to his work. To Nora McMullen Mellon all this was new and difficult. She was homesick from the first and it was only natural that she should make repeated trips to her family in Hertfordshire and in Ireland. These visits became longer and longer, until nine years after their marriage it became known that the Mellons both sought a divorce.

The story of the divorce proceedings is not one which the Greatest Secretary of the Treasury since Alexander Hamilton likes to contemplate. Perhaps realizing this, he was successful at the time in keeping the story out of all except one newspaper. However, the record in an Allegheny County Court, in the State capital at Harrisburg and in the files of the Philadelphia *North American* tells the story—and it is one which involves detectives, kidnapping, dictaphones, and a special law passed by the Pennsylvania Legislature.

The Mellons had two children, Paul and Ailsa, now Mrs. David K. E. Bruce, daughter-in-law of the former Senator Bruce of Maryland. The fight largely centered around their custody.

In 1909, according to the *North American,* Mrs. Mellon entered suit for divorce against her husband, "making serious charges." He objected to answering the charges in open court and consented to a separation agreement by which Mrs. Mellon received an allowance of $60,000 annually, and the custody of the children for seven months a year. She returned to her old home in Hertfordshire.

Mellon, however, according to the *North American,* resented this bargain and got Senator Boise Penrose, then political dictator of Pennsylvania, to pass a bill through the State Legislature, later known as the Scott Divorce Law, giving judges the right to deny women the right of trial by jury in divorce cases. The bill was passed "under cover" and was repealed after the Mellon divorce fight was settled, so that scarcely any one knows of its one-time existence even to this day.

Assured that his name and standing as Pittsburgh's foremost banker would not be besmirched by sordid scandal, Mellon sued for divorce not on the charge of desertion as previously agreed with Mrs. Mellon, but on the charge of infidelity. He charged his wife with misconduct at different times and different places with Alfred George Curphey, an Englishman she had known ever since childhood.

Meanwhile, Mellon had hired detectives to shadow his wife at her home in England. Detectives also scoured Europe for evidence. One of them was Gaston B. Means, later famous as a Department of Justice operative during the Harding scandals and as the author of "The Strange Death of President Harding." Another detective, Barney Devlin, Pittsburgh ex-saloon keeper, "after many weeks of shadowing, went insane," according to the *North American.* That paper, reporting Mrs. Mellon's efforts to keep her children, said:

"She held on to them until hired thugs entered her home, and after beating her and a friend, took the little ones away to a home provided by the banker."

Mrs. Mellon, determined not to relinquish her children, returned to the United States. All the power of the Mellon millions, all the influence of one of the most ruthless political machines which ever dominated any state, was pitted against her. Mellon even had induced the District Attorney of Allegheny County to go to Europe to help the fight against his wife. When Curphey, charged with illicit relations with Mrs.

Mellon, arrived in New York to help her fight the case, he and his friend Captain Kirkbride were arrested on Mellon's orders. Governor Dix of New York, however, refused to honor the Pennsylvania extradition papers.

What Mrs. Mellon faced was a situation wherein she had been publicly accused of infidelity, and wherein she could be forced, under the special law passed by Boise Penrose, to answer those charges in secret. The chances of clearing herself seemed hopeless. However, she demanded a trial not before a master but before a jury in order that the world might know the truth.

At first it looked as if Mrs. Mellon's nerve would force a decision in her favor. Despite the law, October, 1911, was set for a jury trial. Mellon influence overruled this, however, and the Pittsburgh courts appeared inclined to grant Mellon's plea for a secret trial.

The dispute dragged on. Several things happened which dampened Mellon's ardor and made him fear that publicity would besmirch his name, despite the precautions he had taken. One was a powerful argument made by Judge James Gay Gordon of Philadelphia who appeared before a court in Pittsburgh and challenged the constitutionality of the Scott Divorce Act. Another was an incident staged by the reporter of the *North American* who took Mrs. Mellon out to her former home in an effort to see her children. He carried a photographer along, with the idea of getting a "sob" picture of the weeping children clinging to their mother. As Mrs. Mellon got out of her car in front of the Mellon mansion, however, detectives hustled her back into it and manhandled the reporter and photographer. The children barely got a glimpse of their mother.

Mr. Mellon had been prepared for any emergencies but apparently the fight was wearing on his nerves. He finally consented to sue his wife on the grounds of desertion, each of them getting the children for six months of the year. John P. Hunter, Master in the case, filed his report in an Allegheny

County Court on May 25, 1912, and the decree was granted on July 3 of the same year.

Mrs. Mellon has always received the devotion and affection of her two children. They have visited her religiously every year, and, according to their friends, have made several attempts to bring about a reconciliation.

Mr. Mellon, however, seems never to have forgiven his wife. There is only one thing he likes less than being referred to as the country's third richest man, and that is any allusion to his wife or his divorce. When a Washington newspaper, reporting that Paul Mellon had purchased a large Virginian estate on which his mother would live, alluded to the possibility of a reconciliation, Mr. Mellon expressed his disapproval and disgust in no uncertain terms.

*

WHEN Andrew Mellon first arrived in Washington he was disappointed and began methodically marking off the months on his calendar. He looked forward to the forty-eighth month when he would be finished. To-day he could have marked off one hundred and twenty months had he not given up the practice after the twenty-fourth. The reason he gave it up was because he suddenly discovered he liked Washington.

Some people attribute Mr. Mellon's desire to linger on to an ambition to be Secretary of the Treasury longer than any other man. Already he has achieved that record with the possible exception of Albert Gallatin, also a Pennsylvanian, who at the end of the last century served for twelve years. During two of those, however, Gallatin was abroad on a diplomatic mission and Congress declared his cabinet office vacant, thus giving him a net service of ten years which is identical with Mellon's.

Longevity of service, however, is not Mr. Mellon's reason for lingering on. The truth is that despite the criticism and abuse that have been heaped upon his head, Mr. Mellon tremendously enjoys his job. As a private citizen he had become prodigiously bored with seeing everything he touched turn to gold. Having made more money than any but two or three other men in the world, it was no sacrifice for him to quit making more of it. In Pittsburgh he was relatively unknown. In Washington he has been all-powerful. His name was on the lips of every one.

So he has stayed. He has even changed his age in order that he may appear to be more youthful, so that in *Who's Who* from 1918 to 1921 he has listed himself as born in 1852; from 1921 to 1929, as born in 1854; while in *Who's Who* for 1930-31 he puts himself down as born in 1855. Thus in the past thirteen years he has aged by only ten!

And during this time Mr. Mellon has been a reasonably efficient Secretary of the Treasury. Considering his reputation as a rival of Alexander Hamilton, his estimates for national revenue have been amazingly wide of the mark—never within $100,000,000 of being right and $1,132,000,000 off in 1923. But he has had the rich man's usual facility for handling large sums without being staggered at their size. He has kept politics consistently out of his Department, refusing, when he first came in, to discharge competent Democrats merely because they were Democrats, and forcing Harding to fire Elmer Dover, whom the Ohio Gang had first put over on him as an Assistant Secretary of the Treasury.

He has worked hard. He has had little time for his few diversions—walking, riding and golf. He is to be found at his office promptly at nine and he remains there until six or seven. He walks to his office in all kinds of weather and is so methodical that he has figured his total ten-year mileage between the Treasury and his apartment as equal to walking from Washington to San Francisco and halfway back again. He also has estimated that the walk takes him twenty-one minutes if he is not in a hurry or nineteen if he is. On those rare occasions when he takes a taxicab he sometimes has been known to find himself without a cent and has held the driver waiting while he went inside to borrow money from his secretary.

So Mr. Mellon, in one way or another, has come to be looked upon as a saintly and wealthy old gentleman who has dedicated the last remaining years of his life to the public's welfare—first to building up prosperity, and now to salvaging it.

And in the Mellon myth, badly punctured in places as it now is, two facts still remain completely unexposed and unappreciated. One is the fact that Mr. Mellon's tax reduction led to the orgy of speculation which in turn caused the recent crash. The other is the fact that Mr. Mellon, having been repeatedly warned of the impending crash before it fell reverberating around his ears, did nothing to prepare the public for a gradual dénouement.

To Calvin Coolidge is given credit for beguiling the people into believing that stock market values could be pyramided indefinitely and for leading them up to the brink of the crash. But Calvin Coolidge would no more have gone counter to Mr. Mellon's advice than a faithful Mohammedan would have ignored the teachings of the Prophet. He was the mere mouthpiece for Mr. Mellon's bull-market optimism.

Two years before the crash came, experts of the Federal Reserve Board, charged with keeping sound the financial structure of the country, warned that the inflated stock market could not last and urged that the public be told to ease out while the easing was good. Time after time when the Federal Reserve Board, the American Bankers Association, and various business journals announced that speculation had gone far beyond the point of safety, Mr. Mellon either himself or through his White House spokesman, Mr. Coolidge, issued statements contradicting them. He assured the public that all was well and that it could continue buying on margin with impunity and with profit.

When, because of a Federal Reserve Board warning on June 5, 1928, the stock market broke badly, Mr. Mellon, ex officio head of the Board, issued a statement that the break was without significance. When, on January 6, 1929, the Federal Reserve Board issued another formal warning against the increased use of credit for stock market purposes, Mr. Mellon three days later "explained informally" that this was not intended to "bring about a sudden slump in stocks."

And why not?

Mr. Mellon and his family had made a net profit of $300,-000,000 from the increased stock values of Gulf Oil and the Aluminum Company alone. Perhaps he believed that the stocks of these companies had sufficient earnings really to merit this increase. Perhaps he believed that the public was entitled to share in their enhanced value. Other men, however, who had reason to know something about the corporations which they headed, announced that stocks were much too high, and they made those announcements a year before the crash, which left the myth of Coolidge-Mellon prosperity nothing but a mass of smoking ruins.

Mr. Mellon's failure, however, goes far deeper than a mere failure to warn. Not only had he breathed new life into the great stock market bubble every time it showed signs of deflation, but it was he who started the bubble in the first place.

It was Mr. Mellon who advocated the reduction of income taxes in the higher brackets. It was Mr. Mellon who on every conceivable occasion preached the doctrine that this reduction would release funds which would create business prosperity.

It did. The wealthy became more wealthy. They bought more yachts, more country estates, built more golf clubs. But there is a limit even to that which a wealthy man can spend. He can use only one yacht, one country house and not more than three or four golf courses. It was impossible, for instance, for Mr. Mellon to spend on himself alone all of the $1,500,000 he received in reduced taxes; so like every one else, he put it in the stock market.

Meanwhile those not blessed with as much wealth or with as much proportionate tax reduction were expected to buy the products which industry, spurred on by the stock market, was turning out in greater and greater volume. And they did— up to a point.

Encouraged by national advertising to the tune of a billion dollars a year, they bought all that an over-taxed system of installment buying would permit—until their buying power was exhausted.

But since Mr. Mellon's new plan of tax reduction had served to divert money from the pockets of the poor to the pockets of the rich, and thence to the stock market, the saturation point —even under the installment plan—very soon was reached. After which...the deluge!

*

FACTS percolate to the public mind almost as slowly as mountains rise or oceans fall—but nevertheless they do percolate.

The days when Mellon, the Mighty, was viewed as "a sacred personality of whom it is sacrilege to speak save with the most reverent admiration" are now gone.

Gone also are the days when it was considered a "national calamity" if Andrew W. Mellon should leave the Cabinet.

For King Andrew, the Great, ruler of the taxes, the surpluses, the finances, the prosperity of the United States, is now looked upon as the man who stayed too long.

CHAPTER EIGHT

SONS OF THE WILD JACKASS

*C*HE Senate Insurgents are the strongest and weakest element in American national affairs.

Individually they are the strongest.

Collectively they are the weakest.

Individually they are the most righteous and forward-looking men in public office in the capital. They are sincere, law-abiding and intelligent. Collectively they have been without plan or purpose, unorganized and ineffectual.

Individually they fight gallant battles in the public interest. Collectively they are without significance as a potent force in a machine age owned and ruled by an international capitalism.

Mr. Hoover once used the resounding expression "rugged individualism." He had no intention of applying it to the Senate Insurgents. They were furthest from his thought.

But the characterization is a perfect fit. They are the finest type of this ideal. They personify all the noble qualities of character he implied when he used the pat phrase.

And just as completely they demonstrate the pathetic and utter inadequacy of individuals, no matter how admirable, to cope with the colossal economic and political problems of the present day as long as they are nothing more than individuals persisting in an individualistic philosophy.

It is one of the major tragedies of American public affairs to-day that these men, individually so commendable and noteworthy, should collectively be so futile.

Without program, unity or leadership they have floundered about helplessly, making defensive sorties against some particularly vicious transaction but all the time being more and more mired and overwhelmed by the organized and aggressive forces of wealth and reaction.

Peace and disarmament, economic and political justice and equality, they earnestly and sincerely defend and strive for at all times. They alone can be depended upon to vote right on issues.

But to get together and formulate an explicit and comprehensive economic and political program, to organize the independent political movement that is so desperately needed in the United States to-day, that has been beyond them. Against the might and unified power of national and international capitalism they have had nothing to offer but their own individual forthrightness.

They will fearlessly attack the water-power trust and magnificently press for government operation of Muscle Shoals. But through all the long years of this splendid fight there was never an effort made by them to formulate a comprehensive and fundamental national plan to cope with this vital problem. They are for fair rates, just valuations; some of them are even for public ownership. But a definite and specific program that will go to the roots of the problem, they have none.

And this is true of all the other questions. Always they have wasted themselves on halfway measures which, when they do succeed in putting them through, are used by those in power to perpetrate greater abuses.

After enormous effort and labor they finally forced through Congress a reorganization of the Federal Power Commission. Mr. Hoover promptly sabotaged their achievement by appointing complaisant, reactionary mediocrities as commissioners.

With great resourcefulness they defeated Mr. Hoover's attempt to foist a mediocre Southern Republican politician upon the Supreme Court of the United States. It was a resounding victory.

But actually it meant nothing fundamental. True, Mr. Hoover was reluctantly compelled to appoint Justice Owen J. Roberts, a man of high caliber and professional ability. But as far as the underlying economic and political viewpoint of the tribunal was concerned there was no essential difference between the two men.

The ominous and ever-encroaching power of the Court, its conservative and property-conscious point of view, the real issues that the Court presents, were in no way affected by this fight. As a matter of fact the Court was distinctly strengthened by the addition of a forceful personality.

More than twenty years ago, Senator George Norris, the purest and noblest of the Insurgents, then a young man in the House of Representatives, fought a historic battle to free the chamber from boss rule. After an epic struggle he defeated "Uncle Joe" Cannon and the rules were liberalized.

During the past five years the House has been ruled not by one but by three bosses, who together did not make half the man that Cannon was. The rules were never more restrictive and stifling and the House never more inane and moribund.

That they are tenacious and resolute fighters—Senator Norris for ten years has single-handedly maintained the Muscle Shoals battle—is unquestionably inspiring and commendable. It is heartening to know that in the welter of hypocrisy, demagoguery, cowardice and reaction that pervades the capital there are a few honest and honorable men.

But the day when individual probity alone was enough to cope with economic and social forces has long since passed in this country—if it ever existed. Mighty aggregations of wealth dominated by centralized control rule the land and they can be grappled with only by organized mass action, mobilized behind a program of fundamental reform.

The great insufficiency of the Senate Insurgents arises out

of their lack of roots in the underlying economic struggle of the day—the fight for the ownership of the raw material, the machine, and the wealth produced by the worker. The insurgents spring from classes and environments to which this basic struggle is unreal and which, in some instances, are even hostile to it.

In an industrial civilization, an age of the machine, when the greatest issue is that of possessing class against toiling mass, not one of these men is of proletarian origin. They come from small independent farm homes that are so rapidly vanishing from America, the professional class, and a few from the wealthy. But not one of them from the mill or factory.

Nothing could be more significant than this fact. Therein lies the explanation of their futility and inadequacy in the face of modern conditions and problems, despite their splendid personal attributes.

This does not mean that they are unfriendly or unsympathetic toward labor. Far from it. They are the only friends and supporters the American worker has in the national government to-day. What modicum of labor legislation is being agitated and pushed there, they are sponsoring.

But they are devoid of the class consciousness absolutely essential to bring them into rapport with the underlying principles of the economic struggle. Their whole outlook and approach is that of the patriarchal and *laissez faire* era that ended with the victory of the industrial North over the agricultural South in the war of the states.

During the tragic winter of 1930-31 when millions were walking the streets vainly looking for work, when thousands of factories stood idle and warehouses bulged with surplus grain and cotton although hundreds of thousands were hungry and ill-clad, when the whole horrible failure of the Capitalistic Industrial system was starkly revealed, they not only had nothing fundamental to offer as a solution but did not even get together to formulate a plan for temporary relief.

There never was a time when the country was more in need

of an honest, forthright, and intelligent leadership with a definite program and purpose. They, who should have been in the forefront, were passive and empty-handed.

True, the brilliant oratory and industry of young Bob La-Follette exposed the vicious and brutal policy of inaction and starvation of the President and the Red Cross. But beyond that neither he nor the others did anything positive.

Even the sponsoring of such ameliorating devices as the old-age pension and unemployment insurance came not from the Insurgent ranks but from Senator Robert Wagner, the warm-hearted and liberal Tammany Democrat.

The Insurgents could see the need and urgency of a special session of Congress in 1931 to press for important economic and political legislation at a time when the public was aroused and bitter—but get together to force such a session and to formulate a program of vital measures on which to justify it? That they could not do.

Even on that phase of the economic issue they might be expected to know most about, the agricultural problem, they have been without plan or program. Individually they have a variety of nostrums—the equalization fee, the tariff, the debenture, a government subsidy—but nothing of fundamental nature.

On this question, like the others, they were unable to get together. In 1927, following some by-election gains, they returned to the capital announcing their determination to press for "farm relief." They conferred among themselves on a plan of action and legislation on which they could agree.

The reporters and camera men swarmed about their offices. They were interviewed and photographed at length. One picture showed them in a group with Borah between Young Bob and Norris, their arms lovingly entwined.

It was all very encouraging. But utterly nothing came of it. Borah couldn't see the equalization fee, asserting that it was unconstitutional. Nye and some of the others differed with him and insisted upon the fee. Brookhart said that Mellon was at the bottom of the whole trouble and that the farmer must have two billion dollars from the Treasury to put him on his feet.

Each was sincere. Each was earnestly and honestly seeking a solution. But the problem and task were too much for them. They lacked the economic grasp to see through to the essentials. And they were too ruggedly individualistic to be able to get together even on a makeshift.

The discipline of a common cause, the unifying force of a specific and comprehensive economic philosophy and program, the only hope for significant reform in an industrial civilization, is unknown to them. Guerilla fighting they understand and know how to conduct, dramatically and effectively. But beyond raids and hopeless defensive stands they have been unable to coöperate.

Borah can bring an apathetic Senate to its feet in unprecedented applause with a passionate demand for food for the hungry and clothes for the cold. But to initiate or coöperate with a movement directed toward a sweeping economic reorganization that would strike at the causes of unemployment and lift agriculture from bankruptcy he has shown no capacity.

The elder LaFollette fought nobly for over a quarter of a century, endured stoically and heroically the most ferocious attacks, and yet left nothing lasting or important. Even the patch-work reforms he was able to achieve have fallen into the hands of those who fought them and been used by them to their own ends.

The Insurgents readily admit the need for sweeping readjustment of the economic structure. But most of them want to go back to an imaginary era of individual liberty, equality and fraternity, and not forward to the inevitable mass society. They are individualists in an age of the machine and class interests, who belong neither to those who have nor those who haven't, and pathetically seek for a romantic age that never was.

Young Bob and Senator Norris fully understand this and grasp the import and significance of the real economic struggle. They see and deplore the helplessness of their group and its cause. They comprehend thoroughly the desperate need for leadership, organization, discipline, ruthless economic realism. It was Young Bob, with Norris' encouragement, who conceived and prompted the national gathering of Progressive leaders in Washington this spring, the first attempt toward an organized Liberal effort since 1924.

But Norris is worn and wearied by a long life of lone fighting, and no longer has the strength to carry the burden of the new and fiercer struggle. Young Bob is just beginning. Until this year he has been chiefly preoccupied with building sound political ground under his feet in Wisconsin.

Young Bob is the best hope of the Progressive group for other reasons than his youth.

Even at 35 he is to-day the most constructive and cohesive force among the Insurgents. He has the clearest conception of economics among them. In this he is greater than his famous father who, for all his genius, never had a profound grasp of economics. It was Young Bob's work entirely that brought the Insurgents together and, even more important, held them together for many months in 1929-30, when the Smoot-Hawley Tariff Act was under consideration.

Keeping strictly in the background and always focusing on Borah the leadership and limelight, Young Bob, with Norris' wise counsel and aid, did a brilliant job in organizing the Insurgents in their magnificent fight against the vicious act. Each of the group was assigned a section of the measure, each was assisted in obtaining the necessary facts and the data to conduct his fight, and each was ably seconded when he took the floor.

So effectively did the plan work that for months the Insurgents dominated the situation in the Senate and literally rewrote the bill. It was only the last minute betrayal by a few weak-kneed "log-rolling" Democrats that prevented them from gaining a final smashing victory.

But the effort strikingly disclosed their power when they worked together along a definite line of action. Above all it revealed that there was one among them who had the qualities of leadership. This was not the first exceptional bit of work that Young Bob had achieved in his few years of leadership in the Senate, but it was the most significant in indicating what may be expected from him in the future.

His senatorial career was an accident. He had never planned entering public life. He had been his father's closest associate and for many years his secretary and campaign manager. But he did not think of himself as running for office. Philip, the younger son, now Governor of Wisconsin, was the family's choice as the elder LaFollette's successor.

Had the old Senator survived a few more years, Phil would have stepped into his place. He had already been started on his political career, being elected District Attorney of Dane County his first year out of law school.

But when the old Senator, broken by the strain of the 1924 Independent Presidential Campaign, succumbed six months later, Phil was too young to take his place. It was absolutely essential to the Progressive Party in Wisconsin, and to the economic welfare of the LaFollette family, that a LaFollette succeed to the vacant seat.

The Progressive leaders in the State were at logger-heads among themselves. The LaFollettes were openly critical of Blaine, then Progressive Governor. It was generally believed in Wisconsin that the elder LaFollette had planned to discard him as he had done many other Progressives whose ways he disapproved of. Blaine on his part was fully alive to the situation. He had built up a following of his own among the Progressives and was determined not to surrender without a fight.

In this explosive situation, the first thought was to nominate Mrs. LaFollette for her husband's unexpired term. The proposal met with hearty approval throughout the State where she is widely known as the brilliant helpmate of the idolized leader.

But living up to her reputation as a far-sighted and skilful politician she rejected the tempting offer and put Young Bob forward instead. He was just within the constitutional age limit and, because he had been so close to his father, was quite well known throughout the State.

He had made but one public address before he began his campaign and that was as his father's messenger to the Progressive Convention in Cleveland in 1924. On that occasion Young Bob read a message from his father and acquitted himself splendidly.

From the very first speech he made in his own right he was an effective and forceful campaigner. Like his father he has a keen sense of the dramatic and is vivid and fluent in his oratory. He is completely self-possessed when on his feet and, above all, never talks until he is carefully prepared and knows his subject thoroughly—an extremely rare quality among men in public life.

He worked for months on his tariff speeches and they were the outstanding discussions in either branch of Congress on the Smoot-Hawley Act. His smashing attacks upon the President on the food-relief issue, which forced him and the Red Cross, after months of suppressing facts and minimizing conditions, to admit there was widespread distress, were based on weeks of careful study.

When campaigning Young Bob is indefatigable, often making two full-length speeches on the same day in addition to several brief ones. He has actively participated in three campaigns in Wisconsin since his first election in 1925, in addition to making speaking tours on behalf of Insurgents in other states.

To-day he is one of not more than a half-dozen men in the United States Senate who are first rank public speakers. When it is known that he will take the floor, public interest in the capital is second only to that called forth by a speech from Borah.

The most dramatic incident of his senatorial career, so far, was the extemporaneous counter-attack he made against an attempt by an Old Guard wrecking crew, consisting of Senators Moses, Bingham and Reed, to bar the United Press Association from the Senate because its enterprising correspondent had the initiative to unearth secret and embarrassing roll calls. Speaking wholly extemporaneously Young Bob literally chased the three would-be press censors from the Senate floor and completely smashed a neatly laid plot they had cooked up to punish the independent press organization and its correspondent.

Young Bob is one of the most conscientious members of the Senate. He works hard on the floor and in committee. He attends all sessions. On most important legislation he is the Insurgent sentinel in the chamber and their most skilful and resourceful whip in the lobbies and cloak-rooms.

He is particularly effective in this capacity because of his universal popularity and the high respect in which he is held by every one in the Senate. He is not only the favorite of the Insurgents but is respectfully regarded by Republican Old Guarders, Young Turks, and the Democrats.

This is due not to any mincing of words when discussing issues, but to the fact that he never indulges in personalities. He confines himself, always, strictly to issues and principles. Because of his manifest ability the Insurgents have backed him for important committee assignments and, with the secret aid of several friendly Old Guarders, have placed him on three of the major committees of the Senate—Finance, Foreign Relations, and Manufactures. On the latter he is chairman by right of seniority.

Young Bob's greatest handicap is his health. It is only in the last year that he has really begun to come into his own. For years as his father's secretary and during the first few years of his senatorial career he struggled with ill health.

His ailment dates back to his boyhood. When he was first stricken it was not believed that he would recover. After a long convalescence he slowly returned to active life, but his health was always uncertain.

As a result of the strenuous ordeal of two hard campaigns in succeeding years and unremitting attention to his work in the Senate he suffered a recurrence of his ailment and was compelled to convalesce for a time in 1929. By the fall, however, when the tariff bill was taken under consideration he was active again and except for a faint limp and a pallor showed no signs of illness.

He worked unceasingly for ten months in one of the most arduous congressional sessions in many years and then immediately engaged, during a particularly hot summer, in a state-wide campaign in behalf of his brother's gubernatorial candidacy. In addition he made several speaking trips to neighboring states to campaign for Insurgent colleagues. To-day he is in excellent health and apparently fully recovered.

Before his marriage in 1930, his mother made a home for him in the capital in a modest little apartment. They lived quietly and he rarely went out. As when her husband was alive, she has studiously kept herself in the background, aiding and advising with her gifted counsel and scholarship.

Young Mrs. LaFollette, a charming Virginia girl, was the elder LaFollette's secretary and served Young Bob in that capacity. She and the Senator both devote themselves chiefly to their work but occasionally visit friends or go to a dance.

Young Bob is no teetotaler. Among friends he accepts and enjoys an occasional highball or cocktail. He is jolly and boyish in intimate companionship. Like his father he is a meticulous dresser, but less formal. When he first came to the Senate, he affected rather sheiky sideburns but after some raillery from friends he shaved them off.

There is a strong resemblance between him and his father. Like the latter he is below the average height, has the same stocky, powerful build, leonine head, and fighting jaw. He does not wear his father's pompadour and he is devoid of the latter's bristling manner and piercing eye. His brother Phil affects these traits—not altogether successfully at times.

Young Bob is one of the few men in public life in the capital who is really popular among the correspondents. It is not alone because he is unfailingly fair and courteous but because they know he is absolutely sincere, straightforward, and trustworthy. They constantly manifest their esteem by giving him inside tips and confidential information.

He is not the crusader that his father was but he has the qualities of a great leader. Given the health, he is unquestionably destined for a historic rôle in the Nation's affairs.

Senator John J. Blaine is distinctly of the rabble-raiser type.

He is a sincere Progressive, but with him issues are expressed chiefly in personalities. During his three terms as Progressive Governor of Wisconsin he broke with many of the close LaFollette leaders, almost always because of personal differences.

His administrations never swerved from LaFollette policies but somehow he and many of the old Progressives could not get along together. Some of them finally got so angry at him that they opposed him for reëlection. Blaine went out and developed his own Progressive leaders, chiefly among the younger men, and they have served him devotedly.

He is a shrewd politician and early saw the trend of the revolt against Prohibition in Wisconsin. This perspicacity won him his seat in the Senate.

He ran against Senator Irvine L. Lenroot, who was up for reëlection. Lenroot had once been a LaFollette man but had broken with him and had become an Old Guard leader. Lenroot, backed by all the resources of the Conservatives in the State, ran as a dry, trying to minimize the Prohibition question in the campaign. Blaine stressed it vigorously.

The race was very close. Six years before, Lenroot had defeated a powerful Progressive opponent despite the elder LaFollette's personal campaigning. It was conceded that the nomination would be decided by the strength of the wet vote on which Blaine was putting his reliance. There had been no test on the issue in the State and the outcome was unpredictable.

The day before the Primary, Labor Day, with only the morning papers and one edition of the afternoon's being published, the wets ran a full-page advertisement in the State press demanding the defeat of Lenroot as a dry and asserting that "A vote for Blaine is a vote for nickel Beer."

The appeal was irresistible to the parched voters in the large German sections and the next day when the ballots were counted, Blaine had nosed out Lenroot by a few thousand.

In the Senate, Blaine has proved a tenacious, hardy fighter. He will tackle any one and anything. When the Insurgents or the Democrats want a particularly rough-and-tumble job done, either on the floor or in an investigating committee, they call on Blaine. And he never fails them no matter who the subject of attack.

He is an uninspiring speaker, handicapped by a physical disability, due to a boyhood injury on the farm. But what he lacks in oratorical skill he makes up in vigor and outspokenness.

He enjoys muck-raking. Although serving his first term, he has been on three investigating committees, twice as chairman. On all he has taken a leading part. If he were a more skilful prosecutor he would be more effective. But here again, what he wants in skill he makes up in persistence and courage.

Personally he is well liked in the Senate and gets along with the Old Guard pleasantly enough, although he never hesitates to assail them. When Joseph R. Grundy, the Pennsylvania tariff lobbyist, was appointed to the Senate, Blaine stood a few feet away from him on the Senate floor and did what his colleagues on the lobby investigating committee did not have the courage to do—denounced Grundy for his lobbying operations.

Bolting is another of Blaine's oldest and favorite pastimes.

He supported and campaigned for Wilson and, in 1928, repudiated Mr. Hoover and urged the election of his Democratic opponent. In 1932, with all his past objections to Mr. Hoover fully confirmed, there is every prospect that he will do the same if the President is again a candidate.

Blaine is much happier in the Senate than he was as Governor. In the State House he was always having quarrels with Progressive leaders, particularly in the last years of his incumbency, over his appointments and his wet views. The old LaFollette men are drys for the most part and they couldn't stomach Blaine's militant wetness.

But in the Senate he has full scope for "raising hell" without running afoul of his own political associates. And he is thriving on the happy situation and enjoying himself hugely.

Senator Gerald P. Nye of North Dakota is a most earnest, well-meaning, and hard-working young man, but at times, and wholly without wrong intent, he finds it hard to hew strictly to the Progressive line.

Every now and then his Insurgent colleagues have to speak privately to him about staying in the ranks, but it is to his credit that he always listens to their counsel—except where North Dakota beet sugar and wool tariff interests are concerned, and there he has company, several other Insurgents voting with him.

Nye's difficulties arise out of his friendly nature. He hates to antagonize folks.

In 1928 he supported Mr. Hoover although privately he admitted his grave doubts about him. But to have bolted would have distressed good Republican friends, and Nye dislikes disappointing friends. And, besides, he had such signal exemplars, among the Insurgents, as Borah and Brookhart.

While his amiability may occasionally lead Nye into temporary confusion on issues, it has stood him in good stead in gaining committee recognition in the Senate. Republican leaders, cannily taking cognizance of this quality, chose him from among the Insurgents as the latter's representative on the important Committee on Committees, and made him Chairman of the Public Lands Committee.

Like Young Bob, Nye owes his senatorial career to a "lucky break." He was appointed to fill a vacancy by a Governor who expected to run for the seat himself, later, but who died before he could get around to it.

Until he came to Washington, Nye had never held public office and his most important work had been as editor of a small, weekly, country newspaper. He had taken an active but not a leading part in the North Dakota Nonpartisan League movement which, a decade ago, gave the super-patriots such scary, "Bolshy" chills.

In the 1930 campaign, A. C. Townley, once the Nonpartisan League dictator of the State, trying to stage a comeback in a campaign for Congress, was opposed by Nye and other former Nonpartisan Leaguers.

Nye has developed appreciably in many respects in the five years of his service in the Senate. When he first came to the capital, he looked exactly what he was, a small, farm-town, weekly editor. Since then he has laid aside his snappy, longish sideburns and yellow shoes, and has taken on a quiet, cosmopolitan air.

But he has lost none of his agricultural singlemindedness. To Nye, as to most other Insurgents, economic issues mean farm problems. In discussion he will readily concede the importance of industrial factors but they are theoretical to him. His background, environment, and interests are agricultural.

Agriculture is real and alive to him, although that does not make him any more positive about fundamental measures necessary to solve the farmer's difficulties. He believes the tariff would be a boon to the farmer "if it could be made to work."

Nye has essayed the rôle of investigator with not altogether happy results. He has done excellent work but he has encountered circumstances on which his kind of nature does not best thrive. A hard-boiled Blaine or a slashing Senator "Jim" Reed would not have been troubled, but Nye was distressed.

In both his rôles as investigator, he was chairman of the investigating committees. In the first inquiry, uncovering the trail of the Continental Trading Company phase of the Teapot Dome scandal, he was aided by several important factors —the presence and assistance of Senator Thomas Walsh of Montana, and the fact that a group of the keenest correspondents in the press corps covered the proceedings and were constantly back-stopping him with advice, information, and favorable publicity.

The merited recognition and commendation he won for his work in this matter led him into accepting the chairmanship of the special Senate committee appointed to scrutinize 1930 senatorial campaign expenditures. No one else in the Senate wanted the onerous job. It was obviously thankless labor and it was repeatedly rejected until Nye was prevailed upon to take it.

Nye worked hard and indefatigably on the trying assignment. He ferreted out the despicable conspiracy against Senator Norris, the enormous expenditures of the Illinois and Pennsylvania campaigns, and the Klan operations of the Republican senatorial candidate in Kentucky.

But unlike his first and happier investigational experience, Nye did not have the aid of a Walsh nor the daily counsel of friendly reporters. And, above all, he was confronted with tasks and personalities that he was not quite equal to.

Senator "Jim" Reed knew how to handle Illinois and Pennsylvania political operators when he went after them and drove them from the Senate floor. But to Nye, a Mrs. Ruth Hanna McCormick and a "Puddler Jim" Davis, with their endless bag of shyster tricks, were a bit confounding.

At times the skill of these two glib and ingenious politicians in protesting innocence reached such heights of effectiveness that it was doubtful just who was being investigated—they or the Senate Committee.

Then too, both Democratic and Republican leaders surreptitiously threw obstacles in Nye's path in an underhanded effort to raise suspicions against him, tactics they would never have dared attempt with Reed.

Nye has not been given the recognition he deserves for his work in the Campaign Expenditure Investigation. He laid himself open in minor ways to unfair and wholly unwarranted accusations, zealously spread, by whispers and innuendo, by those he was making uncomfortable. But his conduct was above reproach and his work on the campaign investigation much more important than the more widely publicized Continental Trading Company inquiry.

Nye hasn't the promise of leadership that Young Bob has, but he is far the abler of North Dakota's two Senators, and certainly the best likely to come out of that State for a long time.

If Senator Smith Wildman Brookhart, of Iowa, had a more active capacity for deductive reasoning, he might really be the significant figure he modestly likes to think he is.

A two-fisted fighter, with a sincere indignation against injustice and oppression, hard working, and a simple man, he has all the elements that go to make a leader, except that he always wanders off on a tangent in crucial moments.

At the height of the agricultural relief clamor, when the farmers of the Northwest needed only a spark to set them into revolt, Brookhart, among the foremost in fomenting the disaffection, and who of all people should have known better, was easily beguiled into the Hoover camp and without rhyme or reason acclaimed him as the Great Reliever.

Six months later, when Mr. Hoover bluntly rejected drastic relief measures and insisted on an innocuous policy, Brookhart laid his own lack of good sense to Mr. Hoover's wiles.

For years Brookhart has fiercely assaulted the tariff barons as robbers of the down-trodden farmer, and yet to him there was no incongruity in his advocacy of the debenture as a major farm-relief measure. The debenture is merely the tariff in reverse.

His farm-relief schemes all show the influence of this inability to draw obvious conclusions. For years he has studied the agricultural problem in all its ramifications, both in America and abroad. He is unquestionably the best-informed man in the Senate on agricultural statistics.

Yet he has never propounded a farm-relief plan that was not a nostrum, and the only difference between his proposals and those of the professional farm-relievers is that he characteristically does not hesitate to demand billions from the Treasury where the others talk in millions.

This obtuseness once cost him his Senate seat.

The Republican reactionaries of Iowa have always bitterly opposed Brookhart and in 1924 combined with the Democrats in an effort to beat him. The coalition candidate was an insignificant, reactionary, small-town lawyer who was willing to make the run for which no first-class man could be mustered.

To every one's surprise the race proved to be very close. Brookhart, however, was elected by a narrow margin and was so certified to the Senate by Iowa State officers.

But the Old Guard saw a chance to get rid of a disturber and instigated a challenge of his election. The triumphant Coolidge machine was out to destroy insolent insurgency and it determined to make Brookhart pay for his loyalty to La-Follette. Rather a safe and docile Democrat than an unmanageable Republican.

The case was a straight-out put-up job. It succeeded because the Insurgents were badly demoralized by the smashing defeat of the LaFollette-Wheeler Presidential effort and the Democrats, little better in morale, were further unnerved by the temptation of gaining a member.

Like the Republicans, most of the Democrats have no trouble in rising above principle when partisan or local interests are at stake.

The fight was long drawn out. The Insurgents did the best they could but they were badly handicapped by Brookhart's constant restraining them, because this Old Guard leader of that one had advised him that if he did not create too much disturbance everything would come out all right.

Why, in the face of indisputable evidence that he was being jobbed, he should have succumbed to such patent trickery is inexplicable. But he did, and he was tricked out of his seat.

He would have been through except that the Old Guard outdid itself. The steal was too flagrant.

Brookhart promptly returned to Iowa, ran on a vindication issue against the regular Republican candidate who fortunately came up for reëlection then, beat him by a wide margin and came back to the Senate.

In many respects, Brookhart is one of the most interesting of the Insurgent group. He was born in a log cabin on a farm in Missouri, and worked his way laboriously to an education. His official biography characterizes him as a farmer, teacher, lawyer, and soldier, and he put in long years at each.

His military career reaches from 1894 through the World War. Yet he is an opponent of large military expenditures, and one of his most effective appearances in the Senate was an extemporaneous reply he made to the redoubtable "Jim" Reed in which he very soundly deflated a bombastic big-navy speech the latter had belligerently made.

For many years Brookhart was a champion military marksman, with both rifle and pistol, and, in 1912, was Captain of the American Palma Rifle Team which won the world's championship. He was an officer in the Iowa National Guard in the Spanish-American War and on the Mexican border, and a Lieutenant Colonel of Infantry, and Chief Instructor in Marksmanship in several of the largest rifle schools of the country during the World War.

Almost single-handed, and in the face of the customary tradition-bound stupidity of the regular army caste he reorganized the obsolete system of marksmanship training that was in effect in the American army when it entered the World War.

He is built like a burly wrestler, rather short and powerfully muscled. He walks with his head jutted forward and with an aggressive gait. He rarely wears an overcoat and seldom a hat.

His great want is a sense of direction. He means well, is honest and sincere, has a big, warm heart and a head crammed full of facts and figures. But he lacks a good steering gear.

Senator Lynn J. Frazier of North Dakota is living proof that in politics there is money in dirt farming.

Since 1916 he has held important political posts, being three times elected Nonpartisan League Governor of his State and twice elected United States Senator. In all this time he has been an earnest, sincere, progressive public servant.

But it has been as a plodder in the ranks. The initiative and drive have had to come from others. As Governor he followed the Nonpartisan League leadership. When that organization disintegrated he adhered steadfastly to his liberalism but made no effort to create another party.

In the Senate he loyally and devotedly followed LaFollette. He unhesitatingly bolted in 1924 and when two years later the Old Guard was ready to make its peace on the Insurgent's terms he accepted the committee chairmanship that was offered him.

As Chairman of the Senate Indian Affairs Committee he has done excellent work in defending the tragically misgoverned Redman and bringing to light the terrible abuses of the Indian Bureau. But always the push and direction have come from others.

Frazier is a real dirt farmer. He is a graduate of Normal School and the University of North Dakota. Upon finishing school he returned to the family homestead and actively engaged in farming. He left the plow to accept his first gubernatorial nomination.

Despite his long public service, he is awkward and hesitant on his feet. He shuns the limelight and is happiest when he can close his desk in the capital and go back to his farm in North Dakota.

Senator Robert B. Howell of Nebraska, like Frazier, is a

background figure among the Insurgents, but in his quiet, unassuming way he is one of the ablest of the group.

He is a graduate of Annapolis, served as a naval officer during the Spanish-American War and the World War, studied law and civil engineering, and is one of the most experienced and successful directors of publicly owned utilities in the country. For a number of years he was General Manager of Omaha's municipal water, gas and ice plants.

While not of the crusading cast of his colleague, Norris, he has done some very effective work in the Senate. Several years ago he defeated, single-handed, an Old Guard attempt to pay off the century-old French spoliation claims.

Howell has all the virtues of the technical expert—and the drawbacks. His addresses are dull rhetoric but they are exhaustive and thorough studies of the subject he is discussing. During the war debt settlement fights, he submitted masses of illuminating statistics that made those compiled by the Treasury Department look like grammar school additions.

He is a big man physcially, deliberate of motion, meticulous of dress. He keeps up his interest in the Naval Academy, but neither his military education nor service keeps him from supporting disarmament measures and voting against big-navy bills.

A strange mass of contradictions is Senator Bronson Cutting of New Mexico.

Scion of an old and very wealthy New York family, reared on a Long Island estate, educated at Harvard where he was graduated with Phi Beta Kappa honors, he is to-day one of the most intelligent and clear-thinking of the Insurgents.

Yet his first act, when he came to the Senate as an appointee in 1927, was to advocate the seating of Frank Smith of Illinois, who, the Reed investigating committee revealed, had accepted a large campaign contribution from public utility interests while he was a member of the State Public Utility Commission. Cutting contended that the State was the sole judge of its representatives and that the Senate had no right to reject them.

Also, although he now is one of the most thoroughgoing and intelligent Insurgents in Washington, Cutting in New Mexico is boss of one of the tightest little political machines in the country. It has been called the Tammany of the Southwest, but, while it is unquestionably a paternal organization, no judicial or any other scandals are attached to it.

To understand the Cutting organization in New Mexico, it is necessary to appreciate the character of the State's population. A preponderant majority of the voters are of Spanish extraction—not Mexican, but Spanish. They call themselves Spanish-Americans and they speak Spanish.

They have an age-old *patron* tradition. The landed gentry for centuries have administered to the wants of their dependents, including the political.

Cutting, going to New Mexico for his health soon after leaving college, grasped this fact early in his residence there, and realized its possibilities for future political ambitions. He made friends with the young men of the leading Spanish-American families, who, in turn, were attracted to the grave but charming young Easterner in whose Santa Fe mansion they were always received with the most courtly hospitality.

They became devoted supporters and admirers and, bit by bit, Cutting, as the leading publisher of the State, began to take an important rôle in State politics. Over a long period of years, and at a time when it was financially unprofitable to do so, he attacked Albert B. Fall's machine and manner of doing things.

All this time Cutting's influence with the fifty-odd percent of the Spanish-speaking population of the State increased. When the United States entered the World War he patriotically turned from State affairs to serve as Captain of Infantry on the military staff of the American Embassy in London, for which he was awarded the British Military Cross.

Upon his return to the State, he set to work seriously to

develop a loyal political organization. Local leaders soon came to know that if they wanted anything, from a little road-mending to the transfer of an unpopular government agent, *Don* Cutting was the best man to get in touch with.

In 1922, Cutting, as independent in State politics as he has proved to be in the Senate, tested out his theories and carefully nurtured organization and supported a Democratic candidate for Governor against the Fall machine. His ideas proved their worth and his candidate won handsomely.

From then on, he greatly expanded his organizational activities, but always with that rare tact and skill and generosity which are so necessary with and so appreciated by the Spanish race. In 1927, when a vacancy occurred in the Senate, another gubernatorial friend, this time a Republican, appointed him to fill it. When he ran for the full six-year term in 1928, he was elected by a large majority.

To-day he is the State's most esteemed *patron*. What *Don* Cutting does in far-away Washington, his constituents do not bother themselves about. So good and generous and understanding a man could do only what was right.

Cutting's record in the Senate, with the exception of the Smith episode, is one of the very best. His vigorous fight against the customs censorship when the tariff bill was under consideration brought him merited, nationwide commendation. He is proud of his independence and is one of Young Bob's staunchest and most resolute supporters in pressing for organized activity.

With the marriage of Young Bob, Cutting is now the only bachelor among the Insurgents. He is 42 years of age, wealthy, educated, traveled, and with an assured political future. He is one of the most eligible young men in the capital—and also one of the chariest.

Senator Henrik Shipstead, Farmer-Laborite from Minnesota, is the only one of the Insurgent group with an independent label. But he is the least militant among them.

In physique and political affiliations the most favored for

a crusading rôle, he is a cautious political trader and a pompous bore.

His occasional speeches, consisting for the most part of lengthy quotations from learned authorities, are among the most tiresome in the Senate. His greatest achievements in eight years of service in the Senate are a few pieces of local pork.

Shipstead's only approach to anything of an important nature in legislation was the bill he sponsored several years ago to curb labor injunctions. The long, tedious work on the measure he left to others, and it was Norris and several other Insurgents who fought its battles through the Senate Judiciary Committee.

He is also the author of numerous denunciatory but perfectly innocuous resolutions regarding the government's foreign policy, particularly in Latin America. These declamations are sent to committee pigeonholes, where they remain in undisturbed oblivion.

Three or four years ago, either out of irritation at the bombardment of resolutions or in order to call his bluff, the Senate Foreign Relations Committee took him up on his demand for an inquiry into American banking machinations in Nicaragua and made him chairman of a small sub-committee with authority to investigate the matter. After much preparation, and with great pomposity, Shipstead finally got the hearings under way.

The inquiry was a total flop. After a few sessions, at which Nicaraguan émigrés testified, nothing more was heard of the matter. And Shipstead has never assumed any investigational responsibilities since.

He affects great interest and knowledge of the law and foreign affairs. At smart social-political salons, where he appears more frequently than any of the other Insurgents, he likes to air at length, and with heavy solemnity, his erudition on these two subjects.

He is a dentist by profession, but is said to have studied

law in his spare hours for many years. This ambitious labor has not appreciably improved his senatorial qualities. Whether it has made him a better dentist is not known.

Shipstead's evolution as a safe radical is a remarkable and fascinating performance.

At the height of the Northwestern rural disaffection in the early '20's, he jumped into the arena in Minnesota, where he was born and educated, and announced himself as a Farmer-Labor candidate against Frank B. (Nervous Nellie) Kellogg, then Republican Senator from the State.

Kellogg had once been a flaming spokesman of insurgency. But a few years among the flesh pots of Washington had tamed him. Where once he had seen danger at the hands of the wealthy, Kellogg had reached the point, when Shipstead took up the crusade against him, where he would pale and grow faint at the mere mention of the word "Red."

The race was furious and bitter. Kellogg, backed by big business, all aflutter and affrighted by the Radical menace in the form of the big, husky, pompadoured Norwegian dentist, raised the cry of Bolshevism. It was whispered far and wide that Shipstead's election would mean "free love" and "Communism."

Either because of this alluring promise or just plain disgust with the quaking Kellogg, Minnesota turned him out and sent Shipstead to Washington. There he did what his predecessor had not the genius to conceive or accomplish—he ate his Insurgent cake and had it at the same time.

In his voting record, his numerous resolutions, and his infrequent remarks, Shipstead is always militantly Insurgent. But as far as actually disturbing any one or anything is concerned, he is as dangerous as the most regular of the Regulars.

It has been a great scheme and it has served him well. In 1928, when he ran for reëlection, he was no longer a violent and sinister figure. Important Minnesota business interests expressed themselves as perfectly satisfied with his record. Republicans, Democrats, and Farmer-Laborites joined in supporting him with the result that, although Hoover carried the State by a large vote, Shipstead led him by 100,000.

To-day, Shipstead is the lion of the salons and living proof of the fact that it pays to have ideas in politics.

If Senator Burton K. Wheeler of Montana were more industrious and energetic, he could be one of the really great figures in American public life.

As it is, he is one of the ablest and most forceful men in the Senate. But he doesn't begin to do the work that he is capable of and which his exceptional talents should inspire him to do.

He has brilliant mental equipment. He is charming of personality and has a pleasing appearance. He has character, simplicity, and forthrightness. He is a fearless and resourceful fighter. And he is sincerely and passionately moved by human misery.

But he is lazy.

He rarely prepares himself for a fight, depending upon his sharpness of wit and upon his many friends, particularly the correspondents, to supply him with information. They do so eagerly because he is often the only one who will raise an issue, but he could do infinitely more effective work if he would only apply himself personally to preparation.

Wheeler has been a dissident all his political life. Because he comes from Montana, although he was born in Massachusetts and got his law education in Michigan, he is a Democrat. If he had come from a Republican State, he might have been a Republican, but he would have been an Insurgent wherever he had come from.

Wheeler's insurgency arises out of his deep compassion for human distress. Even as a struggling young anticorporation lawyer in the copper barony of Montana, he befriended the impoverished and degraded Indians. At that time there was neither political advantage nor money in his doing so, nor any thought that there ever would be.

Since the World War, however, his Indian friends have been

enfranchised and they repay him with a 100 percent ballot whenever he is up for election. In his first senatorial race in 1922, their support decided the close contest in his favor.

Wheeler has always fought the copper companies which practically own the State. As District Attorney of Butte for five years he befriended the embattled miners and defied "the company." In 1928 he was reëlected Senator over company opposition by a large vote.

Wheeler had been in Washington only a few years when the scandals of the Harding Administration gave him his opportunity to gain national attention. While his upright and austere colleague, Senator Thomas J. Walsh, was ferreting out the oil deals, Wheeler went after Attorney General Harry Daugherty.

In alarm Daugherty and the Ohio Gang instituted a framed prosecution of Wheeler in an effort to discredit his damning investigation. The case was later thrown out of court and Wheeler was thoroughly exonerated of the false charges.

Wheeler's exceptional work and high courage in the Daugherty investigation made him the elder LaFollette's choice as his running mate when he made his independent Presidential campaign in 1924. Wheeler had no hesitancy in casting off party ties and made a nation-wide campaign attacking both old party candidates.

With the campaign over, he returned to Washington and took his former place among the Democrats. They attempted no such "disciplining" as the victorious Coolidge machine inflicted upon bolting Republicans. In 1928 Wheeler earnestly supported Smith and campaigned for him throughout the West.

Wheeler is still a few years under fifty and should play an important rôle in national affairs—if he will bestir himself.

Senator William E. Borah is individualism in all its glory and in all its futility.

In a fight he is without equal in the country to-day in arousing popular enthusiasm and delivering telling blows.

Hoover was the candidate in 1928, but the voice of the Republican Party that year was the voice of Borah.

In a Senate debate he alone can bring the chamber to its feet in spontaneous applause, contrary to all its staid habits and rules. He is capable of the most brilliant parliamentary and tactical strokes.

But to coöperate with others in a sustained and disciplined effort over a long period of time—that Borah is utterly unable to do. He wants to and means to, but he is just not made that way.

The longest period during which he ever worked in harness with his fellow-Insurgents was the 1929-30 tariff fight, and it required all the tact, patience, and persistence of Young Bob and Norris to bring that about. They worked almost as hard maneuvering Borah into the leadership of that fight and keeping him there, as they did combating the egregious measure itself.

What Borah could do in the way of real leadership if, instead of his empty legalism, he had a wide and comprehensive economic grasp, and, instead of the temperament of an incorrigible individualist, he had a capacity for discipline and coöperation, can only be imagined. He could easily give the impetus to a great political movement.

But he won't, because he is Borah. And he will never be any more.

He will raise more hopes and thrill more audiences, but that is all. The persistent labor necessary to create a Liberal Party will have to be done by others, if it is done at all. It is beyond him.

Borah at one time appeared ready to bestir himself. In 1922 he told close friends that the time had come for raising the banners of political revolt.

For a brief period, he was fascinated by the thought. But nothing ever came of it.

If all that had been necessary for realization of this project had been an epic declamation, a resounding pronunciamento, it would have been brilliantly consummated. But to leave his books, his studies, his cool, quiet, shaded office, his horse, his unhampered and comfortable aloofness for the strain and toil and turmoil that an independent campaign would entail was too much for him.

Not that Borah doesn't like the cheers of the mob. There is no one more sensitive to the stimulation of the crowd than he is. When he steps out onto the Senate floor his unconscious glance is always to the galleries.

But having given full play to his stellar histrionic talents and warmed himself with the excited enthusiasm and flattering adulation, Borah is through. He withdraws to the pleasant, regular isolation of his private life to await another dramatic appearance.

He is a genius at gauging the opportuneness of these occasions. He knows just when to step to the footlights. Outwardly all may seem quiet, but Borah senses the undercurrent and he strikes.

He never acts until he is carefully prepared and rehearsed. His speeches are made without notes and his brilliant appearances seem on the spur of the moment but both are always the result of long and studied thought and planning.

Borah never makes a speech that he has not gone over many times in the privacy of his cavernous study in the Senate office building. And he never talks until he has exhausted the subject he addresses himself to.

He is the great advocate. Scintillating of thought, and enthralling of expression, he is without peer as the passionate pleader. He has raised his voice for many splendid causes, peace, disarmament, anti-imperialism, Russian recognition. He has stirringly denounced infamy, demagoguery, incompetence, and corruption in high and low places.

But to enroll in the ranks or even to take the lead in a movement to give practical expression to these meritorious objectives, he is without capacity. Time and again in inspired words he has raised hopes that at last he was preparing to act, only to let the issue subside.

Borah doesn't mean to disappoint. He never feels that he does. And he is always sincerely distressed when he is told so.

When, in 1924, the elder LaFollette attempted to raise a Progressive movement with his independent Presidential campaign, Borah criticized both old parties. But join with the bolters? That was out of his character. He was fulfilling his rôle by denouncing the inadequacies of the reactionary old parties.

People expect too much of Borah. He is the advocate, the mouthpiece. Not the organizer, the commander.

As the pleader of just causes he is supreme. As such he has done noble service. He is the master mass psychologist as an orator. But he is not of the mass.

He is the student type. He likes to bury himself in exhaustive and careful study. If he had not the gift of great oratory, he unquestionably would have been a scientist.

It is this scholar in him that so powerfully modifies his great political talents. The deep satisfaction and peace of quiet and undisturbed study draw him back from the confusion and clamor of public fray.

It has a profound attraction for him, but as a forum, not as a battle-field.

Borah is one of the kindliest and gentlest of men. He never loses his temper. He never gets personal.

He has a rare talent for friendship. When Congress is not in session and he is in the capital, the Senate reporters assemble in his office every day at a fixed hour for the most unusual press conference in the city.

Here affairs and individuals are discussed and chatted over with the utmost candor. No one and no subject is taboo— including the host. He is argued with and challenged freely and frankly.

Once in a great while a news story will result from these daily meetings, but that is not their chief purpose. The newspapermen go because of the comradeship and mental stimulation they derive from Borah.

Borah lives simply and plainly. The only luxury he allows himself is a saddle horse for a daily gallop, no matter what the weather. Until a year ago he never owned an automobile and he used the street cars to go about the city.

He never entertains, never attends social functions, and only rarely goes to official dinners. Mrs. Borah, known as "Little Borah" among her friends, takes a quiet part socially in the elder senatorial and diplomatic set. They have no children and Mrs. Borah personally manages their small household. She is always on the lookout for new recipes for onion soup of which Borah is very fond.

The last three times he has run for reëlection, Borah has been practically without opposition. He has had Democratic opponents but as one of them expressed it, "I am running for the advertisement."

No Presidential campaign rolls around that Borah is not mentioned—in the beginning. He knows he will never be President. But he has no objection to being mentioned.

He could have been Vice President once. Coolidge offered him a place on his ticket in 1924, when he was alarmed by the LaFollette threat. The story is that Borah looked Coolidge straight in the eye and inquired innocently, "Which place, Mr. President?"

Senator George W. Norris of Nebraska is one of the saddest and noblest characters in American history.

His whole public life has been an unceasing struggle for human liberty and progress. He has never hesitated at any sacrifice in the cause he has fought for. Always, simply and fearlessly, he has remained true to his principles, giving everything he has had in their service.

And after almost half a century of struggle he has come to the bitter realization that the political democracy for which he has so long and unstintingly expended himself has been engulfed by an industrial civilization, and the fight he has so gallantly made has been largely futile.

He is still maintaining his ideals; he is still pressing forward. But he knows that he is fighting a hopeless battle and that the competitive individualism he has sought to preserve is no longer possible.

Had he been born fifty years earlier or later, Norris would have been a far more successful figure. Born in 1861, in a mid-western rural environment, he came to manhood imbued with the philosophy and ideals of an agricultural, political democracy, the last vestiges of which were being effaced by a triumphant industrialism while he was a child in the cradle.

He entered the public arena unaware of the real issues at stake. For long years, single-handedly he fought epic battles for political reform, when the economic was the real ruler.

He overthrew Cannonism and has driven corrupt and vicious men from high office. He strove mightily and successfully to extend the government's political sway over economic forces. But it has been all in vain.

The system he left untouched, and therein was his weakness. When he came to a full realization of this fact, he was too tired and spent to begin anew.

But he has gone on, always the resolute and forthright warrior, trying to plug up the holes, stopping a steal here, a scandal and outrage there. For a time, after the 1928 Presidential campaign, he spoke of retiring from the Senate at the end of his term in 1931 and going back to Nebraska, in the hope of achieving something lasting there.

In a smaller arena the accomplishment of a fundamental and vital recasting of the political and economic system he thought might be within the measure of his remaining years and strength. But vicious corporation and political forces conspiring to defeat him left him no alternative but to take up their challenge.

He again ran for the Senate and despite the use of the most

cowardly, scurrilous, and dishonest tactics against him was overwhelmingly nominated and elected.

He is the gentlest and simplest of men, utterly without affectation. Outside of public life he is a recluse. He and Mrs. Norris attend no social functions of any kind.

He loves to read, to walk, and to drive a little automobile he owns. In the summer, when he can leave Washington, he and Mrs. Norris drive to Wisconsin, where, on a small lake in the northern woods, they have a little cabin that he built with his own hands. There they spend their vacation months in the quiet and peace of the forest.

He reads everything, but especially poetry and history. His favorite book is "Cyrano de Bergerac" and the rolling cadences of that indomitable hero's defiances.

It is a common experience for friends to come upon him in his office late in the afternoon with his feet tilted on his desk, reading aloud to himself stirring passages from that beautiful tale of courage and devotion.

> What say you? ... That it is useless? ... Don't I know?
> But valiant hearts contend not for successes!
> It's nobler to defend a hopeless cause!
> ... Who are you all? I count a thousand ... more!
> I know you all now; my enemies of old!
> You're Falsehood ...
> Here! ... Ha! ha! and Compromise,
> And Prejudice, and Cowardice! ...
> Submit?
> No, never! Ah! here's Imbecility! ...
> I know that, in the end, I must succumb,
> I dare you, though, and strike! and strike! and strike!

Well might these words be said of Norris, valiant warrior in the cause of human progress. He, too, has often fought vainly, but always pure of heart, noble of aspiration, and gloriously.

CHAPTER NINE

THE MONKEY HOUSE

THE House of Representatives is the greatest organized inferiority complex in the world.

Contrary to general belief, its major occupation is not legislation but trying to make itself appear important and significant.

The fact that this is patently impossible, the House being constituted as it is, has not deterred that body from its vain pursuit. It is this blind groping for some means of making itself a respected and significant body that is one of the basic causes for the ready subserviency of the House to boss rule.

Conscious of its inability to impress or to function as an independent institution, it has abdicated its power into the hands of bosses, in the hope that they will give it the standing it could not achieve by exercise of its own free will and intelligence.

The Founding Fathers created the House as a vehicle for the more immediate expression of public sentiment than was considered likely in the aloof and exclusive Senate. Their model was the British House of Commons.

The country got more than the Fathers bargained for. The House is expressive, but only of the most stultifying and reactionary forces in the land.

Instead of being the counterpart of the great English legislative body, it is a cross between a troop of monkeys and a herd of sheep.

The four hundred and thirty-five members, with a few exceptions, are the lowest common denominator of the ignorance, prejudices, and inhibitions of their districts. As a result, the House, instead of being a positive factor, is one of the most debasing influences in the government. It rarely functions as an independent legislative body. For the most part it is the willing instrument of vicious partisan and predatory interests.

It has been the most persistent obstacle to intelligent and progressive legislation in the government. It has lent itself to the delaying, defeating, and emasculating of innumerable sound and needed reforms.

In recent times, the House, for nearly a decade, obstructed a solution of the Muscle Shoals problem, except in the interests of private power companies. For almost as many years, it has barred urgently needed changes in congressional sessions contained in the Norris "lame duck" amendment to the Constitution.

And while strangling these and other essential measures, the House has approved colossal tariff steals, voted fat tax cuts to big incomes and huge estates, and appropriated billions of dollars for local pork-barrel projects.

There have been a few brief periods when the House, under the inspiration and leadership of an honest and fearless man, has cast off its bonds and asserted its independence. But these bright moments have been short-lived.

As soon as the courageous member left, the chamber immediately reverted to submission. Twenty years ago Senator Norris, then a young member of the House, led an epic revolt and overturned the current boss, "Uncle Joe" Cannon. The House took its affairs in its own hands and for a little while made history.

But when, a year or so later, Norris went to the Senate, the reaction promptly set in. The House sank steadily to lower

depths of subservience and inanity until, in 1925, it bowed
before one of the stupidest and most mediocre rules it has
yet experienced, the domination of the Longworth-Snell-Tilson
triumvirate.

The House reflects its true nature in its appearance, pro-
cedure, social activities and political operations. When assembled in its chamber it looks and acts like a section of the
bleachers in a bush league town. Its politics would be tragic
if they were not so funny.

Thomas L. Blanton, Democrat, of Texas, after trying for the
Senate and being defeated, ran for his former House seat on
the issue of less expensive congressional funerals. Up and
down the fifty-three wide Texas counties that make up his
district, he crusaded on the question of curbing lavish expenditure in burying deceased House members. He promised that,
if elected, he would put an end to this waste of taxpayers'
money. He won by an overwhelming vote.

Charles O'Connor, Republican, of Oklahoma, leaped to his
feet one day when the House was considering a seed loan bill
and demanded that his State be included in distribution of
this pork.

"This is a grab," he informed his colleagues, "and I don't
endorse it. But if other States are going to get it, I'm going
to have my slice of pie as well. I'm not going back home and
have my people ask me 'Where the hell were you the day
this was voted?'"

The House could not ignore such a plea. Each member
knew whereof Mr. O'Connor spoke. Oklahoma was included
in the bill.

His zeal in securing for the Congressional Library the
world-famous Vollbehr Collection of historic volumes, among
them one of the three extant copies of the Gutenberg Bible,
almost cost Ross A. Collins, Democrat, of Mississippi, his
seat in the 1930 election. Mr. Collins, a man of considerable
scholarship, was vigorously attacked by a less cultured opponent for squandering the "people's money" by getting the

government to pay $1,500,000 for a bunch of foreign books.

So serious did the situation become that Mr. Collins was compelled to explain to his constituents that the large sum was needed in order to get a bible that "Moses wrote" out of the hands of the heathen.

A hill region representative, who used to make his campaign by hiking over his district, repeatedly ran on one issue: "If you don't elect me this time I'll run again." And he did until his hill-billy constituents finally elected him.

The House chamber is a huge, oblong hall filled with rows of long padded benches. On these the members sprawl without place, order, or decorum, the Republicans on one side and the Democrats on the other.

Usually only a small proportion of the members are in attendance. Days will go by with only a handful of members present, droning away in the ugly, unkempt chamber.

House rules permit applause, and in a debate the place takes on the atmosphere of a boxing arena. There are cheers and clapping, boos and catcalls, constant moving about and clatter. If ever anything worth while is said, few can hear it and still fewer pay any attention.

Under the "gag" rules by which the House has permitted itself to be controlled, the bosses of the chamber determine the length of time they will allot to consideration of a bill on the floor. They will give a tariff bill extorting hundreds of millions of dollars in excessive rates a few hours, and an oleomargarine bill a week.

A soldier bonus proposal entailing a hundred million dollars in expenditures and a complete change in government policy, they will restrict to forty minutes' debate, twenty minutes to a side, while a bus regulating bill will be allowed to hold the floor five days. A "lame duck" reform measure, five times passed by the Senate, the bosses prevented from coming up at all for years, and when finally forced by public opinion to permit a vote on it, they emasculated it by a stultifying amendment.

Such demoralizing leadership, Representative Tilson, one of the major Republican bosses, once seriously acclaimed as responsible for the "House's well-earned prestige."

Every important bill that comes before the House must obtain a "rule" for its consideration. The Rules Committee is controlled by the bosses of the House. It determines the flow of the legislative stream.

If its members don't want a piece of legislation to come up they don't give it a rule. Usually they don't even have to bother to do that. The measures are stifled in committee.

But if a bill they are against, for some reason or other, does succeed in fighting its way out of committee, they shelve it in the Rules Committee. Some years ago a Republican chairman of this committee was commonly reported to carry such measures about in his pocket. He was eventually defeated for reëlection. He promptly set himself up as a lobbyist in Washington.

*

Debate in the House is indescribable. It is a shambles of low humor, impossibly absurd assertions made as statements of fact, violent partisanship, clamor, confusion, and burlesque. Members wander about the hall laughing and talking to one another.

A few minutes, often only a few seconds, are allotted to speakers. They rush to the front, roar out a few remarks, and then ask for permission to "extend and revise my remarks."

These later appear in the Appendix of the Record as elaborate addresses. They are then printed at cost in the government's printing plant and mailed free of charge, under the member's postal frank, to his thousands of constituents.

A characteristic example of House debate is to be found in the proceedings on February 16, 1931. The Soldier Bonus Loan Bill, calling for an expenditure of hundreds of millions of dollars, was under consideration. Each side was allowed twenty minutes to present its argument.

The following is a skeletonized summary of the debate that ensued on this important issue.

The SPEAKER. The gentleman from New Jersey (Mr. Bacharach) is entitled to twenty minutes and the gentleman from Oregon (Mr. Hawley) is entitled to twenty minutes.

Mr. HAWLEY. Mr. Speaker, I yield five minutes to the gentleman from Massachusetts (Mr. Treadway).

(Mr. TREADWAY asked and was given unanimous consent to revise and extend his remarks.)

Mr. BACHARACH. Mr. Speaker, I ask unanimous consent that all members have five legislative days in which to extend their remarks on this bill.

The SPEAKER. Is there objection to the request of the gentleman from New Jersey?

There was no objection.

Mr. HAWLEY. Mr. Speaker, I yield three minutes to the gentleman from Illinois (Mr. Chindblom).

Mr. BACHARACH. Mr. Speaker, I yield two minutes to the gentleman from Wisconsin (Mr. Frear).

Mr. BACHARACH. Mr. Speaker, I yield one quarter of a minute to Mr. Rankin of Mississippi.

Mr. RANKIN. Mr. Speaker, I am in favor of paying what the Government owes these veterans now, even though we are compelled to put a wound stripe on the purse of Andrew W. Mellon big enough to be seen from Pittsburgh to Philadelphia. (Applause.)

Mr. BACHARACH. Mr. Speaker, I yield a quarter of a minute to the gentleman from Texas (Mr. Blanton).

Mr. BACHARACH. Mr. Speaker, I yield a quarter of a minute to the gentleman from Texas (Mr. Patman). (Applause.)

Mr. HAWLEY. Mr. Speaker, I yield five minutes to the gentleman from Iowa (Mr. Ramseyer). (Applause.)

Mr. BACHARACH. Mr. Speaker, I yield one minute to the gentleman from New York (Mr. Fish).

Mr. BACHARACH. Mr. Speaker, I yield one minute to the gentleman from Nebraska (Mr. Simmons).

Mr. BACHARACH. Mr. Speaker, I yield one-half minute to the gentleman from New York (Mr. LaGuardia).

Mr. LAGUARDIA. Mr.Speaker, I yield back the balance of my time. I am going to vote for the bill. (Laughter and applause.)

Mr. BACHARACH. Mr. Speaker, I yield one minute to the gentleman from New York (Mr. Crowther).

Mr. CROWTHER....I have not forgotten the promises that were made to them as they marched away from home and fireside to embark for a foreign shore. With reverence we remember those who never came back, and we must keep faith with those who returned to us after their distinguished service under the Stars and Stripes. (Applause.)

Mr. BACHARACH. Mr. Speaker, I yield to the gentleman from Indiana (Mr. Canfield).

Mr. BACHARACH. Mr. Speaker, I yield one-quarter of a minute to the gentleman from Alabama (Mr. Almon).

Mr. HAWLEY. Mr. Speaker, I yield one-half minute to the gentleman from New Jersey (Mr. Fort).

Mr. BACHARACH. Mr. Speaker, I yield the balance of my time (two minutes) to the gentleman from Texas (Mr. Garner).

Verbal tilts in the House are extraordinary performances. Few trouble to confine themselves to the subject under consideration. The wider afield the discussion goes, the more the disputants pride themselves on their erudition.

The following exchange occurred in a debate on prohibition, the most popular subject of controversy in the House.

Mr. SCHAFER of Wisconsin. If He were here in the Nation's capital to-day, attending a wedding feast, and again performed a miracle, would He turn the water into a non-intoxicating beverage?

Mr. SPROUL of Kansas. I do not know what He would do in that regard, but I will say this to the gentleman, that Jesus made it a point to observe the laws of his worldly country.

Mr. LAGUARDIA. He also made it a point to change some of those laws.

Mr. SPROUL of Kansas. No; He did not.

Mr. LAGUARDIA. That is my understanding.

Mr. SPROUL of Kansas. Well, the gentleman is not informed about New Testament Scripture, because He did not do anything of the kind. He broke none of those laws.

Mr. STRONG of Kansas. Might He not do as He did in the temple, if He came into the Halls of Congress now?

Mr. SPROUL of Kansas. He might.

Occasionally when the bosses are purposely dragging deliberations in order to consume time. a member will be allowed a half hour or more to deliver an address. For the most part these are grotesque declamations.

The following extracts are from a speech by Representative Thomas Alva Yon of Florida. He was relating his impressions of a capitol fire and how he did his bit to save the historic structure.

> Mr. Yon. I have listened to the remarks of my good friend and distinguished leader of the opposition, Mr. Tilson, as he opened his remarks with a reference to that famous fable of Aesop's, "Wolf, wolf, when there was no wolf." But, in proceedings, since I have referred to these two of the best friends I have in the House, I want, as one who was fortunate or maybe as the occasion presented itself, to express my feelings, or, in other words, the consternation that overcame my American patriotic soul at the time, and I take no issue with my distinguished colleagues in doing so, for, as I have said before, they are two of my best personal friends. And for Mr. Tilson to hold the position he does as leader of the opposition party, that of a real Florida-cracker Democrat, he has been unusually kind and considerate to me.
>
> But in proceeding I will say that I left my home district on the afternoon of January 1, after driving over a lot of the most delightful and picturesque paved highways and for the next two days over through Georgia, South Carolina, North Carolina and Virginia of the old historic South. And on this drive through Florida I was reminded of Ponce de Leon, De Narvaez and De Soto; through Georgia of James Oglethorpe, Robert Toombs, Sydney Lanier, the poet, and others of the illustrious past; through South Carolina of Francis Marion, John C. Calhoun and others who have added laurels and luster to the Nation's history; through North Carolina I was reminded of the dispute between North and South Carolina as to which belonged the honor of giving the first light of day to the personification of Democracy in America—Andrew Jackson, and thought also of Nathanael Greene, and of a more recent date, Josephus Daniels, Secretary of the Navy in the late war, and he dried the Navy. Through the grand Old Dominion, Virginia, and of Washington, Jefferson, Stonewall Jackson, "Jeb" Stuart, Lee, and a host of others that have added luster, and memory of them should act as a guiding star to future Americans as examples of patriotism and fidelity to Democratic and patriotic

principles, and arrived in the Capital of the greatest Nation on earth just in time to get dinner and walk out on the street in front of my hotel, just in time to hear the fire alarm. To my consternation, I heard the added remark, "The Capitol is on fire." Living down across the Capitol grounds northwest, I looked up and beheld the flames just bursting forth. Imagine the emotion and the consternation that raged in my soul, for it was nearly three years ago when I first came to this city to assume the responsibilities that my people at home had intrusted to me, and from this same abode I trudged up the "Hill" and thought of the greatness and grandeur of this edifice, representative of a great Nation and this thought came to me in all of my excitement on the night of January 3, 1930: That this grand exemplification of the American Nation was on fire.

In my excitement I ran for my topcoat and hat that I might go and help extinguish the blaze, and as I ran up the walk through the grounds that surround the Capitol and reached the ramparts or western approach, never such an emotion or a more patriotic fervor overcame any one. From these western ramparts I looked up and, as the blaze and threat from the flame was whipping toward the magnificent dome, yet and yet, Old Glory in the light of our early evening, by the light of the innumerable illuminations that make an object of beauty of our noble Capitol dome, and in the lightning blaze of a fire that was threatening its foundation, yet with the screeching sound of the sirens of the fire engines from the 27 to 30 fire stations in the District which were shrieking a warning for the right of way, nothing so thrilled me, though, as I looked skyward, and even though the blaze threatened its foundations, I was reminded that it would not give way its duty "To wave o'er the land of the free and the home of the brave." I was restrained to remember of what I had read of the immortal Francis Scott Key as he was held on a ship in view of Fort McHenry when, in his patriotic fervor and after going through the terrible night's vigil, from the early morn's light he could vision Old Glory, and the view inspired him to write those memorable lines: "Oh, say, can you see by the dawn's early light what so proudly we hailed at the twilight's last gleaming," and so forth, or the words of our national anthem, and with a thought of what happened to the Nation's Capitol in 1814 under Gen. Ross and his army of Britishers, I rushed around to the east front about the time the firemen arrived and, after having observed such a threat as I had to the Capitol, I joined in with the gallant firemen and others who felt as I did, to aid in pulling the hose through a smashed main entrance Capitol door that it could be used at the seat of conflagration on the top floor; and I tell you it was no easy job. Pretty soon I ran into a policeman and a Mr. Lieutenant of Police—that, after everything was over, except the moving pictures. I did not see the picture-taking, as I had gone to my place of abode; but there was a fire, but not nearly so much fire as there was smoke afterward. But during the height of the flame I got a thrill I will never forget. I thank you. (Applause.)

The following short dissertation on oleomargarine was delivered by Representative John Davenport Clarke of Delaware County, New York. Mr. Clarke is a lawyer, conservationist, farmer, and former assistant to the Secretary of Mines of the United States Steel Corporation.

Mr. CLARKE. Strange sounds were heard emanating from the old cow barn, mysterious shadows flitted hither and thither, and Rover, the faithful old shepherd dog, had been barking and howling, so I got up and hurried up to the barn to see what the trouble was.

There was the mother cow and the father cow and the roosters and chickens all gathered around a strange little yellow package to look, in mysterious wonderment, at the little stranger in their midst. In a few minutes a long-haired, wild-eyed professor came rushing into the barn to acknowledge the parentage of the little child he called "Oleo."

The professor grabbed the yellow kid, rushed from the barn and it was fortunate he did, for the papa cow was pawing the earth, and roaring, to beat the band, and the mother cow was weeping at this strange child, conceived in fraud, destined to unfairly compete with the healthy, wholesome product of father and mother cow.

The guilty professor hurried to Uncle Sam, acknowledged the child was illegitimate, destined to unfairly compete with healthy, wholesome butter, admitted to Uncle Sam his guilt, and went further and said he was willing to be taxed ten cents a pound on this yellow daughter, "Oleo," for her support.

A bill was instantly prepared to make certain that Uncle Sam got this tax to support Oleo, and all went well until from the mysterious Island of the Pacific the professor found old mother palm oil and a new yellow kid was born.

A lot of step-children gathered in this unholy alliance, there was Miss Cocoanut Oleo and Master "Nutty" Margarine, and other dirty children. They were all hollering that they could not get old mother fat Guernsey from the Packers and insisting on a ten cent tax, and lo, and behold, Miss Palm Oil opened the door for all this strange crowd of bunko artists.

All the Dairy farmer wants is protection for his legitimate dairy product, and all Mr. and Mrs. Dairy Farmer want is that the parents of Miss Oleo do what they agreed to do originally, pay the tax of ten cents a pound, where Miss Oleo, colored in the semblance of butter, enters into our family life in unfair competition with Butter.

Fair play, a square deal and meeting the obligation Oleo's parents freely entered into with Uncle Sam, is all we ask and all this bill is expected to do when it becomes a law.

The House Office Building, where most of the members have their official offices, is like an ant heap. Congressmen are limited to one room apiece, packed in with files, furniture, office help, and what not. Committee chairmen get an extra room or two.

The big bosses have large, finely furnished suites in the capitol itself. To relieve congestion, but primarily to improve appearances, a second House Office Building is being erected across the street at an ultimate cost of $10,000,000. This will double the present office space and give the members working quarters approximating those of the Senators.

In the Seventy-first Congress, Representative Stone of Oklahoma created a sensation by charging his colleagues with nepotism. He declared that members had their wives, children, fathers, fathers-in-law, nieces, and other relatives on the House payroll as secretaries and clerks. Members of the House are allowed $5000 a year for clerical hire.

He announced that he had information showing that one member had a daughter who had drawn over $3000 as a secretary and had spent most of her time in Europe. Many, he said, had their wives on the clerical payroll, and one member had three relatives drawing pay. Another had a fifteen-year-old daughter attending a Washington school who had collected nearly $1000 as a clerk.

Stone demanded legislation to stop such pilfering of the public till, but the House turned a cold shoulder. When he became insistent and took his crusade to the newspapers, many members ostracized him.

Few House members, if defeated after any length of service, return to the small towns from which most of them come. They go to any lengths to remain in the capital. Those who have been servile enough to partisan or business interests get "lame-duck" jobs. Others become lobbyists, open law offices, or go into business in the capital.

Even if they want to return home, their families, particularly their wives, object. The capital is an experience they never get over.

For them, Washington is the promised land. They zealously and punctiliously execute all the inane and laborious social formalities. No one is so exacting in social niceties as a House member and his wife from Podunk.

The House is the standing butt of Washington's jokes. The most common is the story of a visitor to the capital who found, upon arriving at his destination, that he did not have sufficient change to pay his taxi bill.

"That's all right," the driver said, after looking him over carefully. "You can pay me next time. I'll trust you, I can see you are not a Congressman."

No matter how capable the individual may be when he becomes a member of the House, a certain ludicrousness immediately attaches itself to him and continues until he leaves or attains some other office. Every intelligent member admits this privately.

Few really able men remain long in the House. If they do, it is in hope of winning a higher place. The best of them either quit in disgust or despair or run for the Senate, the governorship of their states, judgeships and even mayoralties. The Senate is the chief ambition of every House member.

Even White House secretaryships seem significant in comparison with membership in the House. Coolidge and Hoover had no trouble in taking their pick of House leaders for White House assistants.

The Longworth-Tilson-Snell triumvirate ruled the House solely by brute force.

The combination was totally devoid of parliamentary skill and finesse. In the instances where the scramble for local pork made the House unmanageable, the triumvirate was utterly helpless.

It even happened on several occasions, as during the fight over the last Soldier Bonus Bill, that the three bosses themselves could not get together. Tilson, the most politically obsequious of the three, continued to fawn upon the White House. Longworth and Snell bolted with the pork-seeking majority.

There never was a time in their rule when they could not have been discomfited and even routed if there had been a half dozen men in the House with the courage and force of character to defy them. Repeatedly, at the slightest show of resistance, they were thrown into a panic.

When the Smoot-Hawley Tariff came back from the Senate and some of the northwestern farm group began to murmur, the trio immediately began to talk concessions. It is fair to say that with the tremendous popular resentment against the bill, the farm bloc, if it had possessed the backbone and principles to make a real fight, could have staged a successful revolt.

Instead, being spineless and without convictions, the farm bloc surrendered before the triumvirate could do so, and the latter had nothing to do but enforce another "gag" rule and jam the measure through.

It was only the bankruptcy of the Democratic leadership and the listlessness and lack of unity among the so-called

Progressives that enabled the triumvirate to maintain its authority.

Had the Democrats really been a militant minority and Representative Garner, their floor leader, an aggressive opposition fighter, they could have repeatedly put them on the defensive. But outside of meaningless partisan protests, the Democrats carefully skirted all responsibility and allowed the Republicans undisputed control.

The weakness and incompetence of the triumvirate's leadership greatly increased after the first year of the Hoover Administration. Longworth and Snell distrusted and disliked the President from the very start. For their own and the party's reputation, they supported him, but without zest. The gross blunders and indecisions of the President made it increasingly difficult and distasteful for them to do so.

Tilson is the only one of the three who slavishly followed the White House. On more than one occasion it let him down, but he never swerved in his lugubrious fealty.

"Nick" Longworth was a man of charm and many graces. He was a gifted musician and considerably above the House level in intelligence.

Had he been born of poor parents and forced to win his livelihood, he doubtless would have achieved real distinction. But he came from a very wealthy family and had unearned riches all his life.

His attitude, as a result, was one of surfeited boredom. He never grew serious about anything and his anger was only peevishness. He ate and drank abundantly and well, dressed in luxurious elegance, and viewed his political career as a source of amusement and a means of keeping himself occupied.

In the more than twenty-five years of his congressional service, Longworth never sponsored anything of the slightest importance, and until he was made Speaker in 1925 was known chiefly as the husband of Alice Roosevelt.

He was too intelligent and self-respecting to be blatant or

hypocritical, or to have had any illusions about politics. He never issued demagogic declamations about the glory of the Republican Party or the nobility of the Republican President. That he left for such political trucklers as Tilson.

But he was always regular, and a strait-laced conservative, even if he would occasionally, on an issue of local implications such as the bonus bill, stand on his own views. He was particularly apt to do this when the President attempted to get the House to assume responsibility for killing such legislation, as Hoover tried to do.

Longworth was genuinely liked in Congress. In the Chair he was unfailingly good-natured and courteous, and even when he was bludgeoning the House he was never disagreeable about it. He disliked disturbances and the docility of the House during his leadership made it easy for him to avoid them.

Socially he associated with a small group of wealthy men. In his gay moods he was an amusing entertainer.

He was devoted to his seven-year-old daughter Paulina, and during legislative sessions was her host once a week at the capital.

When he died unexpectedly, some weeks after the close of the Seventy-first Congress, the full significance of his universal popularity in the House was for the first time fully grasped by the Administration and Republican leaders. It was suddenly clear that he alone had been the best hope of the Republicans to retain the Speakership and that, without him, they were desperately handicapped.

His death also disclosed conclusively that his quiet, affable personality had been the dominant force behind the rule of the triumvirate, and that without him Snell and Tilson might have ruled, but the cry "Czarism," that was heard far and wide during the days of Cannon, would have again resounded.

Longworth was as much a "Czar" as Cannon ever was, but far more successful. He ruled, but the House never rebelled. Which explains perhaps why Mr. Hoover paid him the unprecedented honor of attending his funeral in person.

Representative Bertrand Snell of New York is a hard-boiled, reactionary Republican politician of the upstate New York type. He plays the party game but he never wastes breath on turgid effusions about the glories of the Administration.

As chairman of the powerful Rules Committee he had a controlling voice in legislation and in his blunt manner has had no scruples about exercising it. As long as the House would stand for him he wielded the club.

When the Democrats, following their large gains in the 1930 election, hypocritically attacked the "gag" rules under which he operated, he prophesied that if they gained power they would resort to the same devices.

Snell is short, bald, and rotund. Coming from Potsdam, New York, a small country town, and owning a cheese factory, he is known among the reporters as the "Cheese Maker of Potsdam."

He is not popular because of his curt manner. He is very provincial and occasionally displays amusing ignorance about public affairs.

When the Fish resolution for a Red investigation was under consideration he strongly supported it.

> "Is this resolution broad enough to include Fascism?" Representative Huddleston of Alabama demanded of him.
> "Include what?" asked Snell.
> "Fascism, Fascism," retorted Huddleston.
> "I don't know what it is," Snell admitted, "but I guess this covers it, if it is something wrong. I better not discuss it at this time."

Tilson was born in the Union section of Tennessee. In his early youth he went to Connecticut and there made good all his early promise of incorrigible standpatism.

He is massive and lumbering in build. Mentally he has the agility of a flat-bottomed mud scow.

In debate he is easily confounded and discomfited. He conducts a floor fight like a religious revival. When he wins, he leads his side in cheering, waving his big hands wildly above his head.

He is the perfect type of docile party wheelhorse, always sonorously proclaiming the party's virtues, and unquestioningly doing the bidding of his masters.

His zeal in "upholding the hands of the President" on more than one occasion has given Mr. Hoover considerable trouble. He has learned the trick of getting out statements on Sunday night, when news is slack, and issues provocative diatribes attacking the opposition.

One such violent pronouncement during the food relief controversy precipitated a furor in the Senate and almost broke up a compromise which the President was secretly negotiating.

On the soldier bonus question he also undertook to speak for the Administration in one of these Sabbath outbursts. He demanded that the legislation be rejected. The next day the House, under the leadership of Longworth, approved it by a vote of 363 to 39.

Tilson has two ambitions. He wants to go to the Senate and he would like to be Vice President. In both of these aspirations he has been thwarted by J. Henry Roraback, the Republican boss of Connecticut, who does not like him.

The secondary Republican leaders, the committee chairmen and subchairmen, with a few exceptions are mediocre nonentities and drab party hacks. They hold their places solely through dead weight of seniority.

Representative Isaac Bacharach of Atlantic City, wealthy bachelor, is one of the exceptions. He is a ranking subchairman of the fiscally all-powerful Ways and Means Committee and is the ablest among the Republicans on the committee. He is well informed on the government's finances and on occasion does not hesitate to challenge the Administration on such matters.

He is a standpat Republican, but a gentleman notwithstanding. He never slobbers about the virginal chastity of the

Grand Old Party, nor does he grow eulogistic about its leaders. Politics with him is chiefly a pleasant diversion. He is popular and likes nothing better than a gay party.

Representative Willis Hawley of Salem, Oregon, Chairman of the Ways and Means Committee, and Representative William R. Wood of La Fayette, Indiana, chairman of the House Appropriations Committee, head two of the most important and powerful groups in Congress. As such they could have great weight in fiscal legislation, if they had the courage or capacity to exercise their authority. But they are mere figureheads. The bulk of their work is done by clerks, and their orders come from the White House.

When the White House approves, they approve. Should the White House say "no" they reverse themselves in the same breath. On the compromise Soldier Bonus Loan Bill, Hawley in the morning voted in committee to report the measure. By night of the same day, following a sharp call from the White House, he announced that he had acted hastily on "undigested information," and was against the measure.

Wood is even more blatant than Hawley. He wants all Insurgents and dissidents treated rough and tough. When a Senate investigating committee disclosed that Robert Lucas, Executive Director of the Republican National Committee, had secretly distributed vicious and slanderous campaign literature attacking Senator Norris in 1930, Wood roared out his hearty endorsement of such tactics.

Not a Republican leader in the Senate had a word to say in defense of Lucas, but Wood issued statements, through the publicity bureau of the Republican National Committee, upholding him.

Representative Haugen, of Iowa, Chairman of the Agriculture Committee, is a professional farm reliever. He is so ignorant of the fundamentals of economics that he voted for and defended the Smoot-Hawley Tariff Act, the greatest steal ever put over on the American farmer.

Representative Britten, of Illinois, Chairman of the Naval

Affairs Committee, is a big-navy jingoist and one of the most persistent publicity seekers in the capital. The press gallery knows him as "Pop-Gun" Britten. He was once a prizefighter, but now confines his battling to scaling the social ladder. His committee is notorious, even among House committees, for its unrelieved inanity.

Representative George Holden Tinkham, of Boston, is proof that a good man can live down even a Harvard education.

He has been doing so since 1915 through his extraordinary genius in always keeping one step ahead of his constituents' pet prejudices. For the large Negro population in his district he demands free electoral rights—in the Solid South—much to that benighted section's violent indignation.

The Democratic, Roman Catholic Irish that heavily dominate his constituency, he never fails to satisfy with a clamorous wetness and badgering campaign against the Protestant clerical-prohibition hierarchy.

Several years ago, after a victorious newspaper tilt with Bishop Cannon, he was received in his bailiwick as a conquering hero. Since then, whenever things get dull, he issues a blast against the stock-market-playing cleric, and calls upon the Attorney General to proceed against him. For this he never fails to get a resounding cheer from his "Micks," as the Irish are quaintly called in Boston.

Tinkham is as remarkable in appearance as he is in rabble-raising qualities. He is squat and bald and adorned with a stiff, bristling beard that protrudes almost horizontally from his chin. He took to the appendage during an African big-game hunt, when he discovered that by letting his beard grow he saved both effort and money. Since then he has given it no further attention except an occasional trimming to keep it within bounds.

Although he is very wealthy, he is notorious for his tight-fistedness. He lives in a small Washington hotel because he was able to get good terms on a long-time lease and buys his suits in numbers because of a discount from his tailor.

He is a bachelor and a very chary one. His small, un-aired, hotel apartment is crowded with mounted big-game heads, each of which he has carefully named after a hated prohibition cleric, Bishop Cannon, Dr. Clarence True Wilson, Dr. McBride and the others. His greatest pride is conducting a visitor about the place with the lights off and showing him each mounting by flashlight.

Representative James M. Beck, of Philadelphia, has a lofty legal reputation. He is a member of the bar of England, and from 1921 to 1925 was Solicitor General of the United States. He is also a fellow of the Royal Historical Society, of London, a member of the American Philosophical Society, President of the Archeological Society of Washington, and an author of numerous legal tomes.

All this did not, however, prevent him from accepting his seat in the House from the hands of William S. Vare, the Philadelphia political boss who was refused admittance in the U. S. Senate because his election was steeped in fraud and corruption. In succeeding to Vare's place in the House, Beck zealously defended the latter's probity and purity and his right to membership in the Senate. With the Vare case closed, Beck has devoted himself to elaborate and learned anti-pro-hibition discourses which delight the wets and bore the rest of the House.

Representative Hamilton Fish, of New York, is an earnest and honest man who somehow just can't help appearing some-what ridiculous, no matter what he does. If he goes hunting the wily Red then even such a patriotic and standpat Republi-can organ as the New York *Herald Tribune* berates him for asininity. Does he attack Capitalism and bolt to the In-surgents, then the radicals laugh.

Although one of the most serious men in Washington, no one in the capital takes him seriously, least of all the corre-spondents. This is a great trial to "Ham," as he is known about the city. He is a persistent and zealous publicity seeker. Whenever he has anything to say, the press is never scooped.

He sees to it that all the correspondents have plenty of copies. And when he talks, he never stints publicity.

Once he went to see the President, was closeted with him two or three minutes and then distributed to the reporters a twelve-hundred word statement of what he had told the Chief Executive. Mr. Hoover and his small army of secretaries being very jealous of White House publicity have never forgiven "Ham" for putting that fast one over on them.

Fish's shortcomings are really very sad. He is so well meaning and one of the few gentlemen in the House. During the ridiculous Red hearings he alone of the Committee was courteous and dignified in his conduct toward the Communist witnesses.

A friend of Fish's once diagnosed him as a "victim of misspent youth." He pointed out that in his school days Fish was Captain of the Harvard football team and that he had followed this harrowing experience by serving three terms in the New York State Assembly.

Such excesses, the friend insisted, were enough to impair permanently even as good a man as Fish.

*

The Wisconsin Progressive group has degenerated into an apathetic pack of time-servers. As long as the elder LaFollette was alive and ruled the State, they toed the mark in fear of him. He whipped them into action and made them function as an aggressive and purposeful unit.

After his death in 1925, they quickly fell into complete desuetude. For a time they made a half-hearted attempt to continue their activity, but, with the will of their master gone, they broke into petty jealousies and disintegrated. Within a few years the leaders had made their peace with the Republican bosses and were given back the petty committee places they had once honorably forfeited.

Representative John M. Nelson, LaFollette's campaign manager in his Independent Presidential campaign, and once widely known as the militant leader of the House Insurgents, is now the meek chairman of the meaningless Committee on Invalid Pensions. The only purpose this committee serves is to provide a few additional clerical places.

Nelson outwardly still maintains a Progressive pose, but it is a very chary one. He devotes himself to the intricacies of the remote Philippine Independence question. On anything closer to home he preserves a discreet silence.

When approached with the suggestion, following the Republican defeat in the 1930 election, that a movement be organized in the House either to overthrow the Republican leadership or to revise the rules, Nelson turned a cold shoulder. He refused to do anything that would jeopardize his mediocre committee chairmanship.

Had the Wisconsin group gotten together and waged a fight, it could be the balance of power in the House to-day. But not one member of the group made even a gesture toward doing anything, and Nelson and several others were openly hostile to the suggestion that they make an effort. Only one of the group, John Schneider, had the courage to appear at the Progressive Conference held this spring. Nelson and the rest of the delegation scurried to cover when it was called and kept out of sight during its two days of deliberations.

Representative James A. Frear was for many years a loyal follower of the elder LaFollette. For that he, too, was deprived of committee rank. To-day, however, he has won his way back into the favor of Republican leaders and is a satisfied, low-ranking member of the Ways and Means Committee.

Representative John Schafer of Milwaukee is known among his colleagues as the "Roaring Fireman." When he takes the floor the House drops everything and settles back for a never-failing entertainment. He is a rare spectacle even in the House.

Over six feet in height, of vast bulk, and with a huge quid of tobacco in his jaw, he bellows at the top of his voice. In his youth he was a railroad fireman, and he has never gotten over trying to outshout a moving train. When he gets on his feet, he unconsciously reverts to his earlier days when he had to yell to make himself heard.

He, too, was once a fire-eating rebel, but no more. His great missions now are prohibition repeal and veterans' legislation. He never misses an opportunity to denounce the drys and to clamor for more boodle for the service men.

For a time he had the idea of running for the Senate against Young Bob. He broke with the LaFollette organization, following the old Senator's death and, while still vigorously asserting his Progressivism, he leaned more and more to the regulars.

A close race in 1930 and the election of Philip LaFollette as Governor the same year has done much to dampen his senatorial plans, at least for the time being. But he is a young man, only a few years older than Young Bob, and he still aspires.

Representative Paul Kvale, Farmer-Laborite from Minnesota, serving his first full term in the House, is the only one of the Progressives in the House who holds any promise. He was secretary to his father, who was a member for several terms, and upon the latter's death, succeeded to his seat.

Kvale is 34 years old, one of the youngest men in Congress. If he were associated with an active Progressive group, he would be more effective. Alone, he is still too unsure of himself to take the lead or pursue a militant policy.

*

THE six ladies of the House make a real contribution to the chamber. They supply the only tidy touch in the frowsy place.

Having performed this noteworthy service they rest gracefully on their well-deserved laurels. They confine themselves wholly to local affairs, leaving the serious matters of legislation and politics to coarser and more robust hands.

They always give unquestioning obedience to their leaders. They never bolt or assert themselves or ask disturbing questions. They are always cheery and charming; sweet, lovely girls, and such a refining influence.

With the exception of Mrs. Mary Teresa Norton, Democrat of New Jersey, all of the ladies are widows. Three, Mrs. Florence P. Kahn, Republican of California, Mrs. Edith Nourse Rogers, Republican of Massachusetts, and Mrs. Effiegene Wingo, Democrat of Arkansas, are the relicts of former members whose seats they now fill. Mrs. Ruth Pratt, Republican of New York, and Mrs. Ruth Bryan Owen, Democrat of Florida, are also widows but not of House members.

Mrs. Kahn, the dean of the group in length of service, is a docile party hack on the floor, but away from the chamber she is one of the wittiest and cleverest women in Washington. She is a Regular of Regulars, but she takes neither herself nor any of the other politicians seriously.

She has a lusty humor and is famous for her satirical comments. At the height of Vice President Curtis' social precedence war, she encountered him one evening in the elevator of the Mayflower Hotel. As they reached the ground floor he pompously stepped aside to permit her to precede him.

"Oh, no, Mr. Vice President," she gayly protested. "You go first. I know my social onions!"

On another occasion, she was in a dinner group which was discussing the 1932 Presidential campaign. Some one remarked that the Democrats had an excellent chance of winning, if they didn't make any mistakes.

"Well, have we Republicans left them any to make?" she inquired.

She is very popular in the House and when a local bill that she is interested in is before the chamber, she never lacks lusty-voiced members to yell it through for her.

Mrs. Ruth Bryan Owen has heaps of "It." And knows it. Although gray-haired and a grandmother, she is still, in an inimitable manner, a very attractive woman.

Mrs. Owen is by far the ablest member of the Florida delegation. She knows that, too.

She earnestly aspires to the Senate, and it is not beyond possibility that she may achieve her ambition. Which will be a deep disappointment to Mrs. Ruth Hanna McCormick, who thought she was going to lead the feminine invasion of that chamber.

Mrs. Owen is, of course, the daughter of William Jennings Bryan. She is a clever politician. Her emphasis is always on local interest.

She is always pressing some local project. Every year she brings a few talented young people from her district to the capital.

Mrs. Owen has had a colorful career. She has been married twice and is the widow of a British army officer. She accompanied him on arduous colonial service and was a nurse in the British Egypt-Palestine campaign.

Mrs. Ruth Pratt is the beauty of the group. Also a grandmother and gray-haired, she is still slender and lovely. She is very wealthy, dresses with subdued but rich taste, and is a member of the highest social circles. She acquired her wealth through the Pratt Standard Oil family.

She too has Senatorial ambitions. She would also not be averse to being Mayor of New York City or Governor of New York State. The uncertainty of her political future as a Representative from her district makes her ambition regarding these other offices doubly urgent.

Last session, in the interest of her political future in that part of her silk-stocking district which is rapidly becoming a workingman's section, Mrs. Pratt essayed the rôle during the tariff debates of a severe critic of the outrageous sugar schedule. She roundly denounced the extortionate duty and ringingly declared it meant hardship to the lowly.

It was a splendid declamation and she was acclaimed for her outspokenness. But that is as far as she got. When the floor leaders the next day cracked the whip, she hopped back into line.

She meekly voted to enforce a gag rule that prevented

amending the obnoxious sugar rate, and on the final roll call voted for the unchanged bill containing the schedule she had so feelingly assailed a few days earlier. When the Democrats ungallantly twitted her for her reversal, she haughtily stalked out of the chamber.

Mrs. Norton owes her place to the patronage of the hard-boiled Hague Democratic machine of Jersey City. She has two moving aversions and one distinction. She is adamantly against Bolshevism and birth-control, and she was the first woman to be elected to the House on the Democratic ticket.

Mrs. Rogers is prim and Polly-Annish, and a strong believer in the old-fashioned idea that women should be seen and not heard. She is tenderly solicitous of the service men—provided her Great Leader in the White House approves. She will also shed tears over a bonus bill, but if the President says no, she wouldn't think of voting for it. Not even if the Republican House leaders bolt him on the question.

This devoted fealty to Mr. Hoover has caused the little lady much distress and anguish. On a number of occasions she has found herself torn between the demands of party and the demands of the service men. But though the temptation has been great she has never wavered.

She knows her duty to party and friends. Painful and scary though it may be, she never deviates from strictest regularity.

Mrs. Rogers has faith in Massachusetts.

*

WHILE far more colorful and picturesque, the Democrats are as devoid of first rate men as the Republicans. Being the Outs, they affect, on occasion, a high moral tone of righteous indignation, but that is as far as they go. Responsibility for a vigorous opposition policy and program they carefully side-step.

On the tariff, the water power issue, the Norris "lame-duck" measure, the Wagner unemployment bills, and other important legislation, the Democratic leaders of the House have played sly and devious rôles. They attacked the tariff measure as a whole, but very carefully saw to it that the products their States were interested in got good, healthy boosts in rates.

On the power issue, the "lame-duck" and unemployment bills, they left the leadership to others. The independent La-Guardia of New York was the real fighting leader for these measures in the House.

Representative John N. Garner of Texas is a vivid and interesting personality, but as an opposition leader he is guilty of what military men call "fraternizing with the enemy." Between him and Longworth there was a strong friendship.

Garner often went through the motion of bitterly assailing the Longworth leadership and even satirizing him on the floor as "that bald-headed coot." But behind the scenes they understood each other perfectly and were on the best of terms. "Nick" never took exception to what "Jack" said about him.

After a tumultuous battle on the floor in which Garner violently led his hosts in a bitter attack upon the Longworth machine, the two men might have been seen leaving the chamber, chatting and laughing, arm in arm. It was all a sham battle, and often not even a good show.

In debate Garner is without a peer as a rough-and-tumble fighter. There is no one in the House who can cope with him. He is fast as lightning in repartee, and does not mince words or language.

Atacked in rhyme by a Republican for inconsistency in advocating a tariff on mohair when he was denouncing the measure as a whole, Garner, quick as a flash, sprang to his feet and retorted:

> "It's a hell of a poet,
> Who doesn't know a sheep from a goat."

Garner's best work has been his disclosures concerning the astounding record of income tax refunds that has characterized the Mellon administration of the Treasury. He revealed that in the ten years of Mellon's incumbency, more than three billion dollars have been returned or rebated to great corporations, huge estates, and wealthy taxpayers.

Garner affects a careless, slightly disheveled attire and frequently appears unshaven. His snow-white hair and heavy, gray eyebrows are always on end. He has mischievous eyes and a fine face. He lives modestly and quietly in a small residential hotel. He rules his side of the House firmly and the Democrats follow him loyally.

The other three important Democratic floor leaders, John McDuffie of Alabama, Joseph W. Byrns of Tennessee, and Charles R. Crisp are conservative party followers. They are inclined to a more austere aloofness toward their political opponents than their admired chief, but it would never occur to them to challenge his friendliness.

They keep almost wholly in the background. Mr. Crisp is the outstanding parliamentarian of the House, but beyond a reserved discourse now and then he disturbs himself little. Mr. Byrns is Chairman of the Democratic National Congressional Committee and by virtue of political statements to the press gets into print a little more frequently.

It is among the rank and file that is found the full flavor of the Democrats. George Huddleston of Alabama is a fighting crusader for peace and against large military expenditures. Lamar Jeffers, from the same State, is the son of a Captain of the Confederate Army, and himself a wounded veteran of the World War. Mr. Jeffers is a strong "believer in fraternalism" and is a member of several leading fraternities.

John E. Rankin of Mississippi is a slash-bang denouncer and when he gets heated up about Republican iniquity, he is worth going a long way to hear. Percy E. Quin, also from Mississippi, is another fervent orator of unconventional vehemence. When Percy takes the floor the lobbies and cloak rooms empty to hear him.

He labors powerfully and mightily. Back and forth before the chamber he rushes, waving his hands, disarranging his clothes, and pouring out a stream of uproarious observations. The House and galleries enjoy it immensely.

Tom Blanton considers himself the "watch-dog of the Treasury." He never misses a session of the House and is never happier than on unanimous consent calendar days, when an objection by a single member is sufficient to prevent consideration of a bill.

He has had a stormy career. Once he came within a few votes of being thrown out of the House for abusive language he inserted in the Congressional Record. Several years ago he directed a crusade against several District of Columbia Commissioners and the capital's police force. He forced the Commissioners to quit but the police are still functioning as badly as ever.

Loring Black of Brooklyn, New York, supplies the iconoclastic-intelligentzia element among the Democrats. He mocks all that his Southern fellow-Democrats hold sacred, particularly prohibition. Edgar Howard of Nebraska, on the other hand, while also a cynic, is a believer in prohibition.

He carefully records himself in his official biography as a "free" Democrat, and affects the attire of a bygone day, when presumably there were such creatures. He was once secretary to William Jennings Bryan, and his clothes are reminiscent of that proud service. He wears an old-fashioned swallow-tail coat, and his hair hangs down to his shoulders.

Howard is an ardent friend of the Indian and claims that he can speak several of their dialects. He has a broad, homely wit, and talks with an exaggerated slow-motion drawl.

Henry T. Rainey of Illinois, white-haired and patriarchal, is a sincere and intelligent liberal. On a greater and more dignified stage, his fine qualities of character and ability would have made him a significant figure.

But in the House, he is lost in the mob and its clownish antics. He does what he can, but it is largely wasted effort, particularly as his own leaders are indifferent. He is a lawyer by profession but years ago gave it up for the simpler life of a tiller of the soil. He is one of the oldest members in length of service in the House, serving his fourteenth term.

*

FIORELLO LaGUARDIA is in a class by himself.

He is a Republican who once ran on the Socialist ticket, without Socialist approval, and who votes his own judgment. He is indifferent to all parties, and they are chary of him.

In 1926, none of the parties wanted him. He was preparing to run as an Independent when the Republicans, finding themselves hard-pressed in their local campaign, persuaded him to run on their ticket.

He is the most independent fighter in the House. At a time when an election contest was being made against him, he vigorously pressed a fight to liberalize House rules. He was warned that this insurgency might cost him his seat. He promptly sent word to the Republican bosses that he expected his case to be judged on its merits and not on his docility.

LaGuardia is sensational in manner, but he is wholly without pose. His greatest drawback is that he is too diverse. If he concentrated he would be far more impressive.

Unlike most members, LaGuardia violently dislikes the piddling little department errands and office chores that they must take care of. He is happy only when he is on the floor in the midst of a furious battle. Once in the chamber he never leaves until adjournment. He sends out for peanuts and munches them so as not to miss a chance to object or to offer a pertinent amendment.

He has the record in the House for offering amendments. He likes nothing better than to have the leaders challenge him.

Once they refused to allow him to participate in certain secret committee deliberations. "All right," he grimly replied, "but you can't keep me out of the committee of the whole."

In the closing days of the Seventy-first Congress the Hoover Administration covertly attempted to emasculate Senator Wagner's federal-aid labor-exchange bill. The President had repeatedly endorsed the ideas contained in the measure but because a Democrat had initiated it he underhandedly tried to defeat it and later did kill it by a pocket veto.

LaGuardia, by threatening to organize a bolt against the then hard-pressed Republican leaders of the House, forced them to permit the bill to be brought out on the floor. There he soundly trounced the Administration, defeating a meaningless substitute it proposed by a two-to-one vote, and then passing the Wagner bill.

In debate, LaGuardia is vehement and blunt in expression, but he is always fair. And he never talks unless he has the facts. During the tragic Pennsylvania coal strike several years ago, he made a personal tour of inquiry.

He returned to the House, demanded that the chamber be cleared of women, and then in plain, unadorned language told the goggle-eyed members about the horrible conditions he had seen.

When the S-4 was rammed and sunk outside of Boston harbor several years ago, he made an underwater trip on a sister ship in his search for first-hand information on submarine problems.

When police in New York City were arresting and beating up striking New York clothing workers, LaGuardia joined the ranks of the picketers. The police recognized him, however, and would not arrest him.

When the price of meat went sky-high some years ago he wrote a letter to the then Secretary of Agriculture Jardine demanding that the government do something about it. Jardine in reply sent him a pamphlet entitled "The Economical Use of Meat in the Home."

LaGuardia went on the floor of the House and after displaying Jardine's leaflet, drew from his pocket a tiny lamb chop which he declared cost thirty cents, a small roast that he said cost several dollars, and a piece of steak that was even more expensive.

No other Cabinet officer has since tried to get funny with LaGuardia.

LaGuardia's father was the leader of an army band. He was brought up in the barracks at Prescott, Arizona. At the age of twenty he became American Consul General at Budapest.

Right from the start of his career he manifested his independent and unconventional nature. He refused to delay the sailing of an immigration ship, so that an Austrian Archduchess could visit it, and the Austrian Government demanded his dismissal.

LaGuardia realized he wasn't cut out for a diplomatic career and quit the service. He went to New York and became interested in local politics. He was elected President of the Board of Aldermen.

While in this office he attacked the State Legislature for expelling Socialist members. The super-patriotic members retaliated by increasing the salaries of all the aldermen except his. LaGuardia thereafter presided over the council meeting in a khaki shirt.

When he first came to Washington, he decided to attend a White House reception to see what it was like. He put on formal attire but got only as far as the door. There he stopped, looked the place over and then observed aloud: "What the hell am I doing here?" and went home.

Now he gives the White House invitations he receives to children in his district as souvenirs.

He loves to cook. When he is through with his work on the Hill, he frequently puts on an apron and cap and prepares a delicious dinner for friends he has invited. His specialty is spaghetti.

He plays the trombone and is a screamingly funny mimic. His characterizations of some of the House members are masterpieces.

He is serving his seventh term in the House. He is biding his time for more ambitious offices. In 1928 he ran for Mayor of New York City but was defeated.

Recently a youthful admirer wrote LaGuardia and asked his advice as to whether he should be a prize-fighter or a member of the House. LaGuardia wrote back: "Dear Johnny, combine the two and you will be sure to succeed."

CHAPTER TEN

THE COURT JESTER

*C*HARLES GATES DAWES has spent a lifetime aiming at big things but never quite getting there.

He could have been one of the outstanding leaders in the World War. Some whim of character prompted him, then a very green Major, to start his military career living in a private car.

He could have been a great Ambassador to Great Britain. A coarse mid-western sense of humor told him that it was funny to slip ice down a lady's back.

He could have been President of the United States. He preferred to be true to a boyhood friendship instead.

Boyhood friends have played an intimate and peculiar part in the life of Charles G. Dawes. There are not many who have had such friends. One of them became a great industrialist and Governor of his State; another became the Generalissimo of the armies of his country; and a third was thrice candidate for the Presidency of the United States.

Their friendship began when Dawes, a young lawyer in Lincoln, Nebraska, had nothing much to do but sit with his feet on his desk waiting for clients, or else walk over to the office of William Jennings Bryan and help him wait for clients, or finally go out to the university where John J. Pershing was then taking life very seriously as instructor of cadets.

Dawes was then a small, wiry person through whose character ran the traits of intense loyalty, tempestuousness and nerve, opportunism, contradictoriness and love of the limelight. At that early age, the first and last qualities—which are the keys to Dawes' later life—had not yet become predominant. It was Frank O. Lowden who evoked from Dawes the highest expression of loyalty. It was Bryan who planted the first ideas about the value of limelight.

Dawes and Bryan spent a great deal of time together during their early legal days in Nebraska. They even fought out their first case against each other, Bryan representing the Missouri Pacific Railroad, despite his subsequent advocacy of government ownership, and Dawes, later champion of big business, representing the shipper of some horse collars who claimed that he had been overcharged. The amount was $1.27. It is not recorded who won the case.

But Dawes and Bryan did not often get cases of any kind, no matter what the sum at stake, and once, to kill time, Bryan suggested that they stage a public debate on the question of whether a man should be permitted to have more than $100,000.

Dawes dismissed the idea as absurd. Bryan, of course, later changed his own ideas and died a millionaire, but even at this early age young Dawes had very definite views regarding the necessity of wealth.

He was not the son of a poor man. His father, a Brigadier General in the Civil War, was a prosperous lumber dealer in Marietta, Ohio. His brother Rufus was in the gas business. His brother Beman was in the gas and oil business. His brother Henry was President of the Southwestern Gas and Electric Company. It was not unnatural, therefore, that young Charles should follow them. He borrowed money, acquired a gas plant, and while Bryan remained an obscure lawyer back in Lincoln, Dawes, within a few short years, had made what was, for that day and age, a comfortable fortune.

When Dawes returned to Illinois he developed, besides the

gas business, a friendship which he was to cherish more than any other and which finally was to keep him from the Presidency. Frank O. Lowden was then struggling to establish a law practice. He and Dawes became partners in storming Chicago society and in running the Illinois National Guard, occasionally inducing young Lieutenant Pershing to come up on the pretext of giving military advice.

It was through Mark Hanna that Dawes got his first taste of politics. Hanna introduced him to McKinley and persuaded the latter to let the young man—then just turned thirty—manage his campaign in Illinois. This Dawes did with such efficiency and success that McKinley offered him the job of Comptroller of the Currency. Dawes, who had already won some reputation among his friends as an opportunist, jumped at the chance. His friend, Lowden, who was also offered a place in the McKinley Administration, turned it down.

After five years in the Treasury, Dawes, again the opportunist, saw a chance to capitalize his knowledge of finance and the prestige of government office. He went back to Chicago and organized the Central Trust Company of Illinois, of which he has been president ever since. Dawes first wanted Frank Lowden to head the new institution, but Lowden by that time had married into the Pullman family and was busy organizing the American Radiator Company and becoming one of the great industrialists of the Middle West. However, Lowden lent Dawes much of the money with which he started his enterprise, persuaded several of his friends to come in on it, and became a director himself. His help did not go unrewarded. The Central Trust Company is now one of the most powerful and profitable institutions in the Middle West.

By the time Dawes was forty-five years old he had accumulated as much money as he would ever need and was a respected citizen of Chicago. This was as far as he had gone. Aside from five years in what was not a very important office in Washington, he had satisfied none of his thirst for public office, and outside the State of Illinois he was as unknown as any country banker.

Meanwhile, his old friend Bryan had jumped overnight from a musty law office in Nebraska to the Democratic nomination for the Presidency—all because of an oration which took a jaded and deadlocked political convention by storm.

Bryan's sudden rise and the instrument of its achievement were not lost upon Dawes. He recognized that what appeared to most people as a spontaneous burst of oratory had probably been prepared by Bryan for weeks. The "Cross of Gold" speech marked a turning point in Dawes' life and was the inspiration for the "Hell and Maria" outbursts and the Senate scolding, which later made him first page copy throughout the country. From that time on Dawes became not only an opportunist but an actor.

He got a chance to practise at both when the United States entered the World War. It would be unfair to impute these as the only motives for his patriotism. Dawes was a super-patriot and came by it honestly. Not only had his father been a General in the Civil War but one of his great-grandfathers, William Dawes, had accompanied Paul Revere. His manner of riding to war, however, was not that of his famous ancestor. Dawes rode to his first army post at Atlanta, Georgia, in a luxurious private car and continued to live in it at his own expense while carrying out the important duties of a major of engineers. Throughout his army career, he never quite lived down that initial blunder.

Dawes had secured his commission as Major through his old friendship with the young Lieutenant who had since married the daughter of the Senator who controlled army appropriations and now had become General of the Army. Pershing had bigger things in store for his old friend. What he needed was a man who could take over the buying of supplies for the entire army. Each branch of the army was buying against the other. Their competition was boosting prices, and after they got the material, part of it was lying idle in warehouses.

Pershing first asked Frank Lowden to take the job. Lowden, however, urged the appointment on Dawes, and the latter, always the opportunist, jumped at the chance.

The job was one for which Dawes was peculiarly fitted. He stormed and coaxed, he charmed and bullied, and in the end he brought a fair degree of order out of chaos and unquestionably saved millions for the country. He had done an important job well, but, even so, his name could command not one-hundredth the degree of recognition that his old friend Bryan had won after a carefully planned piece of spontaneity at a Chicago political convention.

Returning to the United States, however, Dawes saw his chance. A hostile Republican committee was trying to pick holes in the Democratic management of the War. General Dawes, a tried and trusted Republican, was called to the witness stand, expected to aid the attack. No theatrical producer ever timed his climax more adroitly. Dawes let the committee members prod and poke him with trivial questions until they had put themselves in the position of schoolboy inquisitors. Then he burst forth with his famous "Hell and Maria" speech.

Walking up and down the room, waving his fists under the noses of the committee, the returned Procurement Chief told them that the American army had been winning a war, not keeping books.

"Can't you understand that men were dying under shot and shell?" he exploded. "When we got a call for a carload of ether for the field hospitals, do you think we stopped to put it down in the right column of the proper ledger? Hell and Maria, no—we shot it along!"

It was a touch of Bryan mixed with the explosive eloquence typical of Dawes. It withered the Committee and it trademarked Dawes permanently for the American public. Henceforth he was "Hell and Maria" Dawes.

It worked so well that Dawes tried it again when Harding appointed him Director of the Budget. The plan of government expenditure by budget was an innovation, and in order to launch the idea propitiously Dawes called a meeting of all Cabinet members. It turned out to be one of the historic events of the Washington year. Vehemently demanding economy, Dawes shook his fist under the chin of every Cabinet member present, including the sedate and bewhiskered Charles Evans Hughes. He pranced up and down before them with a broom, demonstrating the thesis that a Navy broom will sweep as well as a War Department broom and that broom-buying must be coördinated.

After all of which, he settled down to the routine of organizing a first-class system of regulating government expenditure, and did it so well that Calvin Coolidge used "economy" as his campaign slogan.

Dawes probably looks back upon his part in the readjustment of reparations as the most constructive work of his career. Although he has given to Owen D. Young complete credit for the terms of what later became known as the Dawes' Plan, it was the Dawes' fireworks that put the plan across. One of his speeches was described by Mr. Young as clarifying the atmosphere of Europe to such degree that without that picturesque salesmanship the plan would have been rejected.

Having worked out a breathing period for Europe, Dawes was obvious Vice-Presidential timber and his nomination surprised no one except Calvin Coolidge. Coolidge had asked Borah to share the ticket with him and resented the fact that the party leaders forced him to accept Dawes. This resentment increased with the Vice-Presidential scolding of the Senate and the nap which defeated the confirmation of Charles Beecher Warren, until Dawes gave up attending Cabinet meetings and the two were the most recognized rivals in the capital.

This Senate scolding was another piece of studied Dawes' stage-play. The Vice-Presidential inauguration is supposed to be a very whispered and surreptitious performance inside the Senate chamber and must not detract from the main show outside. That, however, did not fit in with the Dawes' flair for publicity. He had dictated a speech against senatorial sloth which he showed to his friends, long in advance, and which he delivered in his high rasping voice to the accompaniment of much arm-waving, gavel-pounding, and the mute amazement of Calvin Coolidge. The speech won him the acute and universal enmity of the Senate, whereupon he proceeded to settle down and become what no other Vice President had been in years—a controlling factor in legislation who did not antagonize the Senators. His fairness, his vitality, and his charm made him, before he retired, the most popular man in the capital.

That Dawes was the logical man to defeat Hoover for the Republican nomination in 1928 was recognized by every political soothsayer in the country. That he raised not one finger to secure the nomination was due to what his friends consider the transcending quality of his character—loyalty.

Dawes was in a unique and most favorable position. He had the backing of the Middle West. He had voted for the McNary-Haugen Bill and the farmers believed in him. Despite this, he also had the support of the bankers. Finally, the politicians liked him and all who did not like Hoover—of which there were many—rallied to his support.

But they could not budge Dawes. He knew that Frank O. Lowden wanted the nomination. Frank Lowden was the man with whom he had soldiered in the Illinois National Guard. He was the man who had loaned him the money to start his bank. He was the man who had declined Pershing's wartime offer in his favor. Dawes knew that Lowden wanted the Presidential nomination more than he wanted anything else in life, and Dawes stood pat. If he had permitted his friends to begin organizing for him one year before the nomination, his chances would have been as good as Hoover's.

It was Dawes' characteristic of loyalty to his friends, coupled with his belief that the U.S.A. is operated for the benefit of big business, that got him embroiled in the Lorimer bank scandal, the most inexcusable chapter in Dawes' life. William Lorimer needed money to convince examiners that his La Salle Street Bank had sufficient assets to comply with state banking laws. Dawes gave him a check for $1,250,000. After the bank examiners were satisfied, Lorimer returned the check. Dawes did not consult his Board of Directors. He did not care a snap of the fingers whether or not he was violating the law. Lorimer had asked him for help and Lorimer was his friend.

Later when Lorimer's bank failed, its 4,000 depositors sued Dawes, and an Illinois court fixed his liability at $1,487,854. Friendly judges later pared this down to $100,000.

During the anti-Red hysteria, which big business suffered from after the War, Dawes had organized the Minute Men of America. It was characteristic of him that he did not go to the bottom of any of the issues involved. He did not care to. All he saw was an opportunity to ride a popular cause in a big way. The name of the descendant of William Dawes, co-rider with Paul Revere, had news value, and the Minute Men of America hit the front pages. They waged unrelenting war on organized labor, made the injunction more than ever a thing to be feared, and smashed the Chicago building unions. Incidentally, their first move was to help reëlect the judge who had pared down the amount which Dawes was obliged to pay the depositors of Lorimer's La Salle Street Bank.

Dawes is not without sympathy for his fellow-men. Underneath his affectation of hard-boiledness there is a genuine lush of sentimentality. As a memorial to his son, Rufus F. Dawes, he established a chain of hotels operated at cost, where a man can get a bath for five cents and a meal for a trifling amount more. Dawes himself doled out sandwiches and coffee to long lines of shivering men during one of Chicago's depression winters twenty-five years ago. His philosophy is, first, that the rich should help the poor, and second, that the rich should always be rich and the poor always poor. The idea that there is anything wrong with a system which creates such an abyss between rich and poor, or that anything should be done to change this system does not register with him at all, so that the campaign of 1924 found Vice-Presidential Candidate Dawes making whoopee speeches all over the country against LaFollette and the Red Menace.

Dawes would have liked nothing better than to have gone on being Vice President. He liked the Senate. Its members liked him. Most of all he liked being in Washington with an excuse to be busy, instead of sitting in the ornate office of the Central Trust Company, back in Chicago, which got along just as well whether he was there or not.

So when Hoover was elected President and his own term as Vice President was about to expire, Charley Dawes, as he was called in Washington, began to feel a little sad about leaving, and a little restless about what he would do next. Having nothing better to do, he jumped at a chance to go down to Santo Domingo to recommend budgetary reforms for that country. And then like a gift of the gods, the Ambassadorship to the Court of St. James fell in his lap. Charley was tickled to death.

What increased his glee was the fact that naval negotiations with Great Britain were just beginning, and he would have something really big to put across. He got as enthused about it as a small boy on his way to the circus. The only trouble was that Dawes was not content with sitting in the grandstand; he had to get down in the ring and be a part of the big show. The result was a second-rate piece of clowning.

When he arrived in London, Dawes considered the time ripe for one of his old Hell and Maria-Bill Bryan stunts. He rushed from Southampton to London just in time to catch a train for Scotland and didn't stop until he got to Ramsay MacDonald's front door at Lossiemouth. Ramsay MacDonald was not accustomed to having foreign Ambassadors seek him out at his country home, not even when they came from the United States, and naturally he gathered the impression that Ambassador Dawes had something really important to tell him—in fact, that he was going to invite him to visit the United States. Imagine his surprise, even his chagrin, therefore, when he found the new envoy brought no invitation, but merely had come to discuss naval affairs in general. Naturally, he was not then acquainted with Mr. Dawes' clown acts, and in talking to newspapermen immediately afterward, the Prime Minister was obviously and openly peeved.

London, however, soon got acquainted with them. Dawes found that, as far as naval negotiations were concerned, his Ambassadorial job was a washout. His rôle was that of a glorified messenger boy. He received cables from Secretary of State Stimson, put on his top hat and morning clothes and trotted over to No. 10 Downing Street where he handed the message to MacDonald or Arthur Henderson. Sometimes he got telephone calls to come to the Foreign Office and receive notes, which he in turn cabled back.

The routine got a little boring.

When the London Naval Conference opened, it became more so. Dawes might have played a real part in this. He might have been the super-salesman that he was when he persuaded Europe to accept the Dawes Plan five years before. His colleagues on the American delegation all seemed to think that he could have done it—that is, all except Stimson, and he was too engrossed in his own troubles to take advantage of the ability waiting to be used around him.

So even before the Conference opened, Dawes, being bored, having had the naval limelight turned off, looked around for other avenues of escape from the monotony of being an ambassador. He discovered Ye Cheshire Cheese Tavern. More than one hundred and fifty years before, Dr. Johnson and Boswell had made it famous. Dawes decided to refresh its fame. He came there almost every noon to lunch. Within two days, word of this had spread to all London and a line of American tourists waited outside for an opportunity to lunch in the same room with their Ambassador. The barman made a small fortune by charging a shilling for a guaranteed opportunity to shake hands with him and waiters charged even more for reserving tables near him.

All London laughed. But it laughed louder after the American Ambassador's dinner to the Spanish Infanta.

Dawes has always had a yen for moving picture actors. He once staged a dinner in Washington in honor of Buster Keaton. To the dinner in honor of the Spanish Infanta in London, he invited Leon Errol. However, only one among that large number of pompous and austere-looking personages knew that the American screen comedian was present.

Errol was disguised as a waiter—as a drunken waiter— and he played his part well. He lurched, he stumbled—dishes caromed everywhere. He insulted the guests. He spilled ice down one lady's back and sent a lobster spinning into the lap of the Duke of Norfolk. Finally, he was fired, with mock indignation, by the American Ambassador, who thought the incident highly amusing.

The Spanish Infanta, who was in on the secret, agreed with him. The others did not. The most indignant of all was the Spanish Ambassador, dean of the Diplomatic Corps.

London had scarcely got over this, when Dawes was called down by the Japanese Ambassador for starting to smoke his pipe before the toast to the King. Matsudaira had known Dawes a long time, but he spoke in a very loud and none too friendly voice. Every one heard him.

Apparently not satisfied with being the talk of London, or perhaps it was because the gossip showed signs of diminishing, Dawes managed to stir it up at one of the court levees. London society takes these functions with more solemnity and seriousness than Washington takes a Presidential inaugural. Days are spent practising curtsies. Fortunes are spent on gowns.

Protocol is followed as carefully as if an empire were at stake—two steps before His Majesty—a bow—a step in front of Her Majesty—another bow—and then on to one's appointed place.

Imagine, then, the consternation of the Court when His

Excellency, the American Ambassador, bowed once before King George, and walked on, forgetting Queen Mary completely.

Afterwards he was reminded of his omission.

"Oh," said Charley Dawes, "I'm from the Middle West. We don't pay much attention to women over there."

But the Middle West is not London and London has not got used to Charley Dawes.

But how could it?

Here is a man who reads Greek literature and Nize Baby, the history of the Maya civilization and Snowshoe Al, who is an expert on P. G. Wodehouse and the lost continent of Atlantis—

—A man who denounced LaFollette as a Red and a menace, who organized the Minute Men of the Constitution to war on union labor, yet who established a chain of charitable hotels for unemployed men—

—A man whose hard-headedness is proverbial, but who has written a play for his two adopted children, who plays the flute and the piano, and who has composed music that is performed by Kreisler—

—A man charming and well-bred and yet homely and uncouth—who plays the hurrah-boy, who demands the limelight and gets it by acting—sometimes by ham-acting—yet who has the soul of an artist.

How could any one, more especially the British, understand some one whose chief charm is the contradiction that constantly runs through his life?

CHAPTER ELEVEN

SONNETS AND BEANS

THERE happens to be in this humdrum capital a little man who occasionally lets his thoughts wander back through a land of pagodas and beggars and bronze-bellied images, through stagnant opium dens, a market of prostitutes, and across the pale pearl of the tropic sea where a "palm-tree bends over the sand and offers its heart to the moon."

He goes about his business rather efficiently. He wears cutaway coats and gray striped trousers when the occasion demands. He signs treaties, delivers notes that have been drafted in Paris, and makes speeches along lines dictated by the Quai d'Orsay. But with it all, one cannot escape the feeling that he is a little sad about life, that in a city which thrives on boiled bosoms and inane wit, which devours its social columns before nibbling at its grape-fruit, Ambassador Paul Claudel is distinctly out of place.

He was picked for the post when French prestige in the United States was at a low ebb. The Embassy had been tossed from hand to hand—from Jusserand to Daeschner to Berenger. The war debts had not been settled. One year elapsed during which the Embassy lacked any Ambassador at all.

Then came Claudel, a man whose name is more widely known throughout the world than all the diplomatic corps together.

He has been a failure in Washington. He has been a success in the United States.

Why?

"Make me as one who sows solitude, and may he who hears my speech
Return home troubled and heavy."

Behind Claudel's back, his dinner partners rage at him. He is known as the most silent, the most depressing dinner companion in Washington.

His mind is on the contagious ecstasy of a field of grain in the sunshine or the inspiration of a Chinese temple at dusk.

*

ABOUT 1885 a youngster bearing the imposing name of Paul Louis Charles Claudel entered l'Ecole Libre des Sciences Politiques in Paris. He came from a clannish family that had lived in their native Champagne for generations without leaving it. It was not until she was sixty that Claudel's mother made her first visit to the sea, and, as Claudel himself expresses it, "All this economy of wanderlust was concentrated in me until it burst. I wanted to see the world. And the only way to travel without money was in the consular service."

The graduates of l'Ecole Libre des Sciences Politiques in those days became either consuls or diplomats. Claudel chose the former because it required no personal fortune.

His first post was New York City.

"New York at that time was crushing," he said, when once persuaded to talk. "I do not find it so now. But then, thirty years ago, it was—how can I describe it—half and half. The sky-scrapers were just beginning to be built and the city was a mixture of giant buildings towering over squat roofs. It was better in those days for the visitor to see some other part of America before he came to New York."

Claudel, then at the age of twenty-five, had already begun to write, and his works show the imprint of almost every city he has visited. New York, he described as a "railway terminal, built of houses between tracks...a pier for landing, a great jetty flanked by wharves and warehouses," while Boston, his next post, he described as a city "composed of two parts: the new city pedantic and miserly, like a man, who, displaying his riches and his virtue, yet guards them for himself; and the hill where the old city, like a snail-shell, contains all the windings of traffic, debauchery and hypocrisy."

After a year in Boston, during which he was in charge of the consulate, this rather sensitive and impressionable youngster was transferred to China, and, *en route,* was given permission to visit his home. The journey to New York had been his first trip away from France and he had been absent nearly two years.

"When a young man goes away for the first time," Claudel confessed thirty years later, "he feels that the world should stop. And when I found that my own family had scarcely missed me, I was disappointed."

This disappointment, described with all the sensitive dignity of his twenty-six years, was one of the first sketches Claudel wrote.

"The voyager reënters his home as a guest. He is a stranger to all, and all is strange to him. (Servant, hang up the traveling cloak and do not carry it away. Soon it will be necessary to depart once more.) Seated at the family table he is a suspected guest, ill at ease. No parents; it is never the same! This is a passer-by whom you have received, his ears filled with the fracas of trains and the clamor of the sea, like a man who imagines that he still feels beneath his feet the profound movement that lures him away. He is not the same man whom you conducted to the fateful wharf. The separation has taken place and he has entered upon the exile that follows it!"

Thus young Claudel sailed away to the East and settled down in the southern seaport of Foochow, famous in the days of the old Yankee clippers as the center of the tea trade, but at that time stagnant—warehouses empty and harbor filling up with silt. Consular duties were not heavy, and Claudel spent much of his five years at Foochow in his house-boat drowsing through the canals of China or reading through languid summers in his bungalow in the interior. At Foochow he learned to know the East—its mystery, its philosophy, its religion.

Nearly twenty years in the Orient gave Claudel something which he himself cannot describe. Nor can it be done here. There he learned that Oriental penetration of character and that understanding of human nature which the Chinese express in word pictures. It is this philosophy, also expressed in word pictures, running through Claudel's works that has made him one of the most criticized poets of France, as he is one of the most criticized diplomats in Washington. A furor was raised when it was suggested that the Academy accord him due recognition. His plays can neither be read nor played, his critics contended. His Oriental mannerisms they branded as lyrical frenzy and bold improvisations, which in France, where the classic dominates art, is nothing short of heresy.

The other great influence in Claudel's writing had begun before he came to Foochow. As a student in Paris, he had become a confirmed disciple of his professor of philosophy, an agnostic. But while in search of atmosphere for some poetry one Christmas Eve, Claudel walked into Notre Dame. That was the beginning of what has since been called his "long pilgrimage towards God." Describing that moment years later, Claudel cries:

I remember the darkness where we two were face to face, those gloomy winter afternoons in Notre Dame.

I, all alone below there, lit up the face of the great bronze Christ with a twopenny-halfpenny taper.

All men were then against us, science and reason; and I replied nothing.

Only the faith was in me, and I looked at You in silence like a man who prefers his friend.

I went down in Your sepulcher with You.

Everything that Claudel has ever written has been dominated by the faith that came to him on that Christmas Eve in 1886. Though in his poetic technique he is a determined opportunist, underneath he remains always the Catholic mystic.

Even in his diplomatic life, Claudel has been dominated by his faith. His greatest ambition, after serving twenty-five years in the consular service and as Minister to Brazil and to Denmark, was to become Ambassador in Berlin, from which he wanted to observe modern European Catholicism. However, "Trois Poèmes de Guerre" which he had written during the heat of the European conflict made him *persona non grata* to the German Government and instead he was sent to Japan.

This was just after the Washington Naval Conference, at which the Anglo-Japanese alliance had been dissolved and the French Foreign Office saw the specter of a much more important alliance—the Anglo-American—looming on the horizon. As a counter-balance France decided to woo Japan, and Claudel was sent as chief courtier.

Probably Claudel was the most popular envoy any country has ever sent to Japan. He achieved this popularity by writing a play adapted to the Japanese "No" acting. "This helped me in my diplomacy," he confessed later, "for the Japanese are a little stiff until they know you. But after my play was produced in the Imperial Theatre, I was known in every geisha house as the 'play-writing Ambassador.'"

Having finished his work in Japan, Claudel was selected for the even more difficult mission of strengthening French prestige in the United States. He brought with him a flock of charming children and a wife who perhaps is less tyrannical than the average ruler of a French household. He dropped discreet and timely reminders that France was paying interest on her war debt. He faced batteries of cameras during ceremonies of treaty signing or stood patiently until long after midnight surrounded by the artificial gayety of a fancy dress ball. But always he looked as if he were longing for his houseboat at Foochow and the pale pearl of the tropic sea where "the palm tree bent over the sand and offered its heart to the moon."

Once during the course of an intimate conversation, Claudel was asked if he did not sometimes become bored with the prosaic commercial world of the United States and long to be back in the Orient, but either he was too good an Ambassador to admit it or else is even more adaptable than any one suspects. He said:

"Oh, the Orient is more picturesque, of course, but not more fascinating. What is more fascinating than standing on the twenty-ninth floor of a skyscraper and watching a snow storm blanket New York? What is more fascinating than looking down upon the traffic lights of New York, watching the automobiles, the trucks and the buses all stop as if moved by a giant machine? New York is superb and mighty and I enjoy it.

"America is like the boom-boom-boom of the battle charge. It is the sustained note. It is necessary in music. They say it came from the Negro. I do not know—but America has it. The boom-boom-boom, never varying, never letting down. I see it in your streets—the throb of life—the charge onward.

"You say America is a prosaic commercial world. There is no such word as prosaic in commerce. Commerce is fascinating. I was never so happy as when I was Minister to Brazil during the War, buying supplies for our armies. I was handling beans and lard and pigs. What is prosaic about a bean? It is fascinating.

"I am glad to begin my work in America and to end it here. I am sixty years old. I have been every place. I have seen the world. I have five children. It will some day be time for me to return to my native France. After America, I shall do so. I have bought a place in the Alps, where I shall sit and write and..." he fumbled for the word..."what is the verb for the word 'rotten'?"

"To vegetate," it was suggested.

"No," replied Claudel, the realist, " 'to rot.' And I shall go and sit and write and rot."

CHAPTER TWELVE

LITTLE NEMO,
THE WONDER-WORKER

*D*WIGHT WHITNEY MORROW spent a lifetime getting a reputation as a great liberal only to spend three months in the Senate blasting it.

The revelation caused Justice Brandeis to observe that the world would be much better off if men were less ambitious.

"People should stick to the jobs they really do well," observed the sage of the Supreme Court. "A man who has perfected the art of shoe-making does not turn around and become a blacksmith. Therefore, why does Dwight Morrow, who did a superb job in Mexico, turn around and try to become a United States Senator?"

There is no question that Dwight Whitney Morrow did do a superb job as Ambassador to Mexico. He went there at a time when relations with that country were at their lowest ebb in recent history—at a time when Frank B. Kellogg had informed the Mexican Government that it was on trial before the world, when both governments resorted to the stealing of diplomatic dispatches in order to get something on the other, when the State Department had announced the termination of the smuggling treaty in order to aid revolutionaries to get arms shipments with which to overthrow the Mexican Government, and when the Mexican Government, in retaliation, was sending paid propagandists all through Latin America to poison the wells of public opinion against the United States.

Within a very short time after Mr. Morrow had arrived, he had settled the petroleum dispute. He had helped to settle the religious controversy. He took a stand in direct contradiction to that of his old banking firm in helping the Mexican Government pay its debts. He took a stand in direct contradiction to that of Western United States in maintaining that Mexico was entitled to one-half of the water derived from Boulder Dam. And most important of all, he won the intimate friendship of Mexican government leaders and the confidence of the Mexican people.

There is no question also that Dwight Whitney Morrow has performed superbly and liberally almost every job he has ever tackled.

When Cuba was virtually bankrupt and New York bankers were demanding intervention, Mr. Morrow, representative of J. P. Morgan, Cuba's largest creditor, opposed intervention and extended additional credits to get the island on its feet.

When a honeycomb of corruption was exposed in New Jersey prisons, Mr. Morrow headed a committee which reformed the State penal system, making it one of the most humanitarian in the east.

When it looked as if the peace of the world would be jeopardized by the failure of the London Naval Conference, Mr. Morrow's skill, patience and untiring energy prevented the American Delegation from returning without a treaty.

When he has been called upon to serve on philanthropic boards, to raise money for hospitals or endow libraries, Mr. Morrow has given unstintingly of his time and his effort.

After this record, which among his friends won him the nickname of "Little Wonder-Worker," Mr. Morrow came to the Senate. And in a session in which the issue between liberalism and conservatism was more clear-cut and harder fought than ever before in recent years, Dwight Whitney Morrow never on a single, solitary occasion failed to vote with the reactionaries. Except in regard to prohibition, Herbert Hoover never had cause to worry regarding the side of the roll-call on which he would find the name of the little wonder-worker. His record was written in cold and unchangeable black across the pages of the Senate's roll-call, and on the economic issues this is how it reads:

Water Power:

Voted against the Norris Bill providing for Government operation of Muscle Shoals. Bill passed.

Voted against the Black Amendment to lease Plants Nos. One and Two at Muscle Shoals for the manufacture of nitrates. Amendment failed of two-thirds vote necessary to set aside rules.

Voted against the Black Amendment to give preference to states, counties and municipalities in sale of electric energy from Wilson dam. Amendment failed of two-thirds vote necessary to set aside rules.

Voted against amendment requiring Secretary of War to supply electric energy from Muscle Shoals to nearby communities at rate not to exceed 4 mills per kilowatt hour. Amendment failed of two-thirds vote necessary to set aside rules.

Voted against motion to reconsider the confirmation of the three Federal Power Commissioners who had voted to oust the two chief enemies of the power trust—King and Russell. Motion carried.

Voted against motion to reconsider the confirmation of George Otis Smith, Chairman of the Federal Power Commission. Motion carried.

Voted against motion to request the President to return the confirmation papers on these three Commissioners to the Senate. Motion carried.

Voted against motion to recommit the nominations of the three men to committee. Motion carried.

Paired with Brock of Tennessee against motion to place the nominations back on Senate calendar. Motion carried.

The Tariff:

Voted for the confirmation of Edgar Brossard as member of the Tariff Commission, despite his admitted financial interest in sugar, and despite the fact that although testifying he had taken no part in framing sugar schedules, it was later revealed that he had worked on them secretly every night in the Tariff

Commission until one and two in the morning. Confirmation voted.

Food Relief:

Voted for Reed motion to await results of Red Cross $10,-000,000 drive before voting on Robinson's $25,000,000 food relief appropriation. Motion defeated.

Voted against Robinson motion to appropriate $25,000,000 for human relief. Motion carried.

Bonus:

Voted against Soldier Bonus Loan Bill. Bill passed.

National Defense:

Voted for modernization of battleships. Bill passed.

Voted against Frazier amendment providing that no funds in the War Department appropriation bill could be used for military training in schools or colleges. Amendment defeated.

Like the small boy who has entered school for the first time and has learned nothing except who wields the switch, Mr. Morrow was ever alert to please the master in the White House.

*

MANY people consider it a rare phenomenon that Dwight Morrow, a man of great wealth, should have shown any liberal qualities at all.

They would be right in the case of Henry L. Stimson, scion of a family of great wealth, which for two centuries has been one of the ruling dynasties of New York State. But with Dwight W. Morrow, not at all. Morrow had every reason in the world to be liberal. He was the son, not of a wealthy conservative, but a hard-working college professor. James Elmore Morrow, President of Marshall College, West Virginia, was a man of broad vision, wide sympathies and a contagious buoyancy of spirit. Without the latter he might have become soured by the difficult task of educating five children on an income of $2,400 a year. But he did not. He gave them all college educations and, with the possible exception of Jay J. Morrow, he passed on to all of them an appreciation of the problem of those who struggle, which, after all, is the fundamental basis of liberalism.

Most of them have consistently kept before them that early appreciation, one daughter marrying the Rev. Dr. Edwin L. McIlvaine, Presbyterian clergyman; and another, Miss Alice Morrow, devoting her life to teaching school, now at Robert College, Constantinople.

To the two sons, Jay and Dwight, came the greatest temptation to stray from the liberal foundation implanted by their father. After his graduation from high school at the age of fourteen, young Dwight Morrow clerked for four years in the County Treasurer's Office in Pittsburgh, and then, because the tuition was free and the Morrow resources slender, he took the competitive examination for West Point. Although he stood highest in the examination, the appointment was refused because his brother, Jay, already had entered West Point and the Congressman declined to send two members from the same family.

This turned out to be one of the most fortunate twists of fate in Dwight Morrow's career. His brother's army education made him a typical military officer of the most reactionary school. His high-handed tactics in conducting the Tacna-Arica plebiscite preliminaries caused the State Department to abandon the plebiscite altogether and to postpone any settlement of the boundary controversy between Chile and Peru for two years. No two men could have more dissimilar points of view, and had Dwight gone to West Point, he would probably now be the replica of his elder brother.

Having escaped West Point, young Dwight Morrow entered Amherst. And because he was poor and had to make his own way, he achieved a brilliant record and got one hundred percent return out of his four-year investment. He did the same later when he entered Columbia Law School, graduating so high in his class that he was promptly offered a fifty dollar a month apprenticeship with Reed, Simpson and Thacher, the same firm which now handles the legal work of Soviet Russia in the United States, and from which the present Solicitor of the Justice Department, Thomas D. Thacher, came to Washington.

It was at this time in his life that Dwight Morrow developed the thesis that honesty and unselfishness always pay.

Long afterward at the Sixth Pan-American Conference, which Morrow attended as a delegate, a group of newspapermen suggested to him that, in order to appease Latin Americans, the United States would have to offer some sort of "sop" in the way of arbitration which at least looked as generous on the surface as the arbitration treaties which Mr. Kellogg was negotiating with Europe.

"Sop?" replied Ambassador Morrow excitedly. "We'll offer them no sops. We'll offer them the real thing or nothing. We'll offer to give them just as good an arbitration treaty as any we give Europe, or if we can't do that, we'll explain the reason why. Why should we offer somebody something that doesn't amount to anything and then pretend that it does? 'Sops'," he repeated again. "I don't believe in 'sops'."

This was typical of Morrow in Cuba, in Mexico, at London, and in all his personal and professional relations. In Mexico he did not begin his negotiations over the petroleum law by pretending that the position of American oil companies was right. Other Ambassadors, quite aware of the failings of the oil companies, had taken such a stand. They asked much, prepared to take less. Morrow reversed the process. He nearly took President Calles' breath away by announcing at the start of negotiations that the American oil companies were partly in the wrong. So, he also said, was the Mexican Government. If both sides yielded, an agreement could be reached. It was.

The result, however, was severely criticized by the oil companies. They claimed that Morrow had opposed, rather than championed, their rights. To a certain extent he had. He looked at the problem also from the Mexican point of view. He believed that Mexico, as well as the oil companies, should get a square deal and that it was his duty as American Ambassador to help protect Mexico.

Somewhat the same issue was involved during the London Naval Conference, when Secretary Stimson made his proposal that the United States build one new super-battleship. Although it never even reached the blue-print stage, the vessel was promptly christened the "Henry L. Stimson."

Later, much embarrassed, Mr. Stimson explained that he had put this forward merely as a bargaining move; that he was asking for a great deal in order to be able to reduce his demands; that by throwing out the specter of a giant battleship, he could wangle cruiser concessions from the Japanese.

Mr. Morrow did not approve Mr. Stimson's strategy. He does not work that way. He believes in putting all his cards on the table, and then, by the soundness of his case and an appeal to the fairness of his opponent, getting what he wants.

Mr. Morrow had not worked these things out very clearly in his mind when he first became a young lawyer in New York and when he first went to live in Englewood, New Jersey. But the essential fundamentals, planted by his father, were already there and it was the working out of these ideals that eventually brought Morrow into the firm of J. P. Morgan as one of its partners.

This also was fifty percent coincidence. The coincidence was the fact that Thomas W. Lamont and Henry P. Davison, two powerful partners of the House of Morgan, happened to live in Englewood. The other fifty percent was Dwight Morrow's generous concern for his neighbors and his community.

Lamont and Davison saw a lot of young Morrow and what they saw was a small, wiry, alert little man who was constantly taking on the problems of community leadership which every one else said they hadn't time to do. Obviously a man of somewhat moderate means, obviously a man who had to devote a great deal of his time to making a living, Morrow somehow or other, always found time to put across the things in his community which he thought needed doing.

He took time, for instance, to amalgamate the five local charity organizations into one Civic Association over which he presided for ten years. He took time also to head a committee which built an armory. As President of the Englewood Free Library he raised the money for a handsome new building. He took time to push three bills through the State Legislature in order to abolish the Tri-Township Poorhouse and he headed two hospital drives which made the Englewood Hospital one of the best equipped in the country.   All of this threw him in constant contact with his neighbors, among whom were Lamont and Davison. He served with them on committees and gouged them for large contributions. They were not only impressed with his energy and mental capacity but they reasoned that if he could get large sums of money from them he could perform equal miracles in the business world.

Just eight years after he had entered the firm of Reed, Simpson and Thacher, therefore, he was offered a partnership in the House of Morgan.

Unselfishness, Dwight Morrow found, had paid. He had not exactly reasoned it out that way in advance, and it does not follow that he has reasoned it out that way since. He had merely been true to the ideals with which his rather unusual father had surrounded his boyhood. There is no question that in those days, Morrow was liberal—sincerely and honestly so.

*

FRIENDS have played a large part in the life of Dwight Morrow.

He is a man who makes friends and keeps them, and he has been fortunate in having a few in high places, some in low, upon whose loyalty he could depend, no matter what the circumstances. He has leaned on them heavily and they in turn have leaned upon him.

It was Dean Acheson, a clever young Washington lawyer,

who wrote the reverberating prohibition speech denouncing the Eighteenth Amendment with which Morrow opened his senatorial campaign in New Jersey. It was the late Joseph P. Cotton, who, as Under-Secretary of State, backed to the limit everything Morrow did in Mexico. And it was J. Reuben Clark, a former Under-Secretary of State, who accompanied Morrow to Mexico and helped him negotiate some of his most delicate deals.

Of all the friends, however, who have both leaned upon Morrow and been leaned upon by him, the two most important are Calvin Coolidge, chief leaner, and George Rublee, chiefly leaned-upon.

Morrow and Coolidge had been classmates at Amherst. They had been good friends although not intimate. Coolidge was shy and reticent, Morrow a mixer. He had a sense of humor that made him popular immediately. Coolidge's wit needed long knowing to be appreciated. Morrow was one of the outstanding leaders of his class. Coolidge voted him the man "most likely to succeed." Morrow voted the same of Coolidge.

During the spring of their senior year, they came to know each other better—took long walks together during which they compared notes on life and love, which at that time rested rather heavily upon their slender shoulders.

Some twenty years later, Dwight Morrow contributed materially to the fulfillment of his prediction that Calvin Coolidge was the man of his class most likely to succeed.

Morrow is a man of great enthusiasms. Sometimes his enthusiasm is sound. Sometimes it is merely successful. His enthusiasm for Calvin Coolidge as President was of the latter variety. Morrow got on the Coolidge band-wagon when it was only a push-cart affair shoved around by one or two enthusiasts, of which Morrow was the chief pusher. He organized the "Amherst Coolidge-for-President Committee," before any one outside of his own State had anything but a vague recollection that Coolidge was Governor of Massachusetts. Through money raised almost exclusively by Morrow the club distributed several thousand copies of a volume of Coolidge's speeches called "Have Faith in Massachusetts." More particularly the club concentrated upon distribution of the book to delegates to the Republican National Convention held in Chicago in 1920, where Morrow with usual haphazard and irrepressible enthusiasm gnashed his teeth because the elder statesmen of the G. O. P. refused to consider Coolidge as Presidential timber.

The fact that Morrow aimed high, however, made it fairly easy for Coolidge to get second place on the ticket and there appears to be no question that Calvin Coolidge, although the last to admit it, owed his Vice-Presidential nomination chiefly to the efforts of his old friend and classmate. Therefore, when Morrow, seven years later, decided that he had made far more money than he or his children could ever use and that he would devote the remainder of his life to ambition and public service, it was not unnatural that Calvin Coolidge should have offered him the Ambassadorship to Mexico.

The appointment however constituted no great stroke of generosity on Coolidge's part. American-Mexican affairs were in a desperate state of depression and it appeared that nothing less than a miracle could pull them out. Coolidge needed the best man in the United States for that purpose and, from three big jobs Morrow had put across before, he knew that there probably was no better man available.

These three jobs were the prevention of intervention in Cuba in 1920, the revision of New Jersey's State prison system, and the delineation of the Five-Year Air Program for the United States.

Of these, the Cuban problem, on a much smaller and less complicated scale, was somewhat analagous to that which existed in Mexico. In a few brief and panic-stricken months after the War, the price of sugar had tumbled from the wartime peak of twenty-five cents a pound to the fantastic figure of one and one-half cents. American banking houses had accepted sugar as security at what then seemed like the safe rate of fifteen and eighteen cents a pound and therefore were left high and dry, with millions of bags of almost worthless sugar on their hands. Sugar was a drug on the market. The sugar producers were bankrupt. The dance of the "Sugar Millions" was ended and American banks were faced with the prospect of paying the fiddler.

In such a crisis, it was natural that the bankers should storm the State Department with demands to invoke the Platt Amendment and intervene. As a matter of fact, they had ample excuse for such a request. In addition to the economic crisis, the government of President Zayas had been one of the most corrupt in Cuban history. All during the War, Cuba had been enjoying a period of prosperity similar to that of the Klondike gold-rush days or of the Venezuelan oil boom. Havana boasted more millionaires in proportion to its population than any other city in the world. Its night life was like an opium smoker's dream. Gold fairly flowed through its streets. Yet despite this unbounded prosperity, the Cuban Government was bankrupt. Its school teachers and—what is much more dangerous in any Latin-American country—its army remained unpaid. Finally it could not meet interest payments on its debts to New York bankers.

Of these bankers, the House of Morgan held the largest share of the Cuban debt. And although there were members of the firm who favored intervention, Morrow stood out against it. He argued that the sending of marines to the island would not improve its economic condition but would create a bitterness and resentment which might actually retard economic recovery. Coöperating closely with General Enoch H. Crowder, who had drafted the Cuban electoral law, Morrow granted the Cuban government a $5,000,000 credit with which to pay its own employees and create a financial breathing spell. Simultaneously elections were held under the new Crowder law.

The second important job Dwight Morrow had performed

before his appointment to Mexico also proved him still true to the liberal qualities instilled in his early youth.

In 1916 the corruption of the New Jersey State prisons was exposed. Walter E. Edge, then Governor, had been Chairman of the State Senate Committee on Labor Legislation when Morrow had drafted the New Jersey Workmen's Compensation Act during Woodrow Wilson's governorship, and Edge called upon him to reform the State prison system. Morrow hired research experts and went to work systematically. He spent a year digging into the penal institutions of the State, going back as far as colonial times. He sided with organized labor against the sale of prison-made goods in competition with free labor. And after a year he brought in a report which caused the revision of the State's penal legislation and set up a penal system as modern and humanitarian as any in the eastern United States.

Neither this nor his reorganization of Cuban finance put Morrow in the public eye. Outside the State of New Jersey, in fact outside of Wall Street, he remained practically unknown until he became Chairman of the Aircraft Board. Thanks to the scathing and unquenchable criticism which General William Mitchell, head of the Army Air Corps, had leveled at the army's air policy, the attention of the entire country was upon the Aircraft Board.

Personal publicity was about all the aircraft hearings did for Dwight Morrow, and he did not do much more for them. He worked hard and at a period when he could ill afford the time, but it was work which any other reasonably able executive could have performed just as efficiently.

The most interesting part of Morrow's service as Chairman of the Aircraft Board was the manner in which Coolidge appointed him. Notification of the appointment came merely through reading a Sunday newspaper. Coolidge asked no questions as to whether Morrow had time to do the work or the inclination to do it. Dwight Morrow he considered one whom he could draft at his convenience. So three days after publicly announcing the appointment, he wrote Morrow asking him to come to Washington on a certain day at a certain hour, and when that time arrived he briefly announced to the nine assembled appointees that the future air policy of the United States needed to be established, that he had no money to pay their expenses, but he thanked them for their willingness to serve their country at this time. Then, giving them no time to remonstrate or decline, he withdrew.

*

THE day after Calvin Coolidge announced the appointment of his old friend and classmate as Ambassador to Mexico, Lawrence Todd, of the Federated Press, happened to meet William Green, President of the American Federation of Labor, and one of the self-acclaimed protectors of the Mexican labor movement from capitalist exploitation.

"What," asked Mr. Todd, "do you think of the Morrow appointment?"

"I hear he's a pretty good man," replied Mr. Green.

"What do you think of his connection with J. P. Morgan?" pursued Mr. Todd.

"My God!" replied Mr. Green. "I didn't know he had any connection. I'll have to look into that."

Despite the fact that Mr. Morrow was a partner in the House of Morgan, and despite the fact that the House of Morgan represented the railway bondholders who for years had been trying to collect money from the Mexican Government, Dwight Morrow's reputation as a liberal was then such that his appointment was received with almost universal acclaim.

He went at his new job in a way calculated to fulfill the expectations of his most doting admirers. Starting with the assumption that he knew very little about Mexico and would know comparatively little even if he remained there a full four years, he took with him as a salaried assistant, J. Reuben

Clark, former American agent on the Mexican Claims Commission, later Under-Secretary of State and one of the ablest international experts the State Department has ever produced. With him also went George Rublee, whose only compensation was the pleasure of being with his old friend, Dwight Morrow.

For the last dozen years, these two men, the antithesis of each other in appearance, have been almost inseparable companions. Rublee is nearly seven feet tall and as thin as the proverbial bean pole. He stoops a little, perhaps from the habit of making his own height appear a little less in contrast with the five-feet-five of his boon companion.

Rublee is the son of a Wisconsin newspaper publisher who championed the old Socialist movement in that State and passed on many of his liberal leanings to his son. A man of no wealth, Rublee had practically retired from a lucrative law practice in Washington in order to devote all his time to Dwight Morrow. They became acquainted when Rublee, then a partner of the late Joseph P. Cotton, served with Cotton on the Allied Maritime Transport Council, of which Morrow was also a member. Since that time Rublee has been one of Morrow's most constant advisors and is responsible for many of the moves which have increased the latter's reputation as a great liberal.

For two months before going to Mexico City, therefore, both Morrow and Rublee concentrated upon a long-distance study of the country to which the former was appointed as Ambassador. This study did not consist of delving into books, but of long conferences with people of all walks of life—from labor leaders to bankers, so that before Morrow arrived at his new post he knew more about the Mexican Government than did the career diplomats of the State Department who had been there for years.

Morrow had been carefully warned of two pitfalls. One was the American Colony which is always rabidly anti-Mexican Government and which mingles only with the aristocracy of

the now-defunct Diaz régime. The other was the career personnel of the American Embassy.

The latter, Morrow had been informed, had no sympathy
at all with the Calles régime, never met any of its members
socially and were constantly associated with factions plotting
to stir up revolution against the government.

Morrow handled the career men very tactfully. He let them
go about their ordinary routine of writing reports and attending teas. And he let them keep their desks on the first floor.
But on the second floor he established the real brains of the
American Embassy. Here he and George Rublee and Reuben
Clark established their offices, and here Morrow and his two
advisors began to work out the solutions of the petroleum,
church and agrarian problems which had so long troubled
American-Mexican relations.

Mr. Morrow also had been warned that Arthur Bliss Lane,
Counselor of the American Embassy, was mistrusted and dis-
liked by President Calles. Mr. Lane spoke Spanish beautifully.
Mr. Morrow did not. Mr. Lane had acted as interpreter to
James R. Sheffield, Mr. Morrow's predecessor, and it was only
natural that he should act in the same capacity to the new
Ambassador.

When Ambassador Morrow paid his first call upon President Calles, however, Mr. Lane did not accompany him as
interpreter. Mr. Lane was hurt. President Calles nearly dropped
dead. He recovered with sufficient promptitude to bring
forward his own interpreter and the two settled down to the
most unique visit that an Ambassador Extraordinary has ever
paid to a President of Mexico. It consisted of a breakfast of
ham and eggs, followed by an inspection trip of President
Calles' farm, during the course of which the two men got
no nearer discussing affairs of state than the practicability of
the milking machines newly installed in the Calles' barn.

In this and in a hundred other ways, Morrow established a
foundation of personal friendship before he even brought up
the delicate matter of the petroleum and the religious disputes.

He made it a practice to drop in unexpectedly at Calles' office for a personal chat. Calles even got into the habit of coming around to the American Embassy to see Morrow, an unprecedented thing for the President of any country to do. In the end, Morrow came to be looked upon more as an advisor and friend of the Mexican government than the Ambassador of an all-powerful neighbor.

The manner in which he leaned backward to give a square deal to Mexico more than merited him that position. It even caused Calvin Coolidge to comment: "It was a great victory for us, but greater for Mexico."

The most notable instance in which Morrow championed the Mexican cause was when he opposed the efforts of his old friend and former partner, Thomas W. Lamont, to arrange a settlement of the Mexican railway debt. Mexico owed somewhere around one billion dollars to those who had bought bonds to build the national railway. Lamont, representing the bondholders, offered to settle for about half that. Morrow, friend of the Mexican Government, and actually representing no one except himself, advised against the compromise. He pointed out that Mexico had a great mass of debts which should be settled in a lump arrangement. To settle the railway debt before the others was to give his old firm the House of Morgan preference over the other creditors.

Although President Ortiz Rubio accepted the Lamont compromise, Morrow's influence was so strong with the Mexican Congress that the debt agreement finally was rejected.

*

DWIGHT MORROW's friends have sometimes called him the most spectacular match-maker of the present generation. Certainly he cannot deny the fact that he is the most famous father-in-law in the United States nor the fact that he was solely responsible for introducing Charles A. Lindbergh to his daughter. In fact, even before he invited Colonel Lind-

bergh to Mexico, Morrow had given him ample opportunity
to meet all three daughters, and it was only an extraordinary
lack of feminine curiosity which prevented a meeting.

Coolidge had invited Morrow to dine at the White House
on the state occasion when Lindbergh came back from his
famous trans-Atlantic flight and partook of the Coolidge
frugal hospitality. As Chairman of the Aircraft Board, Morrow saw a great deal of the young aviator both then and afterward. Morrow was a member of the Guggenheim Foundation
for the Promotion of Aeronautics, and it was through him
that Lindbergh joined the staff of the Foundation.

The young flier spent several week-ends at the Morrow
home in Englewood, but always at times when the family was
away. Only once did the trails of Lindbergh and his future
wife cross before their courtship in Mexico City. Mrs. Morrow, returning from Cleveland with Elizabeth and Anne,
discovered her future son-in-law at the telephone. She recognized him and introduced herself. Unlike the hundreds of
government stenographers who drop their work every time
the Lone Eagle steps into the corridors of the State Department, the two Morrow girls were too busy unpacking their
bags to notice him.

Morrow's invitation to Lindbergh to make a non-stop,
good will flight to Mexico City was a part of the Morrow plan
to focus public opinion in the United States and in Mexico on
the more agreeable relations between the two countries rather
than on the petroleum and religious controversies.

It worked admirably. It also succeeded in bringing together
Colonel Lindbergh and the Morrow girls. At first it appeared
that the flying Colonel was in some doubt as to whom he
really cared for. Elizabeth was tall and slim. Anne was built
along the short and stocky lines of both her mother and
father.

At first Lindbergh had little to do with either of them and
when it became necessary for him to choose a partner for a
Mexican reception, he took the younger sister, Constance.

As a result of this indecision the rumor was current in Mexico City that when Lindbergh left he had the names of the two elder sisters twisted and wrote a letter to Anne, thinking it was going to the tall and more beautiful Elizabeth.

Anne was timid, sensitive, poetic, with a soul which reacts to personalities around her like a barometer. Sitting with her at the dinner table it is possible to read in the flashes of pleasure and pain that pass across her face the story of one who suffers agonies even over the idiosyncrasies of her family. Her first essay in college was a description of a man breaking eggs every morning, with exactly the same precision, day after day, breaking them with a certain pride and egotism. It was her father.

Before she was engaged, Anne once told a friend that she would like to have the refusal of Lindbergh. After she was engaged and before the announcement was made, her friends at college said she "cried for a month" trying to decide whether she was doing the right thing. Finally her mother told her she would have to make up her mind definitely; she could not change it after the announcement. Mrs. Morrow, as usual, had her way.

Although devoted friends, it is no secret that Mr. Morrow sometimes has a difficult time with his headstrong young son-in-law. Morrow, older and more experienced in the clash of human relations, believes in smoothing the path of life as far as possible wherever he goes. Lindbergh, hot-tempered and impetuous, sometimes thinks his father-in-law is a temporizer.

It was a conflict such as this which resulted in withholding the news of the birth of the Lindbergh baby. Colonel Lindbergh has come to have a deep-rooted aversion for the press, an aversion which once expressed itself by speeding his propeller in such a way as to throw mud and water over a group of reporters on Bolling Field.

He resented the fact that a crowd of newspapermen were sent by their editors to wait at the gate of the Morrow grounds at Englewood for news of the baby's arrival. He resented this despite the fact that these reporters had no alternative, and despite the fact that among them were one or two who had packed his sandwiches and helped him get away on the famous flight that qualified him for marriage with the Morrow girl. The upshot of this resentment was the fact that when the baby arrived, the reporters, who had waited for days outside the gate, heard nothing of it until telephoned by their own editors.

It later developed that Lindbergh had given strict orders that no news of his son's arrival should be given out, but that Grandfather Morrow, realizing the tremendous interest the public had in the birth, had slipped quietly to the telephone and tipped off the papers.

It took the new father some time to get over this. Even twenty-four hours later, when Mr. Morrow poked his head through the door of the breakfast room, he decided it was best to let his son-in-law cool off a little more.

Morrow's eldest daughter, Elizabeth, has followed the precedent of her Aunt Alice in teaching school. She has hired three assistants and a school building and has established a thriving nursery school for children between the ages of three and six.

Beautiful and vivacious, she is inclined to resent being called Lindbergh's sister-in-law.

Morrow's youngest daughter, Constance, is still in school, while Dwight Jr., his only son, is following his father at Amherst.

Mrs. Lindbergh, older than Dwight Jr., is the exact replica of her mother. Not as pretty as her two sisters, she is quiet, serious and intellectual. Like her mother, she has written verse which has been published in current magazines.

Mrs. Morrow is a graduate of Smith College and has served on its Board of Trustees for many years. She is an excellent speaker and has worked with her husband in almost everything he has done. She also accompanies him on most of his trips, if for no other reason than to make sure that he shaves.

Shaving is the chief *bête noir* of Dwight Morrow's life. When he has to go out a great deal socially and when Mrs. Morrow is present to supplement the entreaties of his valet, Mr. Morrow occasionally will consent to shave. When his wife is not there, however, it is difficult, and when the American delegation was homeward bound from the London Naval Conference—Mrs. Morrow having come back early— her husband spent four days of delicious hermit-like existence, never moving from his cabin, gloating over the luxury of raising a beard.

After the London Naval Conference, Morrow deserved any rest he could give both himself and his harassed beard. The conference had not been Mr. Morrow's show, and he had not been a naval expert; but he had jumped in when it appeared to be headed for the rocks, and without him Mr. Stimson probably would have returned empty-handed.

Morrow was at his best at the London Conference. It was a situation suited to the kind of personal negotiation—of compromise—of trading back and forth—that he had been doing all his life.

He worked long hours and with tremendous concentration. This power of concentration is one of the secrets of Morrow's success. He has the knack of putting everything out of his mind except the one particular problem which he is trying to solve. So intense was this concentration at the London Conference that the Marine orderlies on duty on the floors occupied by the American Delegation at the Ritz frequently had to prevent Morrow from wandering absent-mindedly into any but his own room. Once in his haste to get out of his room, he opened a closet door, walked in and had closed it on himself before he realized where he was.

Whereas other members of the American Delegation took the usual English week-ends in the country from Friday until Monday, Morrow was at his desk in the Ritz all day Saturday and Sunday. He never quit work until midnight, and it was not unusual for him to call newspapermen into conference after eleven o'clock. When he was placed in charge of drafting the text of the Naval Treaty, he drove his committee day and night, even having cold lunches sent in to them in the conference room—something absolutely unheard of in the annals of European diplomacy.

Despite long hours and tremendous concentration, Morrow never lost his punch. He was never worried or nervous, as was Mr. Stimson. No matter how long he worked or what he did, he always came back with a bounce.

Constantly at his right hand during the London Conference was his old friend George Rublee. Rublee it was who drafted the treaty outlawing submarine warfare and who drafted the preliminary text of the Naval Treaty, long before any of the other delegates had thought about its necessity. Rublee it was also who sold Morrow the idea, which the latter sold to Stimson, that a consultative pact was absolutely essential if a five-power pact, instead of a three-power agreement, was to be signed at London.

There was no question in the minds of any who intimately followed the London negotiations that the treaty finally negotiated was the work of Morrow, Rublee and Reed, almost to the exclusion of all other members of the American delegation.

*

DWIGHT MORROW came to the Senate almost direct from the London Conference. He came with this tremendous record of liberal and broad-minded achievement which had won him the nickname of "Little Wonder-Worker." He came with a record which shows that even at a period when he was rolling up a vast fortune, he had always given his time to unselfish causes, so much so that once after Morrow had missed an important business meeting, J. P. Morgan remarked:

"Dwight, if you'll get off that Amherst Board of Trustees, I'll give you a present of $100,000."

Try as hard as his critics will, it is almost impossible to find

an important flaw in Morrow's background of liberal achievement before he came to the Senate. He gave certain indica-
tions of impending reactionism when he headed the drive
to oust Alexander Meiklejohn as President of Amherst, but
this was chiefly because his own father managed to support a
large family on a college president's salary of only $2,400,
while Meiklejohn, with a much larger honorarium, was head
over heels in debt.

There is no question that Dwight Morrow has old-
fashioned and conservative ideas about the necessity of a man
living within his own income. There is no question also that
long association with great wealth has given him a respect
for regularity.

None of these, however, was sufficient to warn Dwight
Morrow's admirers of the disappointment in store for them
when their "Little Wonder-Worker" took the oath of office
as a United States Senator.

During all of his first session in the Senate, Morrow sat
at his desk, behind a stack of books and papers, a very silent
and very small man in a very noisy and very big room, looking as if he hardly knew what it was all about. On his face
was an expression of anxious eagerness—as if he would like
so much to do something but didn't know what it should be
or how to do it once he had made up his mind.

Once he made the wistful complaint that the clerk of the
Senate had announced the third reading of a bill, but that
he, Morrow, had sat on the floor of the Senate painstakingly
and patiently, listening to everything, and he knew that that
bill had not been read three times. Again when he did not
know how to vote on the question of home liquor raiding,
he decided always on the question of prohibition to watch
Blaine of Wisconsin, and vote as he did. Blaine, he reasoned,
was the wettest member of the Senate, and since he, Morrow,
aspired to a wringing wet leadership in New Jersey, he could
not go wrong by following Blaine.

He was a pathetic figure—so pathetic that he became the

great enigma of the Senate. Why, every one asked, has Dwight Morrow, "the little Wonder-Worker," the great liberal, the man who was to have been the outstanding leader of the Senate—why has he fallen so flat?

The answer is not yet forthcoming. His friends have given several answers—none of them convincing. One is that Morrow's whole life had been spent in personal negotiations and the cloistered seclusion of the banker's office. The din, the confusion, the fast-moving debate of the Senate was new to him. Morrow, they pointed out, was not a trial lawyer. He never appeared in court, never even wrote briefs. His wizardry lay in organizing new enterprises, settling disputes between big firms, preparing financial plans and advising executives. To think fast and on his feet, so necessary in the Senate, was something completely out of his line.

Other friends pointed out that Morrow was playing a waiting game, that he was biding his time, making himself an expert in parliamentary law, and that at the next session of Congress he would take the Senate by storm.

Again it was explained that Mr. Morrow had to be loyal to his chief in the White House.

Unquestionably he was loyal, but the idea that he owed any obligation to Mr. Hoover was dispelled on the day that the President sent his friend Franklin Fort to run against Morrow as the dry Republican candidate in the New Jersey primaries. Mr. Morrow knew this, admitted it during the campaign, and there was no illusion in his mind about any debt or obligation to the White House.

The complete cause of Dwight Morrow's senatorial disappointment probably will remain a mystery. A careful diagnosis, however, indicates some of the factors behind it. One of them may be the fact that, as a Senator, Morrow has lacked the help of his friends. All during Morrow's first session in the Senate, George Rublee, the reliable, was in Colombia settling that country's dispute with American oil companies.

Another factor in Morrow's failure is that he has not been true to his old ideals.

During his diplomatic negotiations, Morrow has been known to lie like an unfaithful wife defending her home. He got such a reputation for this at London that newspapermen compared him to a bird fluttering off in an attempt to divert attention from her young. The result was that the more optimistically Mr. Morrow beat his breast and declared that all was going well, the more pessimistic the press cables read that night.

All of Mr. Morrow's lies in those days were diplomatic ones and told for the purpose of aiding a righteous cause. Perhaps the lie which Morrow, the Senator, has given to the one-time liberal character of Morrow, the Ambassador, is also aimed to aid a righteous cause. But if so, no one has yet discovered it.

Finally, the blinding and dizzy glare of the Senate chamber cannot be compared with the rarefied atmosphere of a banker's office or an ambassador's chancery. In either of the latter it is possible to consult experts and to spend weeks making a decision. It is possible to compromise, to yield a little here and take a little there, and nobody ever knows anything about it. But on the floor of the Senate, one must make up one's mind a dozen times a day, without experts and sometimes without warning. One must vote aye or nay, and by that vote, written in unchangeable black, a Senator shall be judged forever.

Under these circumstances it is sometimes expedient to be irregular in private and regular in public.

That appears to be one of the things Senator Morrow is trying to practise. In the cloak rooms he has congratulated various irregular Senators. To Senator Wheeler of Montana he said that he fully concurred with him regarding the Senate's right to recall the names of the Federal Power Commissioners. He rushed up to Senator Borah to congratulate him on his drought relief speech.

But when the bell rings for a vote, Senator Hastings, Republican reactionary, looks at Senator Morrow. Senator Morrow knows what that look means. And when the roll-call is checked up, the name of the "Little Wonder-Worker" is found on the side of reaction every time.

CHAPTER THIRTEEN

LENIN AND MACHIAVELLI

*E*ARLY in the Hoover Administration, when Henry L. Stimson was a very green and very perspiring Secretary of State, he asked one of his advisors to point out the ablest members of the Diplomatic Corps. The names of two ex-newspapermen were handed him.

Carlos Davila, Ambassador of Chile, once published *La Nacion* of Santiago, a morning newspaper. Orestes Ferrara, Ambassador of Cuba, published *Heraldo de Cuba,* read by Havana's commuters on their way home in the afternoon. In Washington, Davila, forgetting that he has no early morning edition to get off the press, sits at his desk until four in the morning. Except when he has to greet the President on New Year's Day, he sleeps until noon.

Ferarra, also unable to divorce himself from the routine of getting his paper on the street by mid-afternoon, gets up at five. He works at the particular book he is writing—he has published half a dozen—until nine, when he puts on riding breeches and white vest to take his morning exercise in the park. At eleven, still in white vest, but minus the breeches, he is back at his desk.

In appearance, Davila is not a prepossessing person. He has dark hair, a penetrating mischievous eye, a total height of five feet five inches and is decidedly not the ideal dinner partner for the mellifluous and amplitudinous Dolly Curtis Gann, whom the Ambassador once entertained at a dinner that made Washington social history.

Ferrara is exactly the opposite. He is both tall and rotund with a waistline, the result of having the best cook in Washington. In his eyes are all the mischievousness of a small boy plus a contagious humor that could make Dolly Gann laugh at herself and enjoy it. He would be an admirable dinner partner for the Vice-Presidential hostess were it not for the fact that he is much too busy entertaining some of the youngest and most attractive ladies in the capital.

Davila is not particularly well known in social Washington. You seldom find him at those parties which his correct colleagues attend more religiously than they keep office hours. He is the only member of the Diplomatic Corps who has never spent a summer, nor even part of one, in Newport, Bar Harbor or Europe. You may find him at a movie, which he has heard is typical of some form of American life; dining alone on the edge of the swimming pool at Wardman Park; decorating a Christmas tree for his children; or taking a breath of fresh air along Massachusetts Avenue just before dawn, but you will never find him at a conventional place at a conventional hour....

Ferrara, because of the warmth of his Sicilian nature and the excellence of his wine, would be one of the capital's prime diners-out if he were not too busy studying Machiavelli and keeping President Machado out of trouble with the State Department—a job which the Cuban Ambassador does with great precision and success.

Davila happened to become Ambassador to Washington because he was partly responsible for a revolution which created a new government in Chile.

He was able to inspire that revolution because of his control of the press.

He became a newspaperman because he was not able to make a living at law.

Ferrara happened to come to Washington because he also was partly responsible for a revolution.

He happened to participate in that revolution because he was a born individualist, a rebel and an anarchist.

All of which goes back to the root characteristic distinguishing Ambassadors Davila and Ferrara from their colleagues; they are of that rare species of diplomat who has developed the habit of thought.

*

THE results of Davila's mental activity would shock the average diplomat to the extent of dropping his tea-cup. Only a handful of people in Washington know what Davila is up to. They know he goes to New York more frequently than the average diplomat, but they think he is fond of the theater. They know he goes off on long airplane trips to the Middle West and other weird places, but they think he just loves excitement. They know he spends long and stifling hot summers in Washington but they think that is because the capital's climate is just the same as it is in Chile.

As a matter of fact, during one of the long and lazy Washington summers, when most of the Diplomatic Corps was sunning itself on the sands of Bailey's Beach, Davila was arranging a world nitrate monopoly aimed at the countries of some of the envoys who were so contentedly relaxing at Newport. Nitrates happen to be a source from which the Chilean Government derives the bulk of its revenue, and yet the sale of nitrates, due to competition from synthetic fertilizers, has been steadily diminishing. Davila first launched an advertising campaign to prove to the American farmer the value of Chilean nitrates and later negotiated with the Guggenheims to link up all the nitrate plants of Chile under one organization with a vast sales organization in the United States. The scheme grew until it eventually brought about a division of the world's nitrate markets between Germany, France and Chile.

Davila spent another long Washington summer studying Russia. The Soviet Republic is a long way off from Chile and does not particularly concern it. The two governments lack diplomatic relations. However, Davila became absorbed in the five-year plan and the Russian system of government sales as compared with the hit-or-miss system of capitalism which he was watching bring unemployment and starvation in the United States. The result was a detailed report to his government on Russia, which, according to some of his colleagues who have read it, is one of the most complete studies of the Soviet system that has been made.

During other summers, Davila went in for intensive study of the American people. He joined a Chautauqua circuit and delivered lectures under brown tents to people who afterwards took him into their homes and quizzed him interminably on Chile and Dolly Gann. He flew in an open airplane to Texas to attend a Chamber of Commerce meeting, and was collegiate enough to tote a pocket flask to journalism-week at the University of Missouri.

Having learned to know the United States, he wanted the Chilean public to get a more accurate picture of it than the one they receive from the stories of sex, jazz and gang warfare which the press associations daily carry south. So Davila sold the heads of the two great press associations the idea that the U. S. A. was not a cultural desert and that the cultural news of the "Colossus of the North" should be emphasized in the daily dispatches along with the reports on American jazz civilization.

Davila had already Americanized the Chilean press. Chilean newspapers at that time were stodgy affairs, their front pages crowded with advertising and their inner pages stuffed with political essays.

Davila, having been put through all the journalistic paces from police court to politics, became managing editor of *La*

Nacion, and immediately instigated rebellion. Instead of hiring regulars in the newspaper profession, he picked his reporters from every walk of life. He got an engineer to handle economic and financial news. He picked a painter to write dramatics. And, after working with his fresh and pliable staff until three in the morning regularly for a month, he sent his newsboys out on the streets one day selling a paper, which except for the Spanish language, was an exact replica of a modern American daily. Advertisements were banished from the front page. Cable news was featured instead of political essays. A dramatic page, a financial section, and sporting pages had been added.

Santiago gasped a little and then read *La Nacion* with avidity. Eventually every other newspaper in Chile followed suit, and Davila eventually did himself one better by establishing the first American tabloid on the South-American continent.

Having revolutionized Chilean journalism, Davila turned his attention to revolutionizing governments. The Ambassador is rather philosophical about revolution now, but at that time he was young, intolerant and quick on the trigger.

Chile was then governed by a Parliament of twelve heterogeneous and combative parties plus a President who was perpetually engaged in going in every direction at once in order to please all of them. Chilean credit abroad was wavering. Chilean claims to Tacna-Arica had become the football of politics. Labor strikes disrupted the country.

Davila spread the groundwork of public opinion that led up to the revolution. The four newspapers of Santiago pretty well dominate Chile, and, of the four, Davila controlled two. His friend Carlos Silva Vildosola controlled the others, and together they drove home the idea that parliamentary government was ineffective and extravagant.

The revolution and dictatorship which followed came nearer to resembling the Russian experiment than the Italian. It was a government of the left, and in this government Davila was offered the post of Minister of Foreign Affairs. He declined it in order to come to Washington. Why he declined no one exactly knows, except that Davila's appetite to know more about the United States had been whetted by the American newspapers he had been studying, and, in addition, he nursed a latent ambition to settle the Tacna-Arica dispute which had been poisoning Chilean-Peruvian relations for forty years.

Regarding this dispute Ambassador Davila had some practical ideas. He argued that since the two provinces of Tacna and Arica were nothing more than stretches of arid sand, the issue at stake was not territorial. He further reasoned that since the Chilean-Peruvian Boundary Commission had spent 2,000,000 pesos in trying to fix a boundary between two provinces which yielded only 400,000 pesos in taxes, the issue was not material. He concluded, therefore, that the issue was one of national honor and that it could not be settled until Chile and Peru forgot their worries about such ethereal and immaterial questions.

So once again, through his own paper and his colleague, Vildosola, Davila launched a program to mold public opinion in favor of Chilean-Peruvian friendship. The two countries had been gloating over severed diplomatic relations for eighteen years. Under Davila's leadership, however, they agreed to exchange envoys. This meant an increase in trade, which was exactly what Davila had been hoping for. Peru had never before sold so much sugar to Chile, and Chile had never before sold so much nitrate to her northern neighbor.

Davila and Frank B. Kellogg, sitting silent in Washington, merely watched the two publics realize that their mutual good will was essential to prosperity. After that the settlement of Tacna-Arica was easy.

*

There are not many men who could represent President Machado and at the same time retain both their own self-respect and the respect of many of Machado's enemies. That

Ambassador Orestes Ferrara can do all three is a tribute to his sense of humor and his frankness. Ferrara is his own harshest critic. He has no illusions about himself nor his President. Referring to the criticism he got for promoting the Pan-American Conference at Havana in 1928, he once remarked:

"Whenever I do anything particularly worth while and righteous, I get criticized for it. Whenever I do anything for which I should be ashamed—and that is more times than I can remember—every one applauds."

Ambassador Ferrara holds no particular brief for President Machado. He admits that his faults are legion. Neither does he hold any brief for himself. But he makes his faults amusing and so he is forgiven.

Ferrara was once the antithesis of Machado—also almost the antithesis of what he himself now is. Born in Sicily, he probably would have been a member of the Black Hand had he not been too intellectual. Expelled from two or three universities, he joined an anarchist cult instead. Anarchism and adventure—probably the latter—took him to Crete to aid the Greeks in their rebellion against the Turks. Then, his appetite for revolution whetted, Ferrara came to New York and joined a filibustering expedition supporting the rebels who had been keeping Spain in continual hot water on the Island of Cuba. Two attempts to land arms failed, but the third succeeded, and Ferrara got to Cuba just in time to ride the crest of the revolutionary wave to fame, wealth and conservatism. When he arrived he was twenty years old. His sole assets were a thirst for excitement, a love of rebellion, a body that could withstand any hardship and a temper that later forced him into fourteen duels. At the end of the Spanish-American War, Ferrara was twenty-two years old, held the rank of Colonel, was Governor of a province, and had started on the path of conservatism and respectability.

To-day he is a millionaire, fat, charming, the best judge of wine in Washington, and the only man in the Diplomatic

Corps who can consume his own Bacardi cocktails, vodka and hors d'œuvres, two platters of spaghetti with a bottle of burgundy and then be equal to a day's work.

As to how he made his money, Ferrara always has a twinkle in his eye when he explains that he took advantage of sugar when sugar was profitable. It was in those lucky and affluent days that Ferrara founded *Heraldo de Cuba,* now the only newspaper in Havana which has not been periodically and consistently banned by Machado. Ferrara is always proud of his old newspaper days, although silent about the present contempt with which his paper is generally held in Cuba. He is also proud of the fact that he still holds the post of Professor of Law and Government at the University of Havana, despite the fact that the University of Havana has been closed by Machado for three years, more or less, and despite the fact that Ferrara has scarcely lectured there in a decade.

Whatever his philosophy or his foibles, Ferrara is without peer as a diplomat. One fact alone is sufficient evidence. In the face of an American press almost universally hostile to Machado, and in the face of a bitterly critical Senate which has sent various of its own members on political filibustering expeditions to the Island, Ferrara continues to make Henry L. Stimson and the Hoover Administration sign on the dotted line in support of his President. Should Mr. Stimson waver for one moment, Machado would be out.

It is Ferrara's job, however, to see that Stimson does not waver and he does his job well.

To those who really know him, the old spark of revolution still flares occasionally in Ferrara's breast, but being an Ambassador he works it out of his system more discreetly than in the days when he was twenty, with Crete and Cuba to conquer. Sometimes he will talk a little more disapprovingly than an envoy should of the high-handed methods his President uses to destroy labor unions or assassinate his opponents. Sometimes he will reminisce a little regretfully about the hectic days of his youth, as if he wished that rebellious period were back again. Almost every day he will go over to the Italian Embassy to fence with Marchetti, or roll the rugs up in his own room with any one who is a semi-equal match for him— which is rare.

But for the most part the Ambassador works out the last lingering traces of his rebellious youth in writing. Some of his books are anything but rebellious, such as the *Causes and Pretexts of the World War, Lessons of the War and Peace Conference,* or *Pan-American Commercial Relations.* But when he gets into the *Private Letters of Machiavelli* or the *Life of Machiavelli,* Ferrara is once more, at least on paper, his old rebellious, domineering, devil-may-care self.

CHAPTER FOURTEEN

THE VESTAL VIRGINS

*I*T may have been his long experience among subject peoples in the Far East, where size of retinue is the mark of rank, that gave him the taste, but throughout his public service Herbert Hoover has always surrounded himself with a small army of personal servitors.

As head of the semi-military food and relief organizations and as Secretary of Commerce, he had a corps of aides about him. In the White House this trait has resulted in the creation of a new institution, the Presidential Secretariat.

This body of assistants has been a never-ending source of wonder, confusion and despair to politicians and newspapermen. Its purpose was apparently to facilitate and improve the dispatch of Presidential business. As it has functioned in actual practice the exact opposite has been the case.

Unquestionably a considerable measure of the President's press and political difficulties have arisen from the inadequacies of members of this staff. Time and again important visitors have been antagonized by tactless handling by one or another of these secretaries.

With the press corps, the Secretariat, with one exception, is a by-word for unreliability. Among political leaders mention of it brings snorts of derision and disdain.

But with all their blunders and incompetence the wide-

302

spread disrepute of the secretaries is not altogether their own fault. Unquestionably they are mediocrities, selected chiefly for their docility and submissiveness. But they have an impossible task.

Mr. Hoover makes unfulfillable demands on them. The secretary dealing with the press, with the best will in the world, is bound to antagonize the correspondents when the President secretly plays favorites, or puts on him the responsibility for withholding or manipulating facts.

The reputation of the political secretary, unenviable enough to begin with, is not enhanced when he is called upon to bring about the defeat of such a measure as the Wagner Unemployment Exchange Bill or find lucrative Federal jobs for unsavory lame-ducks.

Not a little of the Secretariat's troubles in the past also rose out of the fact that their activities overlapped and they were covertly jealous of one another's standing with the President. Theoretically, each has a separate field of operation. But their duties intertwine and not infrequently the President will further muddle matters by entrusting some detail to Lawrence Richey, who has been with him in a confidential capacity for more than twelve years and is his most dependable assistant.

With the retirement of George Akerson, who dealt with the press and visitors during the first two years of the President's incumbency, a good deal of the friction in the staff has been eliminated. Between Richey and Akerson there was a longstanding feud for the President's favor. There is no particular love lost between Richey and Walter Newton, the political aide, but as there is less contact between them, and, since Newton plans eventually to return to politics, they get along without the strain that was always current in the relations beween Akerson and Richey.

For a long time after Mr. Hoover took office, his secretarial entourage was a deep perplexity to the politicians. They were at sea as to who was the most important and had the most weight with him. They knew Richey had been with him the longest and was his most confidential aide, but Akerson made large claims regarding his importance to the President, and Newton had been a House leader.

But gradually it became apparent that if any one really wanted to get to the President, or wanted to get things done promptly and with reasonable competence, the man to see was Richey. He was dependable, when he gave his word, and he had sure and effective access to the President.

This became all the more definite as Akerson began to pass out of the picture. Bit by bit Richey loomed up as the ablest and most significant member of the staff, and with Akerson's departure he has become *the* important secretary.

To-day, those in the know when on business at the White House seek out Richey. He is the least apparent of the staff, but he is by far the most potent.

In numbers, the Secretariat has varied between three and four. This does not include Mrs. Hoover's secretarial personnel. She has at least three of her own, all women. In addition, during the winter social season, the President and Mrs. Hoover command the services of some wealthy and socially informed career diplomat to deal with the delicate and tenuous problems of ceremony and precedence.

The second to serve in this capacity, F. Lamont Belin, former First Secretary to the London Embassy, got so disgusted with the impossible task of trying to please the Hoover whims that he quit both the State Department and the White House.

The first secretarial aggregation consisted of Richey, Akerson, French Strother, and James Francis Burke. The last three have departed, Akerson and Strother after several years' work, Burke after only a few months' activities.

There has always been considerable mystery as to just what Burke's duties were and the extent of his connection. When the President took office Burke came in with the new Secretariat. He had a desk in one of the then-existent outer offices and busied himself with the President's affairs.

He had many political callers, wrote letters on official White

House stationery and used a White House automobile to go about in. Yet, he was not on the Executive payroll and, in reply to inquiries, it was explained that he was serving the President without reward and solely out of love and reverence.

Knowing him as they do, this always provoked ribald jests from the reporters. But Burke's altruism seemed to serve him well. He dressed in the height of fashion, with a marked English cut to his dashing attire, and he lived in the capital's most expensive and fashionable hotel.

But when Mrs. Mabel Walker Willebrandt, after retiring from the Department of Justice, began publishing her prohibition enforcement memoirs and disclosed that her famous harangue against Al Smith before the Methodist prelates during the 1928 campaign had been inspired by "Jimmie" Burke, although he himself is a Catholic, he rapidly began to fade from the White House scene.

His daily appearances became infrequent and soon he was not about at all. When some months later, Mr. Hoover had the ill-fated Claudius Huston installed as Republican National Chairman, the occasion was also used to kick "Jimmie" upstairs by making him General Counsel of the Republican National Committee, a place he still holds.

The most reliable conjecture about Burke's tenure at the White House is that he tried to crash the gate for a secretarial job. The President was seeking a secretary to handle political matters. Whether the Willebrandt disclosures wilted "Jimmie's" chances or the President turned him down for other reasons, he was not chosen, and he departed. Soon, thereafter, Newton was selected for this place, giving up his seat in the House to accept it.

A few weeks after Mr. Hoover and his Secretariat moved in, a complete remodeling of the executive offices got under way. New offices were added, old ones enlarged and enhanced, and the old vestibule made into a lobby, much after the order of those in the latest hospitals, chaste and not too comfortable.

The dispatch with which the work was begun indicated

that it had been planned long before the newcomers took up their residence. The basement, which, since the erection of the structure, had been used only as a storeroom was converted into offices to take care of the largely increased clerical personnel.

The White House telegraph operators, who previously had been located in the ante-room off *the* Secretary's office, were installed downstairs. The executive files, mailing room and mimeographing apparatus were also moved below.

Room for the new lobby, with its white columns, new carpets and severe benches, was obtained by eliminating several large and little-used offices. One was made part of the new lobby and another was converted into an enlarged lounge for the press.

The rug on which Alice Roosevelt stood when she was married in the White House to Nicholas Longworth graces the floor of the press room. But it has long since lost its sheen and nap. However, the place is quite an improvement over what the reporters used to have for many years when they were crowded into a little cubby-hole.

At most only one card game could be played at a time in the old quarters and even then the players had to move whenever some one wanted to use the telephone. Now there is plenty of room for several card and chess games, as well as desks on which to fling wraps and hats.

The amber-tinted walls of the new room are now hung with solemnly autographed likenesses of Harding, Coolidge, J. Bascom Slemp, and other departed immortals, and numerous group pictures of the correspondents at various festive gambols, arrayed in uncomfortable evening attire and not a few of them showing signs of being exhilarated with something more powerful than wit and humor.

The lobby, besides being much more commodious than the old vestibule, also serves by its stateliness to impress the thousands of tourists who come there the year round for a peek inside and to wangle tickets for a view of the lower corridor and East Room of the White House.

The photographers, who had to sit around on the visitors' chairs in the old building, have also been accommodated. This they have Akerson to thank for. As if foreseeing his eventual business connection with the motion picture industry, Akerson from the first was solicitous of the cameramen's welfare. He couldn't find room for them inside the executive offices, so he had a nearby gardener's storeroom fixed up as a lounge for them.

But no sooner was the establishment remodeled and in working order than a fire broke out in a defective flue in one of the secretarial offices and the whole structure was gutted. The work had to be done all over again. After three months of discomfort in temporary offices, the place was completely rebuilt in every detail, with one addition, an air-cooling system such as every good movie house has for hot weather.

In keeping with all these refurbished surroundings, the White House police were elevated to newer dignities and the secret service staff somewhat increased. First Sergeant George Dalrymple, who has served for 32 years in the executive offices, was raised to the rank of Captain, and Sergeant Ernest Seamen, who has been about the place 28 years, was made First Lieutenant. They and the rest of the uniformed police were also given smarter attires. The White House has its own police force, with its own uniform.

Among the secret service men assigned to the White House are several of the most picturesque and interesting personalities in the capital. Richard Jervis, chief of the Presidential detail, has guarded White House incumbents since 1910. Edward Starling, the next oldest in length of service, was a "crony" of Coolidge's. He is a statuesque, delightful Kentuckian, who, when on duty, is always the cynosure of the women visitors, particularly the young adorables.

Jervis and Starling are treasure-troves of Presidential lore. They are both well-educated and able men and if they should ever turn to writing their experiences they could tell enormously illuminating tales.

Uniformed police and secret service men are on duty about the executive residence all the time. The former guard the property from intruders and the latter the person of the President. A detail of secret service men accompanies the President wherever he goes and is always by his side. Coolidge, in his walks and vacation trips, made quite a comrade of Starling. He not infrequently invited him to his early morning breakfast. Hoover maintains complete aloofness from his guards. He deals with them wholly through Richey.

"Larry" Richey is far more than a secretary to Mr. Hoover. He is his confidential agent, the major domo of his private affairs, his solacing friend, and his comforting advisor. Between the two men there is a deep and binding understanding.

Richey joined the President's service shortly after the latter became Food Administrator. Hoover wanted a confidential assistant and investigator and Mark L. Requa, a California politician, recommended Richey. The two men met, had a brief talk, and have never separated.

Until he went into the White House, Richey was little known and quite a mysterious figure. He was always in the background and only a few of the correspondents even knew him by sight. He still keeps out of the forefront in the White House, and little is known of his actual activities, but time has clearly disclosed his influence and importance. He is the man closest to the President, and that takes in everybody in or out of Washington.

Politicians and newspapermen are common types in the history of Presidential secretaries but a man of Richey's career is a distinct departure. The major part of his life until he became associated with the President he was a detective and secret service agent. And since he joined the President, practically all his work has been of a confidential nature.

He began his secret service career as a youngster of thirteen. The government was running down some counterfeiters near his home town in Pennsylvania and they wanted a boy to shadow the headquarters of the gang. Young "Larry" eagerly responded to the opportunity, and, disguised as a newsboy, gathered the information the agents wanted.

On the night that they made their raid, he courageously clambered through a window of the house the counterfeiters were using and crawled through the dark to open a door so the agents could enter. This fine piece of work brought him an appointment to the secret service and by the time he was sixteen years of age he was one of William J. Burns' ablest operators.

For a number of years he led an exciting and adventurous life, chasing counterfeiters, smugglers and crooks throughout the land. He has a reputation for being cool and steady in danger. He is under middle height in size and heavily built, but very agile and powerful.

There is nothing of the policeman about him, either in appearance or expression. He is well informed and dresses with dignity and taste. And he is unquestionably a very able and efficient worker.

When he left the government service, after being attached to President Roosevelt's secret service guard for summer duty for several years, he went into business for himself. He managed a gold mine in the West and spent some time in Alaska on a mining venture. He then became an investigator for *Everybody's Magazine* during its muck-raking days, doing the detective work for such writers as Harvey O'Higgins, C. P. Connolly, and Judge Ben B. Lindsey. Following this he became a private investigator for business and insurance concerns and had developed this into a lucrative practice when he met Hoover and entered his service.

In this work of many years' standing he has given his chief unfailing devotion. No one has ever heard from his lips a word of question or criticism of the man he works for. As a matter of fact, no one has ever gained any information from Richey that he should not have imparted. Which is a great deal more than can be said for some of the other members of the Secretariat.

They have friends to whom they are not adverse to relating their troubles. But if Richey has any such confidants, no one in Washington has yet discovered them. Yet, despite his reticence, the newspapermen consider him the most reliable man on the White House staff. When he does reply to their inquiries, they know that he has answered them truthfully.

William Hard, who worked with Richey when he was a reporter on a Chicago newspaper and the latter was doing the sleuthing for the same publication, graphically portrayed the man in an article he wrote soon after Richey entered the White House and public curiosity about him was aroused.

> "Lawrence Richey," Hard said, "is, in a way, the mystery man of this administration. He is the very core and marrow of Mr. Hoover's activities and has been for twelve years. . . . Mr. Richey has two outstanding qualities. One is that he is a dynamo. The other is that he is a well. Mr. Hoover comes along and tosses things into the well. He can then go away and forget them. He can forget them twice. He can forget them because he knows that the dynamo will attend to them, and he can forget them because he knows that there is no bucket in the world that can draw them up out of Larry Richey. It took Mr. Hoover fifteen minutes to know that Mr. Richey was the man that he wanted most closely, confidentially beside him in Washington. . . ."

Throughout Hoover's work as Food Administrator, Richey was his third hand. When he retired from this office and went into private life Richey went with him. When Hoover became Secretary of Commerce, Richey again entered the government service with the title of Assistant to the Secretary. Mr. Hoover had his secretaries, but "Larry" was his confidential assistant.

His chief job was keeping an eye on the personnel of the rapidly expanding Department. When a situation needed "correcting," it was Richey who did the job neatly, quietly and with dispatch. No hint of scandal or trouble leaked out of the Department. What changes occurred were always silently effected. This all-pervading system had a powerful influence on the Commerce Department. No other branch of the government functioned as effectively and smoothly.

But it was not alone to departmental affairs that Richey gave attention. When Mr. Hoover was interested in certain legislation, Richey conferred with the right men on the Hill. When opposition developed, he called on the erring statesmen and pointed out wherein they were wrong and also how friendly and eager to serve them the great and powerful Department was.

With this wealth of background in dealing with crooks, businessmen, politicians, editors, newspapermen and government officials, Richey was naturally of enormous help to Hoover in his Presidential campaign. Always in the background, he was nevertheless very active. Mr. Hoover designated him as his personal representative at the Republican National Campaign Headquarters and there was little that transpired there that Richey did not know about. And what Richey knows Mr. Hoover knows.

As a result of Richey's work Hoover was able to keep a constant check on what the campaign office did. He appreciably reduced the number of blunders committed by Dr. Hubert Work, the Campaign Manager Mr. Hoover himself selected, and he was also able to suppress some of the worst manifestations of the fierce friction that raged among Republican leaders throughout the campaign.

A high point in this under-cover wrangling was the remark made to newspapermen by Senator George Moses, as he quitted one heated conference he had with Dr. Work. "Well, boys," Moses breezily observed, "at last I have found the man who can beat Hoover."

Richey's activities in behalf of Mr. Hoover's political ambitions date back, according to many in Washington and California, to years before the 1928 campaign. It is declared by these individuals that as far back as 1920, when Mr. Hoover first aspired to the office, Richey was sent abroad to take care of sundry files and records. Certain it is that he did go to England and Europe about that time. Of course, no one knows what was the nature of his business.

In the White House it has always been Richey who has executed the delicate and confidential missions. At the very moment when Akerson was blatantly assuring the reporters that Mr. Hoover would invite whom he saw fit to his dinner table and would apologize to no one for doing so, Richey was calling on Senator Hiram Johnson, of California, with the President's regrets and explaining to him the mysteries of the "inadvertence" that had resulted in Johnson's not being asked to come with the rest of his colleagues on the Senate Foreign Relations Committee to a state dinner.

Because of the mystery surrounding him and his background of sleuthing, Richey was not popular when he first went into the White House. The politicians and correspondents were suspicious of him. Akerson with his swagger, glad-handing and bulkier presence was widely known and generally liked.

But as time wore on, it became increasingly apparent that it was Richey, in the background, who was the abler man and the more dependable. Richey also became more known and better esteemed. No one has ever ascertained just what he does, but he now mingles more, and people have found him a pleasant companion.

Richey is in his early forties. He is part Italian. His father's name was Ricci. He is very fond of the outdoors and greatly enjoys fishing. He has a camp in Western Maryland, near Hagerstown, and likes to have small groups of the President's intimates as his guests.

There is no man who knows Herbert Hoover as Richey does. He knows more about him and his personal affairs than any one else in the world. He could, if he wanted to, tell much that would be of interesting historical value. But those who know him best say he never will. He is one of the few men in Washington who believe in keeping secrets.

The explanation as to why Walter Newton, a Republican

Representative of ten years' service from a safely Republican Minnesota district and a ranking House leader, should have given up his political career to become one of a staff of White House secretaries is to be found in the deep hidden contempt that all but a few members of the House hold for it.

There was no more money in making the change. And, politically, the opportunities were highly problematical. It was only the desire to get into a more dignified atmosphere that could have prompted Newton to give up his seat and take a desk in the Executive Offices.

His work there has had to do with the political. He has been anything but a shining success.

In the House, his lobbying activities on behalf of the President for and against legislation evoke bitter resentment among his former colleagues, and, in the Senate, the mere mention of his name in connection with a measure is always certain to send up the temperature of three-fourths of the chamber.

Whether rightfully or wrongfully, he is given the odium for some prize political blunders. One of these is the deal by which Senator Frederick Sackett of Kentucky, dull, reactionary and certain of overwhelming defeat, obtained the post of Ambassador to Germany. Apparently in return for not running and being defeated, Sackett was given the important diplomatic office and Representative John M. Robsion, a lank, blatant hill-billy, was put up as the senatorial candidate instead. Robsion got a sound trouncing and the President lost the State to the Democrats, to say nothing about a choice diplomatic job to an undeserving lame-duck.

Hoover's selection of Newton as his political Secretary was a deep shock to his liberal friends. But they soon got over being disillusioned as even worse appointments followed one another in succession.

The President's apologetic supporters disapprove of Newton because he is so patently a hard-boiled political operator. They don't object to the hard-boiled politics, but he is so distastefully that type. Newton's whole viewpoint is expressed in a remark he made concerning a certain government official who was selecting his assistants from among non-political experts. "Say," Newton observed, "doesn't he know we are in politics? Those are good jobs he's giving away."

Doubtless, the enormous demand under which he has labored since the 1930 election to find places for lame-ducks has made him supersensitive to vacant government posts. He just hates to see one go by him without being plugged up with a pleading lame-duck.

Throughout his long service in the House, Newton was a steady, party hack of unquestioning regularity. Coming from an agricultural section he declaimed much about the ills of agriculture and voted ever-higher industrial tariffs as sound measures for relieving those distresses. Such farm-relief devices as the debenture and equalization fee, he solemnly inveighed against as evil and injurious, not because he knew much about them but because the White House was against them and he never went counter to a Republican President.

Newton is large and lumbering in size. He dresses in backwoods taste. He has a large, ungainly mouth, and plowman's hands. He is a slow and unimaginative thinker. On his feet he is loud and trite. As one of the floor leaders of the House he always responded to the party lash which was easy for him, as this course furnished him with ready-made convictions.

He early clambered on the Hoover band wagon and beat the tom-toms for him. During the campaign, he had charge of the speakers in the western headquarters, and filled the corn belt with clamor about the virtues of the Republican champion. He did the same four years previous for Coolidge.

When he resigned from the House and joined the Secretariat, it was widely conjectured that he contemplated running for Senator Schall's seat. Schall thought this, too, for a while, and was bitterly hostile to the White House. But when the campaign came around in 1930, Newton kept hands off, which was one of the wisest things he ever did. Minnesota was overwhelmingly anti-Hoover that year, as the balloting showed, and what the voters would have done to Newton, straight from the White House, would hardly have been worth tabulating.

Newton undoubtedly would like to go to the Senate. But the campaign for the next vacancy is a long way off, and even then there has been nothing in his close association with Mr. Hoover to give him grounds for encouragement in this ambition. The best guess in the capital is that he will wind up in some soft government berth, such as a Federal Judgeship.

Akerson and Strother went their own ways in the middle of Mr. Hoover's term. Akerson frankly told his press friends that he was leaving while the leaving was good.

As the voluntarily retiring Secretary of an incumbent President he had a great deal more commercial value than as the former Secretary of an ex-President. So George, despite his boyish delight in the trappings and glitter of his job, cast about him and angled up a $25,000 post with the movie people, to whom he had extended many favors during his work with Mr. Hoover.

As Press Secretary, Akerson had his marked shortcomings. Of course, he had a difficult place to fill, called upon as he was to defend Mr. Hoover's administration. But George added his share to the difficulties by an incorrigible procrastination.

This rose out of his inability to say "no" to any one and his reluctance to admit that he was not the most important man near Mr. Hoover. On more than one occasion this bit of egotism on Akerson's part proved extremely embarrassing to some of his press intimates.

When the President was organizing the American delegation to the London Naval Conference, there was considerable conjecture in the papers as to who the two Senate members would be. From Senate sources the tip went out that they were Senator David Reed, of Pennsylvania, and Senator Joseph Robinson, of Arkansas.

Akerson airily denied this. He assured his press friends that there was nothing to the rumor. The next day, following the publication of the denial stories, the President announced the appointment of the two Senators.

Even more delectable was the instance of Akerson's tipping off close newspaper friends that the President's choice for Chief Justice to succeed Taft was Associate Justice Stone. Exactly an hour later, just long enough for the correspondents to rush off inside dope messages to their papers and for one local Washington paper to prepare an "extra" layout announcing Stone's appointment, George came out of the President's office to announce that Charles Evans Hughes had been named.

Akerson's real talent lay in "planting" a story. On more than one occasion he took away the headlines from the hostile Senate and focused favorable attention on the White House.

Akerson labored earnestly in the last months of his incumbency to persuade the President to assume a bellicose attitude toward the snarling Senate. The President awkwardly tried it several times, to George's proud satisfaction, but the results were not such as to inspire a man of Mr. Hoover's character to keep it up. The Senate, to his pained surprise, failed to be alarmed and fiercely fought back.

In the White House, Akerson started off with great plans. Press relations were to be reorganized on a more liberal and dignified basis and there would be news every day. But, like all the other glowing promises of the Hoover Administration, nothing came of them.

After things started on their downward course, Akerson, with all his loyalty to "the Chief," had no illusion of the true state of affairs. Coming from newspaper ranks himself he clearly saw the trend of conditions. And what he missed himself, his press friends candidly told him about. So when the opportunity offered, he got out. And his friends, for his sake, were glad to see him go.

Strother occupied himself with the "literary" end of the President's work. He prepared material for his speeches, indited some of them, wrote proclamations, and also took care of some correspondence. Before he joined the Secretariat he was Editor of *World's Work* and among other things had written a volume called "Fighting German Spies."

In manner he was quiet and pleasant and little was seen of him. He kept himself aloof from the political phases of the White House. When the President announced that Strother was retiring, in accordance with his wishes that he be allowed to leave after two years' service, it was a surprise to correspondents. Strother's explanation of his resignation was that he desired to retire to his Long Island home and engage in a life-long ambition to write fiction.

To the ironical comment of his friends that he ought to do very well after his two years of intensive practice in the White House, he good-naturedly replied that he was sure his experience would prove helpful.

When Strother's retirement was announced, Hoover intimated that the place might remain vacant. But only a few weeks elapsed before a successor was named. It was explained that, unlike Strother, he would not rank as a Secretary. He would be merely an "executive clerk." The pay, however, would be the same.

The newcomer, George A. Hastings, of New York, was unknown in Washington. Nobody had ever heard of him before. He was announced as a former newspaperman and welfare worker, an exotic combination if there ever was one.

First inquiries about him in New York produced photographs showing a plump, moon-like face adorned with an extensive Buffalo Bill goatee and mustache. The publication of this picture brought word from the White House that Mr. Hastings had dispensed with the hirsute display since the photograph had been taken.

Further inquiries also produced some illuminating facts about his newspaper labors. Mr. Hastings had worked for such potent and powerful organs as the Malone *Farmer,* the Mount Vernon *Argus,* and the Yonkers *Statesman,* all of New York State.

From these important journalistic connections he graduated into social welfare work. He was associated with the State Charities Aid Society of New York and was secretary of the New York State Committee on Mental Hygiene. He was also an instructor in the extension division of Columbia University and in 1930, when the White House staged its Child Welfare Conference, he was publicity agent for the Committee on Dependency and Neglect.

Presumably, on the basis of his work at the Conference, Mr. Hastings won White House recognition. Since joining the Secretariat he has kept sedulously in the background, as becomes every well-trained Presidential "ghost" writer.

When, early in 1931, Akerson announced his resignation to go with the movie industry, the President's friends immediately began to belabor him with advice about a successor. He was told that he desperately needed a man of sound political judgment and wide contacts, pleasant and reliable personality and who knew the press and how to deal intelligently with it.

Frank R. Kent, of the Baltimore *Sun,* one of the President's newspaper admirers, devoted one of his columns to enumerating the qualifications that the new secretary should possess. Summed up they called for a composite about as follows: the political guile and skill of a J. Bascom Slemp, the publicity adroitness of a Charles Michelson, the charm and vivacity of a Jimmy Walker, and the integrity of Caesar's wife.

For two months Mr. Hoover worked on the problem and then picked one of the most tractable, stodgy and partisan trained seals of the Washington press corps.

Every suggestion that had been urged upon him for an oustandingly able man the President disregarded. Theodore G. Joslin, for many years the Washington Correspondent of the Boston *Transcript,* whom he named, made even Newton stand out as a strong figure in contrast.

Without political experience, intellectually mediocre, pompous and ponderous in manner, this was the man Mr. Hoover chose as his personal assistant.

Unquestionably, he fits in perfectly with the White House atmosphere as it exists to-day, which is doubtless why Mr. Hoover selected him.

Joslin, as Press Secretary, has concentrated on "humanizing" the President. Under his ministrations, the President has grimly and laboriously strained to arouse popular appeal. Boy heroes, girl heroes, visiting delegates, tourists and what not are invited to the White House. Its private lawns have been thrown open and the populace, which previously had been coldly held back, are now wheedled to come in. Messages of condolences, congratulations and good wishes pour forth far and wide.

No opportunity is overlooked to squeeze out "human interest" copy. Joslin counts the day lost that he has not peddled a sob story to those correspondents willing to listen. He has told them about the number of telephone calls made by the White House, and about Chili Fish, a Seminole brave, who was made Chief for a day. That the press and public have been cynically derisive has not daunted "Ted." Being totally devoid of humor, he is unaware of the silliness of the spectacle. He has continued working as stodgily and seriously at this effort as once he labored grinding out administration propaganda in his dispatches.

While the sarcasm of the correspondents has not abated Joslin's zeal it has created a growing rift between them. His officiousness has been bitterly resented and more than one of them have told him in no uncertain terms to mend his manners.

The situation between them has reached the point where Joslin complains: "I can't talk to newspapermen, any more." When, shortly after this wail, he undertook to admonish a well-known correspondent for "lack of respect due my position" a violent scene ensued right in the White House offices. Joslin came off a decided second best in the altercation. The entire press corps was aroused. The next day Joslin made his peace with the reporter, while the whole capital laughed.

Akerson always enjoyed the good-natured raillery of the correspondents. He never lost contact with his newspaper ante-cedents. But Joslin seems to have completely discarded all press background upon joining the White House staff.

He is as touchy as a sore thumb and gets highly indignant about a flippant remark. He also seems to be in a state of profound concern about the security of his job. In appealing to one correspondent about his handling of a statement re-leased by Joslin, and about which there was considerable con-fusion, Joslin pleaded with him not to write the story as the re-porter intended, as "it will get me in bad."

Joslin's incumbency has brought one improvement to the White House. He is punctual in his hours and appointments, something Akerson never was able to achieve.

When Joslin's appointment was made known by the Presi-dent, some of the correspondents recalled a brief Republican apostasy on the new Secretary's part toward the close of the 1930 campaign. Files were examined and much to the amuse-ment of the entire capital the following extract was brought to light.

"Political currents," Joslin wrote, "are bearing the Republi-can Party down the River of Doubt.... There is plenty of evi-dence that the Republican Party is not as strong as it was two years ago.... President Hoover has lost prestige."

Which prompted the comment from one of Joslin's Grid-iron Club colleagues—"This is the first time I have ever known any one to climb on board a sinking ship."

CHAPTER FIFTEEN

THE PRESS

*A*S long as the preponderant majority of American newspapers are trivial, reactionary and subservient, the work of the Washington press corps will reflect these debasing influences.

Even if a large proportion of the correspondents were of a high caliber they could do little. Only a fractional minority are their own masters.

The throttle hand on news is not in Washington, where it transpires, but on the owner's desk. The business or partisan interest that owns the publication determines what shall and what shall not be written, and how.

The reporter working for a paper dominated by water power, financial, or political interests writes what these interests want to appear and not what he knows is the truth. If by any chance he should be so foolhardy or careless as to disregard their views he is very soon looking for another job.

On the Washington staff of the ultra-conservative and stand-pat Republican papers of the Curtis group are some of the ablest and most intelligent newspapermen in Washington. If permitted to, they could produce one of the soundest news reports emanating from the capital.

But they don't. They write not what they know but what the viciously partisan and reactionary policy of their employer dictates.

Does the Senate challenge a miserable Presidential appointment, insist that starving farmers and the unemployed be fed? Then it is obstructive and playing politics, so far as the Curtis papers are concerned and the news stories that its Washington correspondents write must take that slant.

The same thing takes place every day in the Washington bureaus of scores of other papers.

The staff of the Los Angeles *Times* will take a news story about Senator Johnson and deliberately twist it into a distorted editorialized attack upon him. The very rich and reactionary owner of the *Times* does not like the forthright and independent Hiram Johnson.

In the New York *Herald Tribune* a sound trouncing administered to the Republican President by the Senate will appear magically transformed into a glowing victory for him.

On the day that a District of Columbia Federal Judge halted an attempt by great water-power interests to emasculate the decade-old Federal Water Power Act, the very wealthy and very dull Washington *Star,* with more than thirty-six pages that day, carried not a line about this enormously important decision handed down within a dozen blocks of its doors.

Throughout the splendid and impartial investigation that the Federal Trade Commission has been making for several years into the offensive propaganda and financial operations of the water-power industry only a few papers have consistently covered these vitally important disclosures.

When the Washington foreign correspondent of the Chicago *Daily News* in writing about the abortive court martial of General Smedley D. Butler inferentially criticized the Hoover Administration's stupidity in the affair, he was promptly warned by his editor to change his attitude.

When President Hoover, in transmitting to Congress the Wickersham Commission's Prohibition Report, made what was for him an amazingly positive declaration on the wet-and-dry question and the following day decided that it would be best to weasel a little for the benefit of protesting wet politicians, he had the impeccable correspondent of the New York *Times* sent for and suggested a helpful little story along such lines.

The *Times,* always accommodating to the White House— what with its dinner and week-end invitations to Mr. Ochs and his Washington correspondent—graciously reciprocated past favors and others to come and carried the story next morning on its front page, carefully suppressing the real source of its information and how it obtained the story.

This is but one of many instances in which the *Times* has allowed itself to be used as a willing vehicle for Presidential politics and propaganda. The press corps of the capital still talks about the astounding news story—really an editorial— that the *Times* carried shortly after the President's return from his South American good-will tour.

The Baltimore *Sun* and a few other independent papers had carried stories, related by the reporters on the trip, of a strict censorship that the Hoover party had enforced on them while on the high seas. The *Times,* apropos of no news development, suddenly printed this editorial denial, carried as a news story under a Washington dateline, pooh-poohing the charge.

The *Times* had a correspondent on this trip. He like the other reporters received a copy of the following instructions:

20 December, 1928.

Memorandum for all Press Correspondents
Effective Immediately.
1. Four typewritten, double-spaced copies of each dispatch will be required.
2. The O.K. system will continue as heretofore.
3. One copy will be returned to its author when the message has been dispatched. Receipt of this copy, marked with the time of receipt in radio room and time actually sent, will constitute the correspondent's check on his dispatch.

GEORGE BARR BAKER

No reference of any kind was made in the *Times* story, denying the existence of a censorship, to this order issued to the reporters when they embarked on the U.S.S. *Utah*. The Hoover staff tried to explain away the censorship by asserting that it was required by naval regulations. Yet, the man who read the reporters' copy and forced them repeatedly to make changes in it, and even to withhold sending stories entirely, was Baker, a civilian, who was one of the Hoover staff and not connected with the navy. None of this pertinent information was contained in the *Times* story.

There are many stories that the great majority of correspondents do not dare handle at all, or, if they do, must deliberately suppress or play down important and significant facts.

The correspondents of such slavishly administration papers as the Philadelphia *Inquirer,* the Portland *Evening Express,* the Providence *Evening Bulletin,* the Cincinnati *Times-Star,* Indianapolis *Star,* the Chicago *Daily News,* the Pittsburgh *Post-Gazette,* and the Washington *Post,* don't dare write anything critical of the President.

No matter how damning the facts, the correspondents of these papers must suppress or distort them where the President or the administration is concerned. On jeopardy of their jobs, they dare not be truthful and outspoken.

That, despite these handicaps and hazards, there are honest and conscientious correspondents who, disregarding economic risks, dare uncover and tackle dangerous stories, is to the everlasting glory of the profession they so gallantly and thanklessly serve.

But such reporters are a minority. With the staffs of the handful of independent papers and news agencies still remaining in the country, these correspondents constitute the most steadfastly wholesome, enlightened, and constructive force in the nation's capital.

They play an important, often a controlling part, in every decent endeavor initiated and pressed in national affairs. Not an exposé of corruption, demagoguery, and infamy, not a meritorious investigation or fight upon a "deal" or for progressive legislation that this small band does not render invaluable service.

The instances where their initiative, quick-wittedness, daring and persistence have supplied members of Congress with vital facts and material with which to win major contests are innumerable.

It was this group that uncovered the facts that led to the authorizing of the Reed Campaign Fund Investigating Committee which cost William S. Vare of Pennsylvania and Frank L. Smith of Illinois their Senate seats.

It was this group that energized the successful fight in the Senate against the confirmation of Judge John J. Parker of North Carolina to the United States Supreme Court, one of the shabbiest appointments in the history of that tribunal and one which Mr. Hoover by every device tried to foist upon it.

It was this group that was responsible for repeal of the century-old secrecy rule of the Senate and forcing into the open heretofore secret deliberations and ballots on executive appointments. It was this reform that made such fights as the successful Parker challenge possible.

It was this group that exposed the peculiar tariff activities of Senator Bingham of Connecticut, with the result that he was censured by a formal vote of the Senate.

It was this group that forced the President to withdraw an undesirable selection as chairman of the new Federal Power Commission and which has been the back-bone of the long and bitter fight in the Senate against the covert and reactionary water-power policy of the administration.

The President and his press claque are correct when they whimperingly cry out against these and numerous other instances of aggravating press initiative and conscientiousness. These reporters are guilty. And they are enormously proud of it.

Theirs is the most honorable record of public service in the capital. The few correspondents who are free to do so proudly admit their participation. The others cherish their satisfaction and pride in secret and are protected by their comrades.

But honorable and brilliant as is this record, it is the work of a minority. It is wholly out of keeping with the temper of American journalism. It is unwanted, resented, and penalized, except on the few newspapers that still own their own souls.

More accurately representative of the American press to-day is the flabby indifference, the provincial and petty ignorance, the smug sycophancy and the disgusting timidity of the majority of the correspondents and especially of the "trained seal" group. They are the truer reflections of their masters, and as a result they go further professionally, financially, and socially than their more conscientious and honorable colleagues.

These improvident upholders of their profession's noblest traditions are the younger men, for the most part. Their names are not found among the high-salaried "trained seals." These dignitaries disapprove of such disturbing proclivities.

Mark Sullivan of the New York *Herald Tribune,* the President's most facile elucidator and defender; Richard V. Oulahan of the New York *Times,* the debonair and socially prominent "dean" of the corps; Theodore G. Joslin, who, before his appointment as Secretary to President Hoover, was Washington correspondent of the Boston *Transcript,* and renowned among his associates for his breath-taking ingenuity in salving any one of Republican nomenclature; Frederic William Wile, of the Washington *Star* and the Columbia Broadcasting System, eulogizer *par excellence;* Leroy Vernon of the Chicago *Daily News,* dull, stodgy and complaisant in heroic proportions; David Lawrence, head of the *United States Daily* and the *Consolidated Press,* super-panegyrist and organizer, who has done so well in these two arts that he operates his own private yacht; all these view with grave disapprobation irreverent raids upon the fabricated reputations and tin haloes of the lofty-placed.

It pains them grievously and some of them speak sadly of the low estate to which the corps has fallen.

In a position to lead in forthright and independent report-ing, these "trained seals" and others of their kind are the severest critics of those who dare to challenge and to speak out about the facts. Their group constitutes one of the most stultifying influences in American national affairs.

The Congressional Directory lists some three hundred and sixty-odd reporters, representing more than three hundred American dailies, a score of foreign newspapers and news agencies, and the staffs of the four major press associations of the United States, The Associated Press, The United Press, The International News Service, and The Universal News Service, the last two Hearst organizations.

These are the officially accredited correspondents. To be officially accredited in the Congressional Directory, the corre-spondent must represent a daily telegraphic newspaper or press association and derive the major portion of his earnings from this source.

Official recognition carries with it admission to the two congressional press galleries, the White House press confer-ences, and the various other department press conferences.

In addition to this large group of accredited newspaper cor-respondents there is a numerous group of writers for trade and business publications, and press agents of various types. They are not listed in the Congressional Directory and despite re-peated efforts by the trade-paper men have been refused admission to the congressional galleries by the newspaper correspondents.

Since the incumbency of President Hoover, the business and trade press has been accorded press privileges at the White House. His conferences have been thrown open to them and no distinction is made between them and the newspaper men.

The press galleries and press conferences have severe rules against lobbying by the reporters and the corps is unfailingly prompt and summary in ejecting any one caught at such activities.

Which is considerably more than can be said for Congress itself, the departments and the White House.

The work and official access it affords offer plenty of opportunity for this sort of secret and lucrative work. But in the last decade only two men have been compelled to give up their gallery standings because of discovery of such forbidden activities.

The congressional galleries are under the immediate direction of committees chosen annually by the correspondents from among their own number. These committees operate under the rules of the two chambers of Congress. The corps is very strict in its rules of admittance.

So much so in fact that no Negro reporter has yet succeeded in gaining membership there.

The several attempts by Negroes representing Negro newspapers to gain admittance have been side-stepped on the technical ground that the applicants did not represent daily telegraphic publications.

Several years ago a Negro reporter for a large Negro publication came to the capital and applied for press gallery membership. For several weeks, in support of his claims for admittance, he filed a large quantity of telegraphic copy to his paper every day.

But it was of no avail. His claim was legitimate but his color was wrong.

A writer for a group of church publications, representing, according to his assertion, several million weekly readers, has also tried repeatedly to gain membership in the galleries and White House press conferences. So far he has not been successful.

He has been particularly anxious to gain admittance to the White House press conferences and on several occasions considerable pressure has been brought to bear there to override the hostile attitude of the reporters.

In 1924, when Coolidge had inveigled the crafty J. Bascom Slemp, Republican chieftain from Virginia, into the White

House as his Secretary, in order to use him to line up the needed Southern Negro delegates to the Republican National Convention that year, a strong drive was made on the White House to gain admittance for this church writer.

It was a campaign year, and Coolidge and Slemp were anxious not to offend so powerful a religious organization. The White House reporters resisted and after a sharp fight had their way.

This church writer has, however, accompanied the President on out-of-town trips. The White House takes the position that on such occasions those accompanying the President go as "guests," albeit heavily paying ones, and that the Executive can "invite" whomsoever he pleases.

The reporters have no personal objection to the writer in the case. They admit that he is friendly, unobtrusive and trustworthy. What they oppose is the principle of allowing a strictly sectarian press admittance to newspaper domains.

One of the most amusing incidents of the Hoover Detroit-Cincinnati-Louisville, inland-waterway-and-electric-light-ballyhoo junket in 1929 was the pairing together by a White House Secretary in the same compartment on the Presidential train of this mild and reserved churchman and one of the most boisterous and accomplished topers of the press corps.

The reporter took with him a large and extensive supply of potables, but the churchman accepted it all with the best of sportsmanship and without complaint. Also, he declined frequent invitations to drink.

When Mr. Hoover went into the White House he informed the reporters that there was to be a new deal in Presidential press relations. The mysterious "Spokesman" of the witching Coolidge era was to be jettisoned. The President henceforth would hold frank and free intercourse with the press, under proper restraints, of course, but still on a much more liberal basis than had been the policy of his predecessor.

So ran the tale, straight from the President himself.

During his campaign he had seen the press at infrequent

intervals and these meetings could just as well have been omitted so far as producing any news was concerned. To outspoken criticism about his press relations in such papers as the Baltimore *Sun* and the St. Louis *Post Dispatch,* the President upon entering the White House let it be known that all was to be changed.

At his personal suggestion a committee of correspondents was carefully hand-picked by his Press Secretary. It met with him and made suggestions. He, in turn, set up three categories of Presidential press releases: direct quotes, attributable information, and non-attributable background information.

It all sounded fine and promising. Within three months Mr. Hoover had completely junked the system.

His press conferences became progressively worse, until today they are more innocuous and futile than even those of the Coolidge régime. Coolidge never called off a conference at the last moment and he always made a pretense of answering questions sent in to him. Hoover frequently refuses to see the press and totally disregards queries.

The correspondents now seldom bother to ask about anything important. They know by experience that if the subject is anything more weighty than a postmastership or some other petty local matter, Mr. Hoover will not answer their questions.

Under the rules set up by the White House all questions must be written out and submitted in advance. The purpose of this arrangement is to give the President time to study inquiries and to obtain any information he might need to answer them.

Mr. Hoover has used this convenience to inform himself as to what the press is interested in, so that he can talk about something else, or, as is most often the case, say nothing at all.

In the first weeks of his incumbency Mr. Hoover attempted to cover up his evasion by saying that he had nothing to talk about because no queries had reached him. This patent falsehood stirred such indignation among the correspondents, who had sent in numerous typewritten questions, that it reached his ears and he dropped the dodge. From then on he has made no attempt to cover up the fact that he will not answer questions dealing with anything of importance.

His press conferences are mere press handout periods. When he has something, the reporters are admitted, listen to him read his prepared statement, and then file out and wait around the outer lobby of the executive offices gossiping among themselves until the inefficient and slow mimeographing service of the White House sends up copies to them.

Another feature of the touted "liberalization" of the White House press relations was the institution of twice-daily meetings between the reporters and a secretary. The purpose of this contact was to afford the correspondents a daily tie-up with the Executive, particularly on local matters.

Here again the reporters soon discovered that the system was being used chiefly to beguile and lull them.

They found that either deliberately or because he did not know and was trying to cover up the facts, the secretary repeatedly misled them on important details. As a result of this slick policy these daily conferences soon fell into disrepute.

The only feature of the Hoover press policy that has proved of any satisfaction to the reporters was the installation of an enlarged press room.

During the fanfare about improved press dealings, The White House Correspondents' Association, for many years a haphazard and informal organization of reporters who regularly covered the White House, was put on a ceremonial basis. The ceremony consisted of collecting a $1 membership fee and issuing an ornate, gold-embossed press card, duly autographed by a White House secretary.

The sole purpose of the Association is to "throw" an annual banquet, which is preceded and followed by numerous private parties given by the reporters and their guests, along the well-established lines for such affairs. Membership in the Association is open to any accredited reporter upon his own application and without any other requirement than paying his dollar. It is all breezy and casual, in the true press manner.

Even the elections of officers of the Association are free and easy. The permanent White House group, which actually runs the organization and arranges its annual frolic, picks a slate, obtains a few nominating signatures, and then announces that, owing to lack of opposition, balloting was dispensed with.

Of course now and then an election fight is precipitated. But only for the purpose of having some excitement.

The correspondents delight in the jangle of a good election scrap and like nothing better than to stage one among themselves just for the fun of a good disturbance. They go through all the motions of hot electioneering and have a great time. The annual presidential contests of the National Press Club are almost always close races.

The famed Gridiron Club is neither promiscuous in its membership nor ebullient in its internal affairs.

It is a select and numbered band. Its active roll is restricted to fifty members who are supposed to be working Washington correspondents.

Actually there are at least a half dozen who are no longer newspapermen. But because they continue to live in the capital they are carried on the active list, much to the anguish of aspiring and long-waiting "trained seals" and bureau managers from whom the club's members are chosen.

Members who leave the city are transferred to an inactive list. In addition, the club has a small group of associate members composed of local professional entertainers who assist in the semi-annual stunt evenings the club stages.

The Gridiron Club has two unwritten rules. No Jews are admitted to its sacred ranks and no reporters are ever present at its revels. Both restrictions have been broken.

Charles Michelson, for many years the brilliant chief of the Washington bureau of the New York *World,* and now the

$25,000-a-year Publicity Director of the Democratic National Committee, who has performed miracles in rejuvenating that long moribund institution, was elected to membership through the influence of one of his staff.

But since then no other Jews have gotten by the holy portals, much to the secret travail of such exalted press figures as "Freddy" Wile and "Dave" Lawrence, both members of the proscribed race.

The famous instance of the club's booting its "no-reporters-present" rule was during the Roosevelt Administration. The President took the opportunity afforded by the supposed secrecy injunction to relieve himself of some forthright views about a hostile Republican leader. He spoke animatedly and frankly.

It was a gorgeous story. Gridironers though they are, good red reportorial blood flows in their veins and some of them just could not resist the temptation. So, much to Teddy's pained surprise, they bolted and wrote.

Since then, however, the rule has been rigidly adhered to. No President has ever said anything worth printing.

Only the press associations, the *United States Daily,* and several of the Washington papers now have reporters permanently assigned to the White House. During the Coolidge Administration and at the beginning of the Hoover incumbency several of the New York City morning papers had men who did nothing but cover the White House. But for some time they have covered it as part of the "downtown run," which includes the various departments and the independent commissions and boards.

White House coverage is a dull, petty routine, especially when Congress is in session. Under Hoover, the White House reporters often first learn of White House news developments when their offices call them and advise them that a message or statement from the President has been received by Congress or by some member of Congress.

When the President goes traveling things pick up. News

is lively, and best of all, the reporters are on the move with generous expense accounts.

Coolidge's practice of picking out a cool, comfortable spot during the summer and settling down for two or three months while Washington stewed and sweltered in its appalling heat greatly endeared him to the correspondents and their wives.

The work was light and by coöperating among themselves it was made lighter. They never spared expense accounts, and being representatives of the great Fourth Estate and Washington correspondents to boot, local society went out of its way to entertain them in the manner to which they would like to be accustomed.

It was great sport and the correspondents looked forward to Coolidge's summer vacations just as eagerly as he did, and enjoyed them even more. With Hoover, however, there have been no such delights. A restless traveler before he entered the White House, he has made only a few hurried trips since then.

Next to the President's conference, that of the Secretary of State is most important and most largely attended. These conferences are held with the Secretary himself or, when he is not in the city, with an assisant. They take place every day except Tuesday, when the Cabinet meets.

Secretary of State Stimson's conferences are no worse and no better than those of his predecessor. Like him, he dodges, evades, denies, and minimizes as often and as much as he can.

When he first took office, Stimson attempted to be hardboiled and abrupt with the reporters. But he quickly and painfully got over that idea, when the regular State Department press group retorted in kind and, figuratively speaking, cuffed him a few resounding news smacks across the nose.

Next in interest to the White House and State Department conferences are those of the Treasury. For the first seven years of his incumbency Mr. Mellon was always flanked by his Under-Secretary when meeting the press. But in recent years the Sainted Gift to the Big Tax Refunders meets the reporters unattended.

He still shows signs of extreme agitation when closely interrogated, but now he does his own evading and enjoys it—when it doesn't get too rough. When that happens, Mr. Mellon becomes flustered and incoherent. Most of the Treasury reporters have grown quite fond of the "Old Man," as they call him, and he in turn has become somewhat more accessible to them.

The press conferences with the Attorney General have improved somewhat since the days of John Garibaldi Sargent, Coolidge's know-nothing-see-nothing-say-nothing choice for that exalted post. Sargent's invariable answer to all press queries was "I'll have to look into that."

If he ever did he never showed any signs that the information had improved his knowledge of what was going on in his Department.

Mr. Mitchell is more conversant with what his Department is doing, but the pall of secrecy about that department's activities is just as dense as it ever was.

One of the conferences, much missed by reporters these days, is that which they once so thoroughly enjoyed with Mrs. Mabel Walker Willebrandt, when she was Assistant Attorney General in charge of prohibition enforcement. The charming lady could almost always be teased into an argument.

She would gently chide the correspondents for their harshness and unfairness to her and the dry cause, and appeal to them tenderly with her large brown eyes to reform and be good boys. More than one of the news men had the experience of visiting her in a hard-boiled temper, bent on mischief, only to come away convinced that he had grieviously wronged the sweet and earnest little lady.

During sessions of Congress, press activity focuses on Capitol Hill, with the White House and the Departments taking secondary rôles. When Congress is in adjournment, news interest shifts to the executive branch. It is then that the President, the Cabinet, and the Little Cabinet, consisting of Assistant Secretaries and Bureau Chiefs, get in their lusty publicity strokes.

The White House conferences, the State Department conferences, and all the other departmental conferences take on new life. Correspondents who rarely go near them during congressional sessions begin coming around regularly. Departmental handouts are carefully scrutinized, where before they were indifferently tossed aside.

Instead of taking the pick of several good stories a day, the Bureau Chiefs and "trained seals" have to scratch around for ideas, an extremely painful process for quite a few of them. The "brain trusts" among certain groups of correspondents intensify their endeavors and hold long "bull sessions" straining and laboring to produce a reasonable suggestion for a story.

These "brain trusts" are informal gatherings of reporters who get together and pool news resources. They are pleasant, friendly coöperatives, rich in comradeship. Rare and tall tales are swapped, most of them far more exciting and truthful than those sent to their papers.

There are three such more or less regular groups. One meets for lunch early in the afternoon in the Press Club. A second consists of a block of press offices on the ninth floor of the Colorado Building, and the third, a group of bureaus on the twelfth floor of the National Press Club Building. The papers of these correspondents do not compete with one another and the men are thus free to coöperate fully.

Another means of news coöperation among the correspondents is the "blacksheet" or carbon copy. It is a convenient means of exchanging news and is done on a coöperative basis. The correspondent who doesn't produce his share is sharply and bluntly called to task.

The correspondents always protect a colleague if he gets

into difficulty while on an assignment. They will file for him over his signature and answer queries from his editor. Sometimes their solicitude has amusing results.

During the Hoover Latin-American good-will tour, one of the correspondents misjudged his entertainment capacity and had to be put to bed. A story broke unexpectedly and three of the reporters, all filing from different cable offices, and thinking they alone were protecting their colleague, sent rush stories to his paper at the rate of $1 per word.

The three stories came to over 3000 words. Each carried the signature of the sleeping correspondent.

The two congressional galleries are much like newspaper "city rooms." They open out into the Senate and House chambers in balconies equipped with writing benches. The Senate gallery, because of the greater importance of the Senate, is larger, better equipped, and far more used than the House gallery.

Both the Western Union and the Postal Telegraph companies have wire connections in the galleries. The press associations have their own telegraph circuits and operators in each gallery. In the Senate gallery they are also allowed railed-off space for their own desks and typewriters.

Each gallery is in charge of a "superintendent" with several assistants. They answer phone calls, see that copy is handled, and furnish writing supplies and reference material. James Preston, the Senate gallery supervisor, has held this post for over thirty years and is one of the most widely known figures in American journalism.

When the chambers are in session, the reporters summon members from the floor by sending for them by pages especially assigned for this purpose. In the Senate, the small back ante-chamber, known as the President's Room, is used for these conferences. In the House, the reporters use the members' lobby.

About a score of women are accredited to the press galleries. Of this number only about half are really active there. These do straight reporting and several of them are among the very ablest, most intelligent and conscientious correspondents in the entire corps.

Ruby Black, head of her own news bureau, is a highly accomplished and indefatigable reporter. She has developed her news service until she now has important papers in a number of states. Before coming to Washington, she taught journalism at the University of Wisconsin and worked on papers in Wisconsin and St. Louis. She is President of Theta Sigma Phi, national women's journalism sorority.

Ruth Finney of the Scripps-Howard Newspaper Alliance is not only a talented writer but an authority on water power, labor and social problems. She has had wide news experience on national affairs, and her work in covering, over a number of years, the bitterly fought Boulder Dam contest, won her the high respect of her fellow-reporters and congressional leaders.

Three other women have stood the test of journalistic work in the capital in the service of the Associated Press and have won the respect of their colleagues for competent and quick reporting of straight news. Sue McNamara and Bess Furman, covering government departments, and Marguerite Young, in the House and Senate press galleries, for several sessions have handled difficult and complicated subjects with skill and intelligence.

There are four classes of news bureaus in the capital: those with a single correspondent representing one newspaper only, those with two or more correspondents representing one newspaper only, those with one or more correspondents representing a string of newspapers, and finally the press associations with large staffs.

In addition, a number of correspondents do work on the side, with the knowledge of their editors, for newspapers not in competition with their own. Quite a few of the correspondents also do special work for weekly and monthly publications. This writing is eagerly sought by most of the reporters as it adds both to their professional prestige and their incomes.

All the anonymous magazine columns giving the lowdown on the capital are done by Washington correspondents whose identity is known to most of the others.

Of the press associations the Associated Press, with thirty-seven men and three women, has the largest staff in Washington. Whatever else the Associated Press may be, it is always lavish in personnel.

In the Senate it has as many reporters as all the other press associations combined. This practice of maintaining numerical superiority is a fundamental tenet of Associated Press news covering policy.

It always covers a story with a pack. Not that this means better coverage. In fact, it rarely does. Almost always the more able, resourceful, and certainly the more liberal and intelligent reporting and writing is done by the numerically weaker, but keener, competition.

As an organization the Associated Press, because of its smug self-satisfaction, is cordially disliked by most of the press corps. Individually the Associated Press reporters, for the most part, are esteemed by their comrades. A few of them, Kirke L. Simpson, general staff writer, Francis M. Stephenson, in charge of the Senate Associated Press staff, C. D. Dickson, director of the House staff, D. Harold Oliver, and James P. Selvage, are deservedly popular and highly respected.

They are able and careful reporters, always scrupulously fair. Simpson is one of the best-read men in Washington, and is by far the most liberal on the Associated Press staff.

Byron Price, chief of the bureau, is cautious, docile, and conservative. Like the entire Associated Press organization, he is under the reactionary and deadening influence of Frank B. Noyes, owner of the ultra-Tory Washington *Star,* and for more than a quarter of a century president of the Associated Press.

The Washington press corps credits Noyes with the inspiration, if not the authorship, of the amazing letter that the Associated Press sent the Senate, over Price's signature, when the Old Guard attempted to discipline the United Press for its exposé of several secret roll-calls on contested nominations. The entire corps, with the exception of the Associated Press, was aroused at this attemtped censorship and rallied behind the United Press.

It was during the debate on the Senate floor over the issue that the Associated Press sent its bleat of hypocritical protest against being penalized for something its competitor had done. The Associated Press, the Price letter said, could have had the story if it had wanted to, but it didn't want to.

Coming as the communication did in the midst of a press censorship fight in which every newspaperman and every newspaper organization had a vital and personal stake, the Associated Press' letter was considered by the press gallery as a stab in the back.

The communication aroused much indignation among Senators and was unquestionably an appreciable factor in the complete and overwhelming defeat of the censorship attempt.

To the honor of the Associated Press staff in the Senate, it was as deeply ashamed of the action of its superiors and as resentful of it as the other correspondents.

The Mexican Bolshevik hegemony story several years ago is another instance of the sort of thing the Associated Press, ever-worshipful and complaisant to official authority, alone of all the press associations was willing to lend itself to.

The story accused Mexico of harboring Communist designs. It gave no authority for this information, other than vague references to reliable sources of information. Coming at a time when, due to the stupidity and bungling of Coolidge and Kellogg, the relations between the United States and Mexico were at the breaking point, the story created a tremendous sensation.

It might conceivably have precipitated a crisis had it not

been disclosed just where the absolutely false story had come from, and the vicious purpose which had prompted it.

Robert E. Olds, Under-Secretary of State to Secretary Kellogg, conceived the story and tried to peddle it to the Washington press. He did so for the deliberate purpose of giving the United States an excuse for high-handed tactics with Mexico. The story was wholly without foundation and when Olds refused to let either himself or the State Department be used as authority, all the press associations with the exception of the Associated Press refused to handle it.

The Associated Press carried the story, suppressing the facts as to the source but giving it the atmosphere and substance of weighty authority.

The Senate letter and the Mexican Bolshevik threat story are not accidents or isolated incidents of unfortunate "breaks." They are characteristic examples of the news policy of the Associated Press. It always plays the administration game.

It is always currying favor and warming up to those in power. Its history is cluttered with instances of unfair, prejudiced and distorted handling of news stories where strikers, radicals, and liberals are concerned. No other press association has such a case record of its correspondents lending themselves to the dissemination of propaganda.

Nothing could be more significant than the fact that the Associated Press is the only press association from whose Washington staff leading members have voluntarily resigned and taken publicity jobs with great business and political organizations. Several of them, including a former bureau manager, are doing press work for a great railroad. Another quit to go with Harry F. Sinclair in the midst of the Teapot Dome leasing scandals. Another, after more than a year of toadying to the Hoover Administration, while a member of the Associated Press staff covering the White House, became publicity agent of the Republican National Committee.

The United Press staff is about half as large as that of the

Associated Press but what it lacks in numbers it many times excels its competitor in capacity and character.

In Lyle Wilson, head of the Senate staff; Thomas L. Stokes, in charge of the House; Paul Mallon, on the White House; Herbert Little, on general assignments; and Louis Jay Heath and Harry W. Frantz, on Latin-American and Far Eastern affairs, the United Press not only has the best among the press association men in these vital posts, but men who are among the very ablest and most trustworthy members of the entire press corps.

These men are outstanding reporters and talented writers. With the generally liberal news policy of the United Press, they have considerable latitude in their work and make excellent use of their opportunities.

Particularly is this true of Frantz and Heath. They are the best informed, most widely traveled and experienced, and enlightened Latin-American authorities in North-American journalism. Their work is little known in the United States but throughout Latin America they are the most widely read foreign writers and their dispatches are considered the most reliable and impartial emanating from this country.

The United Press is predominant in Latin America in the press association field. It serves practically all the important papers there. It has achieved and maintained its supremacy in Latin America by close adherence to unbiased and impartial news reporting.

In the main this policy characterizes its domestic report. It avoids official taint, and is fair to labor and the Insurgents. But on occasion it will temper its realism, as when it killed a story written by its Washington bureau giving the details of the President's secret efforts to modify his dry statement on the Wickersham Commission's Prohibition Report.

The Washington bureau turned the story over to one of the correspondents of the Scripps-Howard Newspaper Alliance, which is affiliated with the United Press, and this organization used it in its papers next day.

The United Press has made great gains in recent years and is serving many wealthy and conservative papers. This unquestionably has had some influence on its news policy.

In style the United Press is sprightly and trenchant. There is more good news writing done daily in the United Press report than is to be found in a week of Associated Press copy. The Associated Press, under Kent Cooper, general manager and a former United Press man, has endeavored to brighten up its news writing, occasionally with ludicrous results.

Until the last few years the United Press was decidedly niggardly in its pay scale. It gave its reporters plenty of opportunity for ambitious enterprise and never stinted work, but was tight-fisted when it came to salaries.

It has become somewhat more liberal, and its Washington staff is more decently paid than it used to be. But there is plenty of room for improvement, particularly among the younger men on the staff. The United Press, also, has the practice of letting out a number of these youngsters at the end of a congressional session. This is a distinctly unfair and cruel policy.

At the close of the Seventy-first Congress five of the younger men were let out. Several of them had wives and babies. One of them was brought from the Middle West, where he had done good work for a number of years. He was brought to the capital in recognition of this competence, and yet, three months later, at the close of Congress, he was dropped from the rolls at a time when press activity in Washington was slack and it was impossible to get another job. The United Press could have easily absorbed these men in its nationwide organization, but it dropped them with a couple of weeks' pay and indifferently set them adrift.

The two Hearst press services, the International News and the Universal jointly have a staff as large as that of the United Press. There are some excellent newspapermen with the Hearst organization in Washington. George Holmes, chief of the International News Service, is an unusually talented writer and among the most competent newspaper executives in the capital.

George Durno, a veteran on White House coverage, Fraser Edwards, on Congress and national politics, and Marion L. Ramsay, on economic questions, particularly water power, are among the leaders in their fields. Ramsay's work on the long and complex investigation by the Federal Trade Commission of the water-power trust is unsurpassed for brilliant reporting.

The Hearst organization in allowing Ramsay free rein on the water-power issue, and in carrying his power stories, has performed a public service approached only, in this field, by the Scripps-Howard papers.

Despite its high percentage of excellent personnel and such signally splendid pieces of constructive journalism as Ramsay's work on the water-power question and the Bingham tariff exposé, the Hearst press service in the capital suffers from the same taint that attaches to Hearst papers generally. It has not the standing in official and political quarters to which the number of its papers and the worthiness of many of its reporters entitle it.

The New York *Times* has the largest individual newspaper bureau in Washington, with ten men and one woman. It is *Times* policy to cover every event of the day in the capital, large or small, with its own writers.

If the regular staff is insufficient, extras are employed. This results in literal duplication of a press association report. If the bureau misses a story that the Associated Press schedules, the *Times* New York news desk notifies the bureau and waits for its story.

Oulahan, chief of the *Times* bureau, is one of about a half-dozen reputed $25,000-a-year men in the press corps.

One of the fundamental attributes of a $25,000-a-year correspondent is that he never write anything challenging or critical of any one in the White House, high society, big business, and finance. No one in any way given to persistent

candor about such personages can hope to attain this lofty
—for the press—financial status.

All the members of this select band of correspondents are
noted for their capacity to see the right side of questions where
high place and influential authority are concerned.

Oulahan does the greater part of his news gathering through
"leg" men on his staff. His writing for the most part is confined to "policy" stories. Policy stories are neatly turned editorials printed in the news columns, with a news atmosphere
about them, but which are actually propaganda for some one
or something that the paper favors.

A choice example of the "policy" story is one from the hand
of Oulahan a year or so ago.

The President was encountering widespread criticism over
the mediocrity and shabbiness of his appointments. To offset
this rising murmur of disapproval, the White House undertook to put out some counter-propaganda. Apparently, as in
the case of the Latin-American censorship story, the *Times*
was willing to assist in this endeavor.

One day a long feature story appeared under Oulahan's
signature telling all about the "new patriots." These latest
model heroes, it developed, were Mr. Hoover's appointees.

Their patriotism, the story explained, arose out of the fact
that they had responded to his command and had left their
private affairs to take the government jobs he gave them.

Washington had heard these Hoover men described as "Boy
Scouts" and "Soft Boils," but "new patriots" was something
new. What, the politicians asked, had become of such one-
time Hoover "patriots" as Mrs. Willebrandt who had carried
his campaign to the Protestant churches? Of Colonel William
Donovan, his intimate advisor during the Presidential race;
Horace Mann, who had done such valiant if mysterious election work in the South; Dr. Hubert Work, his first National
Committee Chairman; and Claudius Houston, his second National Committee Chairman? They too had served, it was
observed. When and why had they ceased being "patriots"?

Oulahan's article made no reference to such disturbing interrogations. In fact that article was the first and last that was ever heard of the "new patriots."

The *Times* does not pay its Washington bureau chief a large salary for his news gathering or news writing ability. What it wants and gets from Oulahan is "front."

He is one of the few really distinguished looking men in Washington. He and Sir Willmott Lewis, the signally able and genial correspondent of the London *Times,* are the only two men in the capital who look like diplomats.

Oulahan is at his best as a host and as presiding officer at a banquet. Then his real talents get free play. He is urbane and decorously sprightly and carries things off with just the desired touch. He is welcomed everywhere in Washington society and particularly at White House and at Cabinet dinner tables. He has a beautiful Georgetown home where he entertains as befits the socially prominent Washington correspondent of the New York *Times.*

All of which is most acceptable to the *Times.* It likes to have its representatives cordially received in the high places.

Oulahan is over sixty years old, and active and vigorous. He is a fair and considerate bureau chief and his staff is devoted to him. They are typical *Times* men, conservative, hard-working reporters, grinding out the day's grist of news in columns where others turn it out in words.

The New York *Herald Tribune* staff is smaller than that of the *Times,* but much more aggressive and alert. This is due to the driving energy and industry of Theodore G. Wallen, who was brought down from the paper's Albany, New York, staff in 1929 and made bureau chief in the capital.

Wallen completely reorganized the bureau. He put an end to news swapping between it and the other New York morning paper bureaus and set the pace on his own staff for hard work. The result has been a measurably improved news report —in quantity. In quality the bureau's product is inclined to be sensational and trivial.

This triviality, in a large measure, is due to the silly over-playing of its Washington news by the *Herald Tribune*. No matter how banal or inconsequential a story is, if Wallen labels it "exclusive" it gets a front page play.

Wallen is one of the higher paid men of the corps but he is still far from the $25,000-a-year class. However, he is un-questionably headed that way. He plays always a safe game and never diverges from the reactionary, big-navy, Republican policies of his paper.

He is personally of strong conservative Republican views and his stories always have that slant. During the London Naval Conference and later during the Senate fight over the treaty, his stories played up strongly the big-navy side, in line with the *Herald Tribune's* attitude. He also never passes up a chance to sneer at the Progressives and by sly adjectives to deride their activities. His paper stupidly approves of this type of small-town partisanship.

There are two members of the *Herald Tribune* staff who are exceptional correspondents. They afford a striking contrast.

John Snure, for many years the paper's Senate reporter, is without peer as an authority on Senate affairs and one of the most resolutely honorable men in the press corps. Despite the fact that he works for a reactionary and partisan publication, he has unswervingly maintained his personal and professional integrity.

Of enormous industry, he covers the Senate all alone, work-ing from morning until late at night. The *Times* has from two to four men on the chamber, but Snure covers it all by himself. And always he does it with rigid fairness and impartiality.

There is not a Senator who does not trust him implicitly. He has more senatorial friendships than any other man cover-ing the chamber. But he always remains true to himself.

Twenty years ago when he first came to the capital, as the correspondent for an Iowa paper, he was the friend and ad-mirer of Albert B. Cummins, Progressive Senator from that state. But he remained a friend of Cummins only as long as Cummins remained true to his liberalism.

When Cummins listened to the soft siren voice that is so persistent in Washington and turned on his progressivism, Snure broke off relations. He is that kind. Which explains why John Snure, superb reporter and honorable man, has never risen to the estate of bureau chief and is not in the $25,000-a-year class.

Mark Sullivan did not come to the capital as an experienced correspondent. Now, however, he is very much of the $25,000-a-year class, and all which that implies.

Sullivan, strangely enough, came to Washington through the instrumentality of Governor Gifford Pinchot, militant liberal and foe of the power trust. A magazine editor friend of Pinchot's wanted a handy young man about his Washington office to look up answers to questions and to write little paragraphs. Pinchot recommended Sullivan, then working on a small Pennsylvania paper. He knew him as a young liberal and a supporter.

But that was a long time ago. To-day, Sullivan is no longer a liberal or a supporter of Pinchot's. In the Governor's 1930 campaign Sullivan wrote unfriendly stories about him and gave support to those who were opposing him.

Sullivan is not a news correspondent in the sense in which that term is generally used. For years his syndicated column has been a Republican propaganda medium. Since the Hoover incumbency it has narrowed even more in scope and become the Presidential press mouthpiece.

Everything Sullivan writes in his syndicate articles is biased by his White House relations. He is in constant direct touch with the President. He is a member of the "medicine-ball cabinet" and is consulted on policy and public statements.

When the President wants to put out an alibi, a defense, or an explanation, Sullivan is the chief channel. His craftily worded dispatches are an exact reproduction of the President's devious mental and political processes.